# ROMAN HELLENISM
## AND THE
## NEW TESTAMENT

FREDERICK C. GRANT

# ROMAN

# HELLENISM

## AND THE

# NEW TESTAMENT

NEW YORK

CHARLES SCRIBNER'S SONS

TO

# ARTHUR DARBY NOCK

# *Foreword*

There is at present a growing interest in the Hellenistic age. It was an age much like our own in many respects, deeply vexed and troubled by similar problems, plagued by wars and universal militarism, by a growing threat of world catastrophe, and by fierce racial animosities and religious bigotry, despite all efforts to overcome them. Ours also is an age misled by false propaganda, struggling to get at the truth of science and philosophy and turning upon all traditional religion the relentless searchlight of historical and literary criticism, not to say the cold analysis of scepticism. Even the widespread superstition of today can be matched by that of the Hellenistic age, when the dense jungle of primitive *Aberglaube*, once bravely swept back by the earliest Greek thinkers, began "reinvading," in Matthew Arnold's phrase, and introduced once more the creeping shadows and the dank, dark mists of occultism, magic, fear of nature's unknown forces—especially the uncontrollable, scarcely predictable daemonic powers of the astral deities. Superstition, fanaticism, emotional disturbance, depressing fear and dismay—this was the darker side of the sunlit promise of economic and political betterment during the happy interval, known as Roman Hellenism, which lay between two grim centuries of constant war at the end of the Roman Republic and the swift decline which began under Commodus and led to the fall of the Roman Empire. The world cried out, as it does again today, for peace, for sanity and mental health, for confidence, for brotherhood and good will, for understanding, for release from age-old fears and terrors, from private malice and public animosity on earth and from malevolence on high. As then, so now: only the gospel of a good God, enthroned above the universe and holding firmly in leash the forces of chaos, a God who really cares for mankind and claims the whole human race as his children, and who promises the blessing of "peace on earth, good will to men" if they will but turn to him with all their hearts—only such a gospel offers hope of a way out of the present impasse. It is our one "live option," if we desire a world fit to live in and to pass on to our children. Hence the relevance to our day of the New Testament, with its deep roots in ancient Judaism, in the Old Testament, and in the best of Hellenism.

The study of the Hellenistic age brings inevitably into sharper focus the true historical significance and bearing of the New Testament, its language, its ideas, and its message. The vague general background of "ancient times" or of "Oriental custom" will not suffice. These early Christian books were written by living men, addressed to living readers, and they spoke upon living issues of their own time. Whatever we can do to recover the relevance of the New Testament to its own period, the first and second centuries, will surely deepen and enrich its relevance for our days. One thing we must avoid at all cost—the attempt to explain the New Testament and its religion by appeal to chance causes, contemporary interests, local movements; for the New Testament is the written deposit of a flooding tide of world-wide religious activity, thought, and aspiration which was surging up from the deeps of ancient life and sweeping into the all-embracing range of its after-effects the whole history of Europe and the West following the first two centuries.

The popular idea that early Christianity was one more "mystery" religion which secretly slipped out of the East as a rival to Mithraism or the cult of Isis and gradually outbid its competitors for popular favour; or that it succeeded where Judaism failed in its appeal to the "God fearers" of the eastern Mediterranean area because it offered more religious satisfaction at far less cost in personal effort (no observance of food laws, no painful, barbarous circumcision, women given the prominence now accorded them in Graeco-Roman society but denied them in the East, and so on)—such simple, sweeping explanations will not do. They miss the massive realities behind the phenomenon of early Christianity. For if we are to understand the New Testament or the religion it enshrines, we must take into account the total background, not only the long development of Hebrew-Jewish religion reflected in the Old Testament but also world history, what we may call the "modern" history of the period known to us as the first century A.D. In fact we cannot even understand the Jewish religious

history of this first century, which formed the immediate background of the New Testament and the rise of Christianity,
unless we take into account the wider background of world
history; and that includes the old Oriental empires, especially
the Persian, and the history of Greece and Rome, and the whole
phenomenon of the rise of a cosmopolitan civilisation in the
area ruled by Rome in the first two centuries of our era. The
New Testament student has need, therefore, for a vast body of
information—historical, literary, archaeological, philosophical,
religious; for there is no telling when some isolated fragment
of a text or some stray record of a religious idea or usage from
far outside the immediate area of Palestine may throw light
upon the book before him. The events and the ideas reported
in the New Testament were by no means purely local. These
things were not "done in a corner" (Acts XXVI. 26) but in the
middle of the wide stage of the Hellenistic world under the
early Roman Empire.

    Wilhelm Windelband began Part II of his famous *Lehrbuch*
for the History of Philosophy, written in Strassburg in 1889–91,
by showing how the intellectual development of Hellenistic
culture arose in three stages: Hellenism, Romanism, Christianity. The third stage represented the fusion and union of the
first two. More recently Professor Werner Jaeger has traced
the Hellenising of Christianity in three stages, especially in its
ethical relations and emphases (see his article, "Paideia Christi,"
in the *Zeitschrift für die neutestamentliche Wissenschaft*, L (1959),
pp. 1–14). This process, beginning early, reached its culmination in the fourth century with Basil of Caesarea, Gregory
Nazianzen, and Gregory of Nyssa; after this, Christianity became the dominant spiritual force in the Roman world-empire.
The highest norm for Christian teaching, as Jaeger correctly
observes, was Holy Scripture, not some external authority;
Holy Scripture contained the whole of Christian *paideia* (p. 10).
And he adds: "Aller antike Humanismus, wenn man von
einem solchen sprechen darf, wie es mir richtig scheint, ist an
dem Gedanken der Nachahmung eines Vorbildes orientiert."[1]
This is a principle not far removed from that described in the
saying of Professor A. N. Whitehead which Sir Richard

---

[1] "All ancient humanism, if one can so describe it—and it seems to me a
proper term—is oriented toward the imitation of some example."

Livingstone took as a text for his book *On Education* (Part II, p. 50): "Moral education is impossible without the habitual vision of greatness." Plato also said something much like it (*Republic*, 401 c). The purely sociological explanation of the rise of Christianity as an accidental fusion of religious forces is as impossible as the old "fortuitous concourse of atoms" which Cicero and the Cambridge Platonists and half the scientists of the nineteenth century criticised the Epicureans and other "atomists" for maintaining.[2]

It must be our aim, then, as students of the New Testament and of early Christian history, thought, worship, theology, ethics, and organisation, to set the record against the total background of the times. Only so can we hope that the full force of its finer nuances will come out clearly and strongly and enable us to interpret the sacred volume adequately and worthily. We do not deny that anyone can read the New Testament, or the Bible as a whole, for himself, and find in it rich spiritual nourishment, bright illumination, a guide to life. But if he is to expound it publicly and officially, and for the benefit of others than himself in the privacy of his own "solitariness," he must be equipped with as much of this fuller knowledge as he can possibly acquire. Naturally this will also enrich his own private study of the New Testament: but his primary aim as a teacher must be "rightly to handle the word of truth" (II Tim. II. 15).

The design of this book is to survey, in Chapters I–III, the Hellenistic heritage of the first century, in religion, education, and philosophy; summarising, in Chapter IV, the total world scene confronting early Christianity, and pointing out, in Chapter V, the unique and all-important factor of acquaintance, on the part of many Greeks and Romans, with the Hebrew Scriptures in the Greek translation, the Septuagint—a factor which can hardly be overrated in the geographical spread of the Church, the intellectual formulation of its message, and the development of both its worship and its theology.

---

[2] The phrase goes back to Cicero. See *De natura deorum*, I. xxiv (§66): *nulla cogente natura, sed concursu quodam fortuito*: "Heaven and earth were formed, not by any compulsive force of nature but by the accidental collision [of atoms]." But what is rejected by science and philosophy is sometimes accepted by the humanities, and history has sometimes been viewed as the adventitious interplay of blind "forces," social, economic, political, and religious.

Chapter VI deals with the most crucial stage in the whole process, the spread of Christianity and the creation of the New Testament: it was early Gentile Christianity which produced the New Testament, and which gave the Church its formal expression in ministry, worship, and creed. Chapter VII deals with the place of Paul in this process, a place sometimes contested or denied, more often exaggerated. I agree with my eminent successor at Union Theological Seminary, Professor W. D. Davies, that Paul was a Pharisee—*always*. Chapter VIII undertakes to summarise the whole and draw the loose threads tight: the New Testament, the Church's book, is the book of the Greek-speaking Gentile Church, the Church of the first three or four generations of Christianity in the Western world, under the early Roman Empire—in the world, that is, of Roman Hellenism. Considering all the factors studied in this wide survey, is it any wonder the early Church viewed its own origin as in "the fulness of the time" (Gal. IV. 4, A.V.)?

The contents of the book formed the substance of my lectures on "The Hellenistic Background of the New Testament" during the academic year 1959–60 when, as a senior Fulbright scholar, I was a guest of Oxford University. Some of the lectures were also delivered at other universities—Cambridge, Bristol, Birmingham, Manchester, Durham, at St Augustine's College in Canterbury, and at William Temple College in Rugby. More recently I gave a brief course on the same subject at Trinity University in San Antonio, Texas. The first chapter, "The Greek Religious Heritage," was used in a lecture at the Metropolitan Museum in New York, in Professor Gilbert Highet's course, "The Classical Tradition." It was also presented to the Oxford Plotinus Society at a meeting in Balliol College. The substance of the chapter "Paul the Pharisee" was delivered as the Mary Fitch Page Lecture for 1960 at the Berkeley Divinity School in New Haven, and is included here by kind permission of the Dean, the Very Rev. Richard Wilmer. The Note on *Religio Licita* was read at the Third International Conference on Patristic Studies, held at Oxford in September 1959, and is included in this volume by the kind consent of the Secretary, the Rev. Dr F. L. Cross, Lady Margaret Professor of Divinity, and of Dr Johannes Irmscher of the Deutsche Akademie der Wissenschaften in Berlin, who is editing the papers for inclusion in the forthcoming volume of *Texte und Untersuchungen*. Other material has appeared in the *Anglican Theological Review*, chiefly in reviews of Professor Martin P. Nilsson's *Geschichte der griechischen Religion* in VOLS. XXX, pp. 64–7, and XXXIV, pp. 11–26. For kind permission to revise, rewrite, and reprint this material I am indebted to the editor, Professor John S. Marshall of the University of the South.

Except where otherwise stated, the Scripture quotations are taken from the Revised Standard Version of the Bible, copyrighted 1946 and 1952 by the Division of Christian Education, National Council of the Churches of Christ in the U.S.A., and used by permission.

# Contents

|                                                                          | PAGE |
|--------------------------------------------------------------------------|------|
| Foreword                                                                 | v    |
| I      The Greek Religious Heritage                                      | 1    |
| II     Greek Education and Religion                                      | 32   |
| III    Syncretism in Philosophy and Religion                            | 54   |
| IV     Hellenism under the Early Roman Empire                            | 81   |
| V      The Jewish Bible in the Graeco-Roman World                        | 99   |
| VI     The Gospel in the Early Gentile Churches                         | 113  |
| VII    Paul the Pharisee                                                 | 132  |
| VIII   The Emergence of Early Christian Doctrine                        | 148  |
| Appendix: A Note on *Religio Licita*                                     | 172  |
| Chronology: From the Death of Plato to the Building of Hagia Sophia      | 179  |
| For Further Reading                                                      | 188  |
| Index                                                                    | 209  |

# Chapter I

# The Greek Religious Heritage

One summer day, nearly twenty-seven centuries ago—it was the year 735 B.C. to be exact—a small expedition of Greek colonists was crossing the blue Ionian Sea and approaching the island of Sicily. The main body of the colonists came from Chalcis in western Euboea,[1] but some of them must have come from the island of Naxos, in the Cyclades, for the city they founded in Sicily bore that name. Their official leader, sent out by the mother city, was Thucles; but when they had landed and established their settlement, that summer long ago, they erected an altar in honour of their divine leader and ἀρχηγέτης, the god Apollo. This altar was still standing in Thucydides's days, three centuries later, and upon it the sacred deputies (θεωροί) always offered a sacrifice before sailing from Sicily to visit the games or to consult oracles in the homeland, e.g. at Delphi. The walls of their city were evidently built at once for safety's sake; as everyone knew, Naxos was founded a year before Syracuse, its Corinthian rival farther to the south. How well these walls were built is clear from the heavy lower courses which still lie firmly in place after all these long centuries and in spite of repeated destruction of the city.

Far up the cliffs behind the new town was a settlement of Sicels, whose graves have been opened in recent years by the Italian archaeologist Paolo Orsi. Part way up, about 250 metres above the beautiful sheltered bay, later stood Tauromenion, or, as we call it, Taormina, founded in 358 B.C., half a century after the destruction of Naxos by Dionysius of Syracuse at the end of the Peloponnesian War. But it may well have been a settlement of the Siculi long before. The very name is extremely ancient, with parallels elsewhere in the Mediterranean world, notably in Torino (Turin) in northern Italy. Some scholars think the remoter backgrounds of history, here in Taormina,

[1] Thucydides, VI. 3. 1.

include the Minoans. And here the modern student and tourist find an enchanted spot, one of the most interesting cities in the whole world, where every square foot is historic.

At the very top of the shelving cliff of Taormina lies the southward-facing hollow where once stood a Greek theatre, so placed that the audience could both listen to the drama and also rest their eyes, from time to time, by gazing off toward the bright blue sea beyond Schiso, or the curving beach as it swept on toward Catania, or Mount Aetna with its undying grey plume of smoky vapour and its majestic cloak of pure white snow. In time the Romans took possession, and a Roman theatre was erected upon the ruins of the Greek—it likewise destined to fall in ruin when the barbarians overwhelmed the city and destroyed every evidence of the civilisation they detested. Modern archaeologists have uncovered the ruins, and some have endeavoured to restore parts of the ancient theatre; their excavations have disclosed the foundation and footings of a building even older than the Greek or Hellenistic theatre. It was a shrine, or possibly a small temple; the heavy blocks of squared stone are still *in situ*, and their line veers off about 45° from the axis of the theatre. Is it possible that this shrine once belonged to the original Naxians, a temple built so high up that from it one could almost look over the horizon and see the Greek homeland? But this is not all. Not far from the theatre, down the hill to the north and just outside the Messina gate, stands the Church of San Pancrazio, one wall of which was once a side wall of the cella in the Hellenistic or Roman temple of Zeus Sarapis. The stonework is magnificent, and is still in good condition.[2]

Now all this fascinating scene with its long history is not only an illustration but also a symbol—a parable in stone—of the long story of ancient Greek and Roman religion, both of which were founded upon the ruins of earlier cults, and both of which retained within themselves the traces of far more ancient ideas and practices. Like nature's own chart of geology on a cliff in the Helderberg, north-west of Albany, where the stratification records many millions of years of terrestrial change, so here at Taormina we find the record and the symbol of fifteen

[2] See the illustration in Maria Santangelo's *Taormina and Its Environs*, Rome 1951, p. 72.

centuries and more of ancient Mediterranean religious history. But it also symbolises the difficulties which face the student of those religions: the ruins are commingled, and must be extracted one from the other, and with great difficulty reconstructed in their pristine form and with their original significance.[3]

For a long time it was held that the earliest stage of Greek religion is reflected in Homer. When Lord Macaulay wrote his famous essay on Milton (1825), he made two assumptions: that the purest poetry is the most ancient—an inference from the converse, the most ancient is the purest—and that "as civilisation advances, poetry almost necessarily declines" (and with it, apparently, religion!); and that "the first inhabitants of Greece . . . worshipped one invisible Deity", and that "the necessity of having something more definite to adore produced, in a few centuries, the innumerable crowd of Gods and Goddesses."[4] Both these assumptions are challenged today, and the second is most certainly wrong. When half a century later Mr Gladstone pursued Homeric researches in his huge study at Hawarden, with its three desks—one for political correspondence, one for ecclesiastical, the third for Homer—he also described the world of the Greek epic as *juventus mundi* (the world's youth) and the religion of Homer as a survival of primitive monotheism, which had been influenced by polytheistic ideas derived from Egypt.[5] It was the era of Max Müller and the Aryan theory of Indo-European origins, in language, religion, and culture generally. And it was the era which just preceded the rise of modern archaeology.

Between these older views and the outlook of today "there is a great gulf fixed." A number of vastly important discoveries have changed the whole outlook. Schliemann's excavations at Mycenae, Tiryns, and Troy, and Sir Arthur Evans's lifelong work in Crete added whole long chapters to the early history of Mediterranean religion, prior to the Greeks, and pushed its origins back by several centuries. Horace was right: "There were many men of valour before Agamemnon"; and, we may

[3] See my *Ancient Roman Religion*, New York 1957, p. xi.
[4] Everyman's Library edition, pp. 153, 165.
[5] *The Time and Place of Homer*, 1876, p. 245.

add, there were many men of religion. Instead of the blue-eyed, light-haired Aryans sweeping westward from India and southward from the Danube into early Greece, bringing with them pure and noble ideas of religion, we have the Minoans and Mycenaeans; instead of Homer being the earliest poet of the Greek people, he turns out to be a poet of the latest phase in a long transitional culture lying between a prehistoric "heroic" age and the beginnings of recorded Greek history. Instead of reflecting the common faith and practice of early Hellas, Homer's background is the one-sided, aristocratic, somewhat sceptical, already rather antiquated religion of ninth- or eighth-century Ionia. Alongside the bright and beautiful but sometimes melancholy and uncertain outlook of Homer is the far more dismal world of the average Greek, with his dark chthonic (subterranean) deities and heroes and his reliance upon far more obscure and more secret rites than those of the Homeric hecatomb with its roistering feast and accompanying games. In brief, as we now view the earliest stages of Greek religion, it was the poets—Homer, Hesiod, Pindar, Aeschylus, Sophocles, Euripides—who rolled back the dark surrounding realm of *Aberglaube*, superstition, and "primitive" cultus, and introduced a sunnier and saner view of the gods, the world, and human destiny.[6] But the religion of the poets was a fragile creation, and in the end the primeval superstition returned—like a forest creeping back relentlessly across a clearing which has ceased to be cultivated.

When the Greek peoples emerge over the horizon of prehistory, they are still at the stage of "primitive" religion—though what we mean by "primitive" is not quite clear. "Primitive" may of course mean what men thought and believed ten thousand years ago, or a hundred thousand, or a million. Perhaps we should simply say "prehistoric," and add, "no doubt at the latest level of prehistory." In any event, the earliest stage of Greek religion known to us is based upon a still earlier and more "primitive" stage, common to most of the early civilisations, and characterised by certain widely held beliefs, *motifs*, and practices: e.g. the need, and the possibility, of obtaining supernormal power, and the need, and the possibility, of cleansing after contact with what is defiling. In

---

[6] See Wilhelm Nestle, *Griechische Religiosität*, Berlin 1930–3, VOL. I, ch. I.

his great *Geschichte der griechischen Religion,*[7] Professor Martin P. Nilsson of Lund traced the long course of later influence and mutual involution of these two concepts, derived from the antecedent "primitive" religion of the early Greek world. Their strong and world-wide re-emergence in the Hellenistic and Hellenistic-Roman periods is one of the most notable features of that fascinating stage in the history of ancient religion.

Along with these basic urges, deeper than any rational conception or explanation of them, went many curious rites, including sacrifice, sacred meals, sleeping and dreaming in sacred places, the burial of grain or small pigs or jars of wine, and their later removal—practices for which Sir James Frazer and others of the "anthropological" school in the history of religions have found parallels all over the world. There were gross superstitions too—the cap of darkness, the efficacy of spells, even the terrible effectiveness of human sacrifice. The antecedents of early Greek religion were no different from those of many other ancient peoples in East and West. But the Greek miracle consisted in this: these darker elements were done away or put out of sight—at least for several centuries—and religion was humanised, rationalised, and moralised. That is to say, the best that men could think and hope for themselves or their fellows, in the highly civilised Greek city-state, was applied to religion, to their relations with the gods. Ethics and theology advanced *pari passu*, as they likewise did in ancient Israel: a higher conception of man required a nobler conception of God, a higher conception of God required a nobler conception of man and of human duty and mutual obligation.

The various phenomena which are studied in the history of religions are not all of equal importance, and certainly not all of the same antiquity. Chiefly we are concerned with: (*a*) *rites*, usually the most "primitive" element in a religion, and sometimes (as in the ancient Roman religion) characterising it throughout its history; (*b*) *mythology*, especially in the Greek religion (the Romans simply borrowed their myths from the Greeks). As a rule myths came later than rites, though not always, and had an important role in developing primitive rites into settled

[7] Two vols. Munich, 1940, 1950; 2nd ed. of VOL. I, 1955.

*cults*; myths were sometimes transferred from place to place, person to person; they also often influenced one another, and so did the cults; (*c*) *legend and history*. As myth was sometimes the earliest history (so Euhemerus and the Stoics held), it often gave way to legendary narratives, especially of founders, deliverers, heroes, early kings and leaders, migrations, colonisations, and so on; and since it was religious in content, such history was usually looked upon as sacred; (*d*) *theology*, which often resulted from criticism of the myths and the legends, usually under the influence of philosophical inquiry; but the beginnings of theology go farther back, to the onset of any rational thinking about the gods—e.g. that of Hesiod. The later Greeks assumed that Homer had a "theology," much as "theology" has been read into the Old Testament, the Koran, and other sacred books—of course with some justification, if a broad enough definition of theology is used; (*e*) *ethics*, which also developed, side by side with theology, out of "primitive" notions or standards of right and wrong, especially in communal relations, under changing conditions of society, and under constant criticism and the pressure of discussion, personal conviction, and need. Ethics is also reflected in Homer and Hesiod, indeed ethics seems to have flourished widely in the archaic age, but achieved its highest development in the later poets and the philosophers; finally, (*f*) *personal devotion*, what we call piety, what the Germans and others call *Religiosität*, religiousness (not "religiosity"); the hymns and prayers addressed to the gods and heroes were probably the earliest expressions of this personal devotion. Many persons think—I believe rightly—that personal piety reached its highest pre-Christian expression in the mysteries, for example those of Isis, where the individual (e.g. Apuleius) sought salvation and moral strength through union with or devotion to the deity—though one must not overlook earlier examples, some reflected even in Euripides. This piety sometimes went to extremes, even pathological extremes, as in Aristides the second-century Sophist, but it was also influenced by philosophy and rational thinking and was thus chastened and disciplined and deepened—as in the glorious prayer at the end of the *Poimandres*,[8] which ought to be set to music and sung in six parts like the Russian *Cherubic Anthem*.

[8] In the Hermetic Writings, Tractate I.

Holy is God, the Father of all!

Holy is God, whose will is performed by his own [divine]
    Powers!

Holy is God, who wills to be known, and is known by those
    who belong to him!

  Holy art thou, who by the Word hast created all things
    that exist!

  Holy art thou, of whom all Nature has produced the
    image!

  Holy art thou, whom Nature has not formed!

  Holy art thou, who art mightier than all power!

  Holy art thou, who dost excel every excellence!

  Holy art thou, who art above all praise!

Accept our spiritual and pure sacrifices [cf. Rom. xii. 1],
which are offered thee from [a pure] heart and soul [cf.
Ps. xxiv; Jn. iv. 24] that yearns after thee, Thou who art
inexpressible, unutterable, to be named only in the
silence. . . .

The ancient literature must be read closely, when we look for
traces of personal religion. For example, in Mime IV of Herodas
the god Asclepius has "brushed away" an illness "with the
gentle touch of [his] hand."[9] In Aeschylus's great *Prometheus*, the
suffering Titan suffers both *with* and *for* mankind, "the creatures of a day." He is like Euripides's Heracles, "mankind's
helper and mighty friend."[10] In Virgil, the suggestions of divine
gentleness sound almost like the Bible—but they have to be
looked for, and a hasty reader may not catch them at all. In
the *Metamorphoses* of Apuleius, Lucius says to the goddess Isis,
"Your hand alone can disentangle the hopelessly knotted skeins
of Fate, terminate every spell of bad weather, and restrain the
stars from harmful conjunction."[11] That is personal faith, not a
public discovery. Or take, for example, a prayer to Asclepius in
an inscription from second-century Attica: "These are the
words of thy loving servant, O Asclepius, child of Leto's Son:
How shall I come into thy golden house, O blessed one, O
God whom I long for, unless thy heart is favourable to me, and
thou art willing to heal me and restore me again to thy shrine,

---

[9] See my *Hellenistic Religions*, New York 1953, pp. 4–6.
[10] *Herc. Furens*, 1252.     [11] *Hellenistic Religions*, pp. 136–44.

that I may behold my god who is brighter than the earth in springtime? Thou alone, O divine and blessed one, art mighty. It is thou, who lovest compassion, whom the supreme gods have granted as a mighty boon to mortals, a refuge from their sorrows."[12] Over the entrance to the temple at Epidaurus was another inscription:

> Pure must he be who enters the fragrant temple;
> purity means to think nothing but holy thoughts.[13]

Or recall the saying of Porphyry: "To the gods, the best of first fruits are a pure mind and a soul undisturbed by passion."[14] Many of these phrases can be matched from Christian, Jewish, or Buddhist hymns and prayers.

It is sometimes said that Christianity gave the world a deeper consciousness of sin than the Greeks had possessed. But this is questionable. It gave men a different kind of awareness, and an awareness of other kinds of sin, an awareness due in part to the Hebraic inheritance of early Christianity. For example, pederasty was not viewed among the Greeks and Romans with the abhorrence felt by Jews and Christians. But for most sins, the Greek aversion and sense of guilt was as great as the Christian, though often it lacked the feeling of assurance of forgiveness which the Christian conscience possessed. One must distinguish between the sense of finitude and the sense of sin; yet both are inherited, sin and finitude. It is only the sins of an individual which are within his power to prevent or to undo. The Christian, of course, insists that he can do neither, as sin, like finitude, is inherited (original sin); and as for undoing them, his chief hope is repentance, restitution (when possible), and restoration by the forgiveness and the grace of God, mediated or proclaimed by the ministry of forgiveness and restoration of the Church or religious community. But there are parallels to both the sense of finitude and the sense of sin in ancient Greek thought; there was a growing sense of sin abroad in the world, in paganism, in Judaism, and (when it arrived)

---

[12] *Corpus inscriptionum atticarum,* ed. W. Dittenberger, Berlin 1873, VOL. III, p. 171 a. See L. R. Farnell, *Greek Hero Cults,* Oxford 1921, p. 277.

[13] Quoted by Clement of Alexandria, *Stromata,* v. i. 13.   See A. J. Festugière, *Personal Religion among the Greeks,* Berkeley 1954.

[14] *De abstinentia,* II. 61.

in Christianity, from the second century B.C. onwards. Yet one must read carefully and not overstate the case. When Plato said: "The unexamined life is not worth living," was he thinking of daily self-examination, as Seneca practised it centuries later? It is possible. But it is also possible that we have simply mistranslated the sentence: "A life without inquiry is not worth living."[15] This sounds somewhat more like Plato.

Furthermore, the conception of sin with which Christianity began—as it is reflected in the New Testament—was the ancient and really "primitive" conception and feeling of social pollution and defilement or sickness rather than the later medieval and post-medieval conception of purely individual guilt, which must be measured and punished before the bar of justice. In the Epistle to the Hebrews, in the New Testament, Christ is the great high priest who cleanses his people from pollution (Heb. 1. 3b, etc.)[16] rather than the omnipotent Judge at the Last Judgment, as in much medieval art and ecclesiastical sculpture. The later emphases on "justification" and "absolution" (these are, of course, legal terms) should not becloud the issue and obscure the genuinely ancient, more realistic, and far profounder Greek conception of sin in biological terms, which we also find in the Bible. Half the theological difficulties that have arisen over the doctrine of the Atonement, in the course of the history of Christian theology, have been the result of trying to state or to analyse or to interpret a biological conception—which can be illustrated from a hundred passages in ancient Greek literature—in the language of later Roman, medieval, and modern law.[17]

Next to the religion of the Bible, that of the ancient Greeks is the best documented in the world—but even so there are dark lacunae in our knowledge. Yet it is possible to make out, running through the records, certain main features which

[15] *Apology*, 38 *a*. So Liddell and Scott, *Greek Lexicon*, new edition. A life which does not explore its own meaning and significance, conditions, and limitations, for example the way Socrates went about asking uncomfortable questions, is barbarous—what Hobbes called "solitary, poor, nasty, brutish, and short." This was part of Plato's defence of the whole career of Socrates.

[16] See my commentary on Hebrews in Harper's Annotated Bible Series, or in *The R.S.V. Bible Commentary*, New York and Edinburgh 1962.

[17] See the article on "Atonement" in the new edition (1962) of the *Encyclopedia Americana*, and my *Basic Christian Beliefs*, New York and Edinburgh 1960, Ch. III.

characterise the Greek religion as a whole, clearly recognisable down to the fifth century B.C., and never wholly lost—we must remember that Greek religion existed for at least fifteen centuries and has survivals which exist to this day. First of all there was a quality of genuine humility. The wise counsel of the Delphic oracle was quoted everywhere and always: "Know yourself" (γνῶθι σεαυτόν), recognise that you are a mortal, do not presume upon special privileges in dealing with the gods; whatever your wealth or birth, "do nothing over-much" (μηδὲν ἄγαν); remember the famous examples of over-weening pride and self-confidence, the tragic figures of men and women who trampled upon the ancient virtues of reverence, shamefastness, awe, fear of the gods, and wronged their fellow mortals, and so by their ὕβρις brought upon themselves a fate above measure (ὑπὲρ μοῖραν), and were punished both in this life and in the next by the all-seeing gods.

Another quality which runs through much of ancient Greek religion is sobriety. The ancient Greeks were not at all the light-hearted, cheerful, ever-optimistic devotees of sensuous enjoyment, basking in perennial sunshine, as pictured by the enthusiasts for romantic classicism (more romantic than classical) at the end of the eighteenth century; rather, they were a very sober, industrious, and, if not godly, certainly a very sensitive people, who deeply felt the limitations and frustrations of our human situation. Indeed, Herodotus's theory of "the envy of the gods" was never wholly overcome. What the Anglican Prayer Book calls "holy fear" was a deeply ingrained attitude. If you took seriously the conception of the gods handed down in the traditional religion, you would be inclined to tread softly in their presence; you would not call undue attention to yourself; certainly you would not try to emulate them, and live like a god upon earth, for this would swiftly and surely earn their scorn and contempt, as if you were attempting to rival them. The Sophists, of course, did much to break down this ancient awe or reticence, but it was never wholly eradicated from the Greek soul. The Polish scholar Thaddeus Zielinski has insisted that "no other people ever loved its gods as the Greeks loved theirs";[18] but it is certainly possible for men to love God and *therefore* fear to trespass against him—the "envy of the gods"

[18] *The Religion of Ancient Greece*, trans. G. R. Noyes, Oxford 1926.

was only an extreme and picturesque way of posting a warning against human pride.

There was also a sense of fate, a realisation that certain things simply must be, and it is no use complaining or protesting: ὅ δεῖ γενέσθαι will surely come to pass with irresistible, inevitable power. Even the gods are enmeshed inside this network of inescapable necessity, prescribed by the dark-visaged Fate or Moira who stands behind the throne of God in many another religion known to history. This feeling, already present in Homer, provided a ground for the widespread belief in astrology and stellar determinism which swept westward from Babylon in the second century B.C. and later, and was all but universal during the opening centuries of the Roman Empire. It still survives: you can buy astrological almanacs, magazines, and guide-books at almost any subway station in New York. It had its good side: people did not "kick against the pricks" of an unhappy or unavoidable destiny, e.g. hopeless poverty, or physical injury, or irreparable personal loss. But it also had its evil side: for people accepted whatever came, without protest, and weakly submitted, enduring rather than attempting to remove political and social evils.

Another feature of ancient Greek religion was a certain quality of this-worldliness. Happiness must be found here and now, if anywhere, any time; the after life is gloomy and uninviting. In the unforgettable words of Homer, one "would rather be a slave upon earth, even with a churlish master, than reign in the realm of the dead" (*Odyssey*, xi. 488 ff.). But we recall that a similar note is sounded in the Old Testament: "The dead do not praise the Lord, nor do any that go down to silence" (Ps. cxv. 17). Nevertheless, out of this dark background of traditional religion, in both cases, there arose the hope of a blessed immortality, in the one instance as a result of the teachings of philosophy (chiefly of Plato) and the anticipations encouraged by the mysteries, in the other partly as a result of philosophy (as in the Wisdom of Solomon, a book strongly influenced by Greek thought), but more emphatically as a result of the heroic martyrdom of men who trusted God utterly, and threw away their lives in his cause (as in the Book of Daniel, and in II and IV Maccabees).

Thus the mysteries, especially those of Demeter at Eleusis,

guaranteed this happier future in the other world, but not immortality itself—which was taken for granted, from Homer down. "Glorious indeed is that mystery vouchsafed by the blessed gods, for death is no ill for mortals but rather a good."[19] As Pindar wrote, "Blessed is he who has seen these things and then goes beneath the earth; for he knows the end of life, and its Zeus-given beginning."[20] Or Sophocles, "Thrice-blessed are they who have seen these rites and then go to the house of Hades, for they alone have [true] life there—all others have only woe."[21] Or Aristophanes, "To us alone [in Hades] is there a sun and a joyful light—to us who have been initiated, and who live toward friends and strangers [alike] with reverence for the gods" (*Frogs*, 454 ff.). The later mysteries, e.g. those of Isis or Mithras, probably offered no more: a blissful rather than a sad and regretful state in the after life, but not the gift of immortality itself; except that, as Sophocles said, "they alone have life that is truly life" and deserves the name, "the others have only woe."

Finally, even by the end of the fifth century, but especially in the fourth, philosophy had begun to deal with the theoretical problems of religion and ethics, e.g. the problem of evil, the injustices of life both personal and social, the apparent triumph of evil and violence—a problem set all the more grimly in the forefront of the religious consciousness as the long Thirty Years War between Athens and Sparta drew to a close, a war utterly suicidal and dysgenic for Greece and for Sicily and Magna Graecia, a war from which Greece never recovered, a war which shook the very foundations of Greek religion. It is against this background (one may read its details in Thucydides) that Plato's heroic effort to maintain the justice of the gods must be studied, both in his *Republic* and in the later *Laws*; it is also against this background that his defence of Socrates must be viewed, and his belief in immortality—in spite of Socrates's martyrdom: indeed, it is the character of Socrates that provides his weightiest argument for immortality.

---

[19] The inscription of an Eleusinian hierophant, 94–91 B.C.; *Ephem. Archaeol.*, III (1883), p. 81, 8; quoted in C. H. Moore, *Religious Thought of the Greeks*, Cambridge, Mass. 1925, p. 71.

[20] Fragment 137; Moore, p. 71; Nilsson, *Geschichte der griechischen Religion*, VOL. I, p. 638.

[21] Fragment 753; Moore, p. 71. The language is almost identical with Pindar's; can it be traditional cult language?

This reflective trait in Greek religion was a fundamental characteristic, and one that proved inseparable from it and its influence, all down the later ages during which the Greek influence continued. For early Christianity, this feature was of paramount importance: it resulted in Christianity becoming, as Dean Inge remarked, "a philosophical religion from its beginning." The bond between religion and philosophy, and the later culmination of religious thinking in a system of theology (or in several systems) was wholly inevitable —granted the Greek genius and its fertilising energies.

At the same time it is noteworthy that Greek religion itself never produced anything like a Bible—though in later centuries Homer was often viewed as inspired—nor did it produce a church or a creed or a system of dogma or a body of eschatological beliefs, either cosmic or terrestrial. Without a transcendental deity who is one, sole, and supreme, the Creator God, it was impossible that the religious history of classical Greece should move along the lines of the Hebrew, Jewish, early Christian, and ancient Catholic development. In spite of later use made of the heroic epos—the victory at Troy— or of the repulse of the Persians in 490 and 480 B.C., there was no unifying *Heilsgeschichte* or sacred national history stressing divine guidance, such as the Jews possessed in the Old Testament and the Christians in the Old Testament supplemented by the New, the one beginning with the call of Abraham and the Exodus from Egypt, the other including the Resurrection of Christ and the beginning of the New Age. What would an ancient Greek have made of an oracle like the one in Zechariah XIV. 9, so dear to both Jew and Christian? "The Lord will become King over all the earth; on that day the Lord will be one and his name one." Greek religion never became a "book religion," like Judaism, Christianity, or Islam.

It is another feature of the history of Greek religion which is of paramount importance for later religious history that the type of Greek religion which was spread abroad by Alexander's conquests was chiefly the disillusioned fourth-century variety, not the vigorous, healthy faith of the seventh, sixth, and fifth centuries.[22] The internal weakness of fourth-century religion

[22] For its influence on Roman religion, see now Professor Kurt Latte's *Römische Religionsgeschichte*, Munich 1960, especially Ch. X.

was partly due to the work of the Sophists, but more especially to the exhaustion and collapse which followed the long fratricidal-suicidal Peloponnesian War, itself the background of the disillusionment and scepticism of the Sophistic movement. However, it must not be assumed that the end of the Peloponnesian War and the inauguration of the Hellenistic Age—a profound historical crisis followed by a consequent shift in social forces—marked a total change in Greek religion. Under the powerful influence of contact with the East after Alexander, especially with Egypt (not so much with Babylon or Persia), various tendencies which had long been native to Greek religion began to flourish with renewed vigour. We must not forget the ancient and "primitive" conceptions of power and holiness, with which Greek religion emerged from its barbarous pre-history; or the magical rites, the sacrifices, dances, oracles, amulets, the beliefs about the dead—who were dangerous, under certain conditions, especially when left unburied or untended, but could be placated and appeased; or the beliefs about daemons, friendly and unfriendly, centaurs, satyrs, Pan and the nymphs, all of which belonged to the lowest and most ancient stratum of inherited religious beliefs and practices, and survived right down through the classical age though often relegated to dark corners, at least by the educated. One might say, of course, that this is not a peculiarity of the Greek religion, but of the Greek view of the world, within which religion functioned; but it was religion which did most, it would seem, to keep this view of the world alive. Thus Greek religion represented a combination of surviving elements of Minoan, Mycenaean, and perhaps even earlier religious beliefs and practices with those of the immigrant stocks, Ionian, Dorian, and so on—as well as the later Homeric. The gods were partly indigenous, partly borrowed, partly Ouranian or Olympic, partly chthonic and subterranean. Some were relatively late arrivals, like Aphrodite, who came apparently from the East. One of the latest was Dionysus, who came from Thrace via Asia Minor, bringing with him the mystery cult which he inspired and in its wake the Orphic movement with a doctrine of individual salvation, a body of sacred scriptures, and a vivid eschatology. But the origins of Dionysiac worship and of Orphism go back to the archaic period (seventh century).

Hence, in spite of the old-fashioned tendency to limit the data for a study of Greek religion to the writings of the philosophers and poets, or to the architecture and sculpture of the fifth century, we must remember its darker and more mysterious phases; and we must remind ourselves that these were not later additions to Greek religion, but were old enough to have formed part of its very structure. What the Hellenistic age did was to shift the centre of gravity, so that certain old features became more prominent, others less so, while some wholly new features were added.

Probably the most important characteristic of the Hellenistic age, which began in the fourth century,[23] was the decline of the ancient Greek city-state, with its close-knit social bonds, its local cultus, and its devotion to the gods and heroes. The consequence—or possibly in some degree the cause—was a growth of individualism, of religious independence: the state no longer decreed the worship which the individual was permitted to render; men chose their own gods. Conversion, as Professor Nock has reminded us,[24] became a possibility. The foreign nations, especially the far older nations of the East, had gods which must be recognised by travellers and traders and foreign residents in their lands; and often one could recognise a familiar divine face under the strange disguise of a foreign vestment, crown, or throne: the identification of the Greek gods with foreign deities became common. Finally, the foreign gods made their way to Greek lands—though some of them were conspicuously unable to gain admission. The widest open door was in western Asia Minor and the islands of the Aegean, which were under the control of the Ptolemies for just long enough to permit the cult of Isis, for example, to gain a foothold. The westward march of the Persian Mithras, on the other hand, bypassed Greece, and left almost no traces in Hellas. The Greeks had older and better mysteries of their own.

One should not think of the Hellenistic age as wholly sceptical and non-religious. Thousands of inscriptions and

[23] I agree with Professor Hermann Bengtson that this new age began even before the time of Alexander. See his *Griechische Geschichte*, Munich 1950, new edition 1960.
[24] See his *Conversion: The Old and the New in Religion from Alexander the Great to Augustine of Hippo*, Oxford 1933.

papyri, in addition to the literary testimony, prove the contrary. It was a very religious age—in some respects almost too religious—uncritical, superstitious, and ever receptive to new ideas from whatever source. (A typical scene is Paul's visit to Athens, described in Acts xvii. See also xiv. 8–18.) Belief in the penalties of the underworld, and in ways of mitigating or escaping them, was widespread. The philosophers might argue against superstition, or proclaim the justice of the gods, however long delayed, or ridicule the sale of formulas of cleansing; but all this made no difference to the ordinary person. Astrology had been known in Greece for a long time, but it made new advances in the Hellenistic age; under the Roman Empire it became ubiquitous and all but universal. The inevitable accompaniment was a wide variety of magical or theurgic devices for escaping the rigid, iron-clad mechanism of destiny. Scepticism produced Euhemerism, the theory that the gods, like the heroes, had once been powerful, famous men upon earth, founders of cities, conquerors of nations, discoverers of the arts, law-givers and promoters of civilisation, who in recognition of their merits and their services to mankind had been made into gods and worshipped. Meanwhile, private piety, as seen in such attractive persons as Plutarch, flourished and abounded here and there. One of the finest examples of this piety is the cult of Agdistis in Philadelphia, in western Asia Minor; here the highest kind of moral discipline was attached to an ancient cult—which was now celebrated in a private house, as it would appear.[25] Phrygian religion produced confessions of sin and formulas of absolution or forgiveness. Finally, it should be recognised that the Oriental cults often taught a high standard of ethics.[26]

When we turn to ancient Roman religion, we are struck by an enormous contrast with the Greek. It was an ancient agricultural religion which was later adapted to city life, and then finally to the control of an empire—but it never wholly outgrew its original features as the local cultus of the old

[25] See my *Hellenistic Religions*, pp. 28–30; A. D. Nock, *Conversion*, pp. 216 f.; and other references given in my volume.

[26] See for example the Isis Aretalogy, translated in my *Hellenistic Religions*, pp. 131 f.

Italian farmers and herdsmen. It was greatly influenced from without, chiefly by the Etruscans and the Greeks; when the full tide of Greek influence had swept over it, bringing in Greek rites, Greek gods, Greek myths, architecture, and sculpture, some features of the old Roman cultus were completely obliterated. At least they were submerged and overlaid with new ideas, so that the best antiquarian experts, men like Varro and Plutarch, could not even guess the original meaning of many a rite and custom, word or office. Of course, in a ritual-istic religion, the meaning or explanation is not all-important: what matters is that the ritual works, and must therefore be continued. As Cicero said, "If we wish to compare our people with foreigners, we find that although in other matters we are only their equals or even their inferiors, in religion, i.e. in the cult of the gods, we are far superior."[27] That is, the chief feature of the traditional Roman religion was its ritual, its "cult of the gods"; the rest was mostly borrowed. When the Emperor Augustus undertook to "restore the republic" and did so first of all by restoring the ancient Roman cults and reopening the long-closed temples and restaffing the ancient priesthoods, he was acting like an ancient Roman—the cultus of the gods was the very essence of the Roman way of life. When he added to this his own private devotion to Apollo, it was a significant choice: in many ways Apollo was the noblest of the Greek gods. Horace's beautiful Ode to Apollo echoes this imperial devotion, and Virgil's exquisite Fourth Eclogue has for its theme, "Thine own Apollo reigns"—*tuus iam regnat Apollo*.[28]

What has been called the "conflict of religions" under the early Roman Empire was not altogether a competitive struggle. Some cults were entirely compatible with others, and one could be inducted or initiated into more than one—just as members of "lodges" in the United States often belong to more than one. This was another feature which differentiated Graeco-Roman religion from the Jewish and the Christian. The fore-most characteristic of pagan religion under the Empire was probably the growing importance of emperor-worship. This

---

[27] *De natura deorum*, II. 3 (§8).
[28] See also Horace's *Carmen Saeculare*, translated in my *Ancient Roman Religion*, pp. 182–4.

went a long way back, to the Ptolemies and Seleucids of the
Hellenistic age, who knew how to bring religion into "the
service of the kings"—to use Professor Nilsson's phrase. Under
the Roman Empire it was undoubtedly a policy of state; the
simple rite of acknowledgment of the benefits of the Roman
peace, of the sovereignty of the emperor, of the good will which
went with Roman rule throughout the world—who could
refuse the pinch of incense and the prayer that went with it,
unless he were a traitor, an insurrectionist, or a long-haired
fanatic dreaming of some impossible utopia? The worship of
the state itself, *Roma*, gradually gave way before the cultus
of the emperor, or was combined with it; and to the very end of
paganism some of the most loyal and devoted citizens failed to
see that this cultus interfered in any way with religious liberty
as they understood it.

Another characteristic of the opening centuries of our era,
especially the second to fourth, was the spread of the Oriental
"mystery religions." It is a popular idea nowadays that the
mysteries taught deep doctrines about the soul and the here-
after, and by their rites conferred immortality upon their
devotees. But, as has already been said of the earlier Greek
mysteries, the evidence is against these interpretations. What
they conveyed was not a body of doctrine but a soul-stirring
emotional experience, as Aristotle had pointed out long before.[29]
Instead of immortality, which was taken for granted in the
ancient world—or at least some kind of temporary survival—
the mysteries promised a happier, more blessed life in the future
world than could possibly be enjoyed by the non-initiate: that
is all. The mysteries of Mithras, for example, could be repeated
once in twenty years, refreshing the soul, purging it of sin,
renewing the spiritual youth of the devotee, and making him a
new person.[30]

As we have already suggested, the spread of astrology was

[29] Fragment 15; see D. Ross, *Works of Aristotle*, VOL. XII; *Select Fragments*, Oxford
1952, p. 87.

[30] The sole inscription (*Corpus inscriptionum latinarum*, VI. 510=H. Dessau,
*Inscriptiones latinae selectae*, 4152, in VOL. II, PT. I, p. 146), which reads *taurobolio
criobolioque in aeternum renatus*, comes from the late fourth century (13 Aug. 376),
and may very likely reflect Christian language—all but the first two words! In
English the inscription reads: "Reborn unto eternity by the blood-bath of the
bull and the ram." Aedesius dedicated an altar in Rome to the Emperors Valens
and Valentinian and on it these words were inscribed. See below, Ch. III.

another outstanding characteristic of late paganism, against which magic on the one hand and theurgy on the other were devised as means of liberating the human spirit from the tread-mill of mechanism, i.e. of mechanistic determinism. Still another feature, and in some ways another kind of liberation, was the growth of solar monotheism, especially in the third century, under the Emperor Aurelian. The victorious, invincible sun—*Sol invictus*—could certainly rescue people caught in the toils of daemonic, sub-lunar powers, and could even help to some extent those under the control of the apparently more distant planetary forces.[31]

Finally, and of permanent importance, the widespread influential development of philosophy under the Empire must be mentioned as characteristic of the time and its religion. Not only Stoicism, which had exerted the greatest influence, as many think, upon the Roman character, and Epicureanism, which had met the mood of the final decades of the declining Republic, but more metaphysical and more religious schools were represented: Eclecticism, Neo-Pythagoreanism, Hermetism, Neoplatonism—these more religious schools of philosophy were "sweeping up the fine gold dust" left by earlier cults and philosophies, as someone has said, and reminting it for further use. The enormous influence of Neoplatonism, for example, upon all later European thought, is certainly a proof of its adaptation to environment, if not of its permanent solution of the problems of metaphysics.

Eventually Christianity won this contest of religions, though the victory was much nearer to a draw than to the total conquest of paganism which old-fashioned writers and orators used to enjoy describing. The conception of a total victory of one culture over another, of one religion over another, is almost always an idealised projection—like the conquest of Canaan as recounted in the Old Testament, which also records the later protests against the "high places," showing that the old Canaanite cults still survived. To this day, traces of the old Graeco-Roman cults survive: the ancient Nereids are now ghosts; the festivals of the gods are sometimes saints' days; the beautiful ancient rite of the Ambarvalia, unforgettably described by Walter Pater in *Marius the Epicurean*, is still (or

[31] See *Hellenistic Religions*, pp. 62 f.

until recently has been) the blessing of the fields and the "beating of the bounds" at Rogationtide; the Pantheon at Rome, perhaps originally dedicated to the astral deities, became a Christian church; the basilicas became Christian houses of worship (like San Clemente in Rome) or baptisteries, or both (like the one at Ostia); the ancient titles were taken over—*Pontifex Maximus* is still one of the titles of the Holy Father; the "mysteries" came to mean the Christian Eucharist rather than pagan cults of initiation and renewal. All these were the result of a slow process of transition, not of a sudden break followed by a fresh beginning. In religious art the process was slower still; as Jean Seznec has shown,[32] the pagan gods survived until the Renaissance—and they certainly were living much later! Magic and divination likewise survived. Benvenuto Cellini describes in his autobiography a mysterious necromantic midnight rite in the Colosseum, when he and two others were able to wake the dead in that vast theatre—the living dead, emperors, the ancient Roman nobility, with multitudes of gladiators who still haunted the place. Astrology survived: among Protestants, Melanchthon was an expert astrologer—to name only one among many.

But all these matters are more or less external. The classical tradition in religion and mysticism goes far deeper. One cannot discuss the rise of Christianity without taking it into account. In spite of opposition and even of antagonism (as Tertullian said, "What has Jerusalem to do with Athens?"), in spite of the persecutions, in spite of centuries of bitterness and suspicion and mutual defamation, the debt of Christianity to the Graeco-Roman world is undeniable. There was also a debt, for a time, on the part of Judaism (witness Philo and Josephus, and the Alexandrian Graeco-Jewish writers); but eventually the influence was thrown off, and the ties with pagan language and literature were broken, though the study of secular literature was never wholly given up.[33] But it was the Christians who became full heirs to the classical tradition. The Christian

[32] Jean Seznec, *The Survival of the Pagan Gods*, trans. Barbara F. Sessions, Bollingen Series VOL. XXXVIII, New York 1953.
[33] As Professor Saul Liebermann has shown; see *Greek in Jewish Palestine*, New York 1942; *Hellenism in Jewish Palestine*, New York 1950.

schools in Alexandria and elsewhere took up at the point where pagan schools left off. Christian preachers and apologists quoted the classical poets—if only, very often, in order to refute them. It was the Christian Church which preserved as much of the ancient literature as has survived, by the slow patient work of copyists and correctors, schoolmasters and librarians, chiefly the parish school-teachers and clergy, and, in the West, the religious orders. They also preserved such Graeco-Jewish works as those of Philo and Josephus. Alas, that much more of the ancient literature was not preserved!—though we should be thankful for what we have.[34]

But the debt goes deeper still. The language of the New Testament, and therefore of early Christian literature generally, of the early Christian liturgy, of hymns and sermons, apologies and expositions of Scripture, was an example of the common or *Koine* Greek of the first century, which in religious circles, especially in Egypt, had already been influenced and coloured by Jewish usage, mainly by way of the Septuagint translation of the Old Testament, made by the Jews of Alexandria from about 250 B.C. This Jewish translation of the Old Testament into Greek was the Bible of the early Church, and influenced its thought and theology as well as its diction. And this translation itself, it may be said, had already been subjected to certain influences from the surrounding Greek world: the anthropomorphisms of the Old Testament were toned down, and God was described in language which made possible the philosophical doctrines of Philo, who was influenced by Plato, the Stoics, and even by Aristotle.

Christianity, as we shall see, took over not only much of the language but also some of the ideas of the late Hellenistic age, e.g. Stoic and Platonic ideas, in the popular form in which they were now a common possession of many, perhaps of most, educated persons in the Roman Empire. "The things that are seen are transient, but the things that are unseen are eternal," said St Paul (II Cor. IV. 18)—this is almost pure Platonism, though we expect, in the second line, a reversal of the present text: "The things that are seen are temporal; *eternal* things are *unseen*." Perhaps it is because St Paul was not really a philo-

---

[34] Experts have estimated that only about one-fourteenth of ancient classical literature has survived.

sopher that he wrote as he did. Or take the Stoic terminology: much of the ethical teaching of the Church was formulated in language already devised for such use by the Stoic teachers. St Ambrose's *De officiis ministrorum* is based upon Cicero's *De officiis*, though Cicero was only half a Stoic. Or take the conception of the *Logos*, the Reason, Mind, or Word of God by which the universe was created, by which it is sustained, and which—or who—became incarnate in Jesus of Nazareth. The Greek influence is clear, up to the last point. Philo, for example, never could have said that "the *Logos* became flesh and dwelt among us . . . we have beheld his glory, glory as of the only Son from the Father" (Jn. 1. 14). That is Christian language, and marks an advance, an innovation. Nevertheless, the basic concepts in Christian theology, from that day to this, were either derived from or influenced by the Hellenic or Hellenistic philosophers. For example, the conception of the nature and person of Christ, set forth in the ecumenical creeds, is by no means the old Jewish prophetic or apocalyptic conception, but one which has been moulded under the influence of Greek philosophy, especially after the time of Philo. As Paul Elmer More insisted, "There is a straight line running from Socrates to the Council of Chalcedon." Dr More, of course, approved that line of connexion. Those who disapprove it—like the old Ritschlians, who wanted to free Christian theology from its bondage to Greek metaphysics, and other more recent theologians, who appear to have no use for history—call it the intrusion of philosophy into the Gospel. Adolf Harnack described Christian dogma as the work of the Greek spirit upon the data of the Gospels. The chief point at present is that, whether they like it or not, Christian scholars recognise the influence of classical thought upon the Christian religion,[35] and the only question is, How early did it begin?

The successive stages in the history of early Christianity are easily recognised, though like all stages or divisions in history they overlap. As we shall see, the earliest stage was that of the Aramaic-speaking Palestinian community of Christian Jews who were followers of Jesus and looked for his return as

[35] See especially Edwin Hatch, *The Influence of Greek Ideas on Christianity*, new edition, Harper's Torchbook Series, New York 1957.

heavenly Messiah or Son of Man to judge mankind and inaugurate the Kingdom of God upon earth. Their theology was apocalyptic, i.e. it moved in the same circle of ideas as the books of Daniel, I Enoch, II Baruch, IV Ezra, and many other writings of that type. A survival of it may be seen in the Revelation of John, the last book in our New Testament. What connexion, if any, these early Palestinian Christians had with the sect which produced the Qumran documents, the so-called Dead Sea Scrolls, is not yet clear. One doubts if they really had any connexion—Judaism was a far more variegated religion in the first century than in the second, or later. This earliest stage of Christianity, which underlies the Gospels and their sources, and is presupposed (rather than explicitly represented) by the rest of the New Testament, seems not to have been influenced by Greek ideas. The oldest surviving Christian liturgical term, *Marána thá*, "Our Lord, come!" is purely Aramaic, and is an apocalyptic prayer, reflected also in the Book of Revelation and the Didache.[36]

A second stage began when, according to the Acts of the Apostles, the persecuted "followers of the Way" were scattered as far as Damascus and Antioch.[37] We assume that some may have gone to Egypt, since the relations between the Jews of Palestine and those in Egypt, especially Alexandria, were very close, and because there was much trade and commerce—and therefore travel—between the two countries. This scattering brought the Christian movement face to face with Graeco-Roman religious ideas and practices, just as the far-flung western Diaspora had already brought the Jews face to face with paganism, ever since a time early in the Hellenistic age, especially in Egypt, Cappadocia, western Asia Minor, and Rome. The necessity for translating not only the religious terms used by Christians but also their religious ideas into Koine Greek, the language of the whole Mediterranean world, now became more pressing than ever. Such a title as "the Man" or "the Son of Man," as applied to the exalted Christ, such a conception as that of the Kingdom of God, or the Resurrection, such a practice as baptism or the eucharist or the laying on of hands now had to be expressed—and to some extent explained

---

[36] I Cor. XVI. 22; Rev. XXII. 20; Didache x. 6.
[37] Acts VIII. I, IX. 2, XI. 19.

—in Greek. The fact that, even to this day, our religious language is basically Greek shows how thoroughly it was done. "The Kingdom of God" is God's βασιλεία in Greek, with the connotation of a realm, more often than it is the Hebrew-Jewish-Aramaic conception of *kingship*, *reign*, or *sovereignty*. "Baptism" is βαπτισμός, "dipping"; "Eucharist" is εὐχαριστία, "thanksgiving," as the beautiful prayer in the early second-century Didache makes clear. "Christ," in Greek χριστός, is an attempt to translate the Hebrew or Aramaic word Messiah (*Mashiakh*, *Meshikha*) which means "Anointed"—though the meaning was surely lost upon most non-Christian Gentiles; in some instances (e.g. Jn. 1. 41) the attempt was abandoned, and a Greek transliteration was adopted, *Messias*; eventually, *Christos* ceased to be a title and became only a part of the proper name, Jesus Christ. The title "Son of Man," for all its obscurity, was simply translated, either as "The Man" or "The Son of Man," no doubt to the further confusion of non-Christian Graeco-Roman readers. Aside from some of the more technical of these terms, the religious vocabulary of the earliest Greek-speaking Christian churches was taken largely from the Septuagint. This religious terminology was thus very largely the creation of Greek-speaking Jews, later borrowed and amplified by the Christians.[38] A good example is the word for *love*, both human and divine: it is ἀγάπη, rather than the older or at least more widely used ἔρως or φιλία. That it was much used by Jewish writers is clear not only from the Septuagint but also from such a popular religious writing as The Testaments of the Twelve Patriarchs. It was during this second stage, of which we are now speaking, viz. that of early pre-Pauline Gentile Christianity, which was already Greek-speaking and largely non-Jewish, that the use of this vocabulary began.

Paul was a cosmopolitan Diaspora Jew who placed an impress upon primitive Christianity which has never since been lost. His religious experience was peculiarly his own, certainly not a normal Jewish religious experience.[39] But it is not true to say that Paul "refounded"—let alone "founded"—Christianity, or "warped it out of shape"; his language and his ideas both presuppose the early Gentile Christianity which was in existence

---

[38] Cf. C. H. Dodd, *The Bible and the Greeks*, London 1935.
[39] See below, Ch. VII.

before his conversion to the new religion. For example, the title "Son of God" was applied to Christ before Paul became a Christian; and this certainly was not a traditional Jewish messianic title, but a Greek title for a divine being, usually for a saviour or benefactor of the human race, like Asclepius or Heracles or Dionysus. It was not the bare term, but the content or meaning poured into it, which distinguished its Christian use from the ordinary Greek and Roman. As all his epistles show, Paul's chief contribution was a far greater stress upon the person of Christ, his pre-existence, his incarnation, his suffering, his death, resurrection and glorification, and the present life of the Church and of Christians "in Christ." That is to say, Paul was a good deal of a mystic. Spiritual realities were all-important, as in his use of the Platonic formula we have already quoted, or in his saying, "To me to live is Christ, . . . to die is gain" (Phil. I. 21)—another saying that can be matched from Greek thought, at least the latter part of it. For Paul, the most important and most transforming of spiritual realities was the new life in Christ, experienced by him and, as he supposed, by all other Christians. For him Christ *was* the Spirit, or *lived in* the Spirit, or *mediated* the Spirit—a mystic can make all three statements, and they need never be logically harmonised. All three are true, in turn, and therefore simultaneously.

Paul's second great contribution was the actual geographical extension of Christianity to Asia Minor and the Aegean basin. How the Church got to Rome we do not know, but it was there before Paul arrived, as his own Epistle to the Romans shows. Peter and Paul were martyred there in A.D. 62 or 64, according to tradition.

The following period, the stage of Christian expansion and development from 65 to 100, included the writing of the Gospels—Greek books, the earliest of which (Mark) sets forth the traditions about Jesus in an order which some scholars describe as "dramatic," i.e. following the canons of Greek dramatic writing.[40] Certainly there is in the story a gradually growing tension, a καταστροφή at the end, and a final solution

---

[40] But see Abp. Philip Carrington, *The Primitive Christian Calendar*, Cambridge 1940, and *According to Mark*, Cambridge, 1952, for another and more probable order, that of the ancient Christian Jewish liturgical year, with whose festivals the gospel lections appear to have corresponded.

in the resurrection of Christ. Luke–Acts is an apologia for Christianity, in historical form, designed to show that Christianity was not inimical to public law and order, and was entitled as a Jewish sect to the same consideration at law that Judaism enjoyed.[41] Its author aimed to write as a Hellenistic historian, as his Prologue suggests (Lk. i. 1–4). Matthew is a didactic arrangement of Jesus' life and teaching; one might almost call it the first religious education text used in the Christian Church.[42] It is written in excellent Greek. John is still another kind of gospel, a sacred drama, a prose poem designed to counteract the growing Gnostic and Docetic teachings of the early second century, according to which the man Jesus was unreal, a phantom deity, a divine aeon who walked the earth briefly and then departed before the hollow shell of his physical body was nailed to the cross—the entire Gospel of John is a protest against this travesty of history. In summary, the whole series of the early canonical gospels (we are not now speaking of the later, non-canonical ones) are Greek books, designed to meet the situation which the Church faced in the Graeco-Roman world after the death of the first generation of Christian leaders, those who hitherto had borne the witness of the oral tradition. The time had now come for the Christian "gospel" *(εὐαγγέλιον)* or "proclamation of the good news of salvation" to be put into writing.[43]

The stages that followed, some of which are reflected even in the New Testament, attest the *rapprochement* (or in one case, the Revelation of John, the antagonism) between Christianity and the world of Graeco-Roman religious thought and culture. The great problem for the historian is to trace the steps of this *rapprochement*.[44] The Apologists, who wished to be considered philosophers; the writers of Christian romances, some of them found in the Apocryphal New Testament; the historians; the letter-writers; the exegetes or expounders of Scripture—all these writers worked more of less in the genres of contemporary

[41] See appendix below, *Religio Licita*.

[42] See my commentary in Harper's Annotated Bible Series, or in *The R.S.V. Bible Commentary*, New York and Edinburgh 1962. Cf. art. "Matthew, Gospel acc. to," in *The Interpreter's Dictionary of the Bible*, New York 1962.

[43] For a fuller account, see my book *The Gospels, Their Origin and Their Growth*, New York 1957; London 1959.

[44] See Robert M. Grant, *The Sword and the Cross*, New York and London 1955.

Graeco-Roman literature. The early Christian literature belongs in the history of Greek literature, as Wilamowitz and von Christ have shown; so likewise the Latin Christian writings belong in the general history of Latin literature. But the Christian writers brought to their work a new element, a new inspiration, quite foreign to the Graeco-Roman world. For one thing, they had a conception of history as linear and headed toward a goal, rather than cyclical and endlessly repetitive. Another was their conception of man as a creature of God, but sinful, disobedient to his Creator, and in conflict with himself—an idea anticipated by the old Orphics, and more faintly even by Plato and certain of the tragedians (as reflected in various examples of high-handed wickedness which they portrayed or took for granted), but never developed to such a degree in earlier Greek literature as it was by the Christians. Still another example was the conception of redemption and divine forgiveness as something which went beyond mere restoration to an earlier but temporarily forfeited state of happiness, and included a total transformation of the "inner" man and a guarantee of his "salvation" in the life to come—i.e. a state of safety, welfare, *salus* or σωτηρία, not a mere act of rescue. These ideas were shared, to a degree, by the Hermetic writers and the Gnostics, for whom salvation consisted in the imparting of secret knowledge about the soul, or the nature of the universe, or the purpose of God. These latter ideas were Greek in origin, for the most part. But no one called them a "gospel," "good news," unless he were trying to supplant or outbid the normal Christian teaching.

What the early Church did, in creating its theology—as distinct from its propagation of the gospel—was to combine the traditional Hebrew-Jewish-Old Testament ideas, derived from the Septuagint, with the Greek current flowing from primitive times and emerging, purified and sparkling, in Pindar and the tragedians and then disappearing like an underground stream for hundreds of years until it re-emerged in the later Hellenistic age. The "mystical" Plato of the Middle Ages and the Italian Renaissance—the Plato of Marsilio Ficino—was a figure derived from private and unofficial interpretation of his writings, not the frigid over-cautious logician of the official Academy. It was this religious interpretation of Plato which underlay large

tracts of patristic theology, especially in the East, and appealed
so strongly to the Middle Ages and the Renaissance. Combined
with this, it is true, were such "mystical" theories as those of
the Pseudo-Dionysius the Areopagite, whose *Heavenly Hier-
archies* formulated the doctrine of angels, i.e. the nine angelic
orders, which remains a part of orthodox theology to this day
in the Roman, Anglican, and Eastern Orthodox Churches.
Combined with it also was the logic of Aristotle—the only part
of his teaching known to the early Middle Ages, and derived
mainly from Latin translations of Arabic translations of Syriac
translations of the original Greek; but by the early decades
of the thirteenth century, manuscripts of the remaining
treatises were available, and "the philosopher" became better
known.[45]

The result was that fusion of Aristotelianism, Platonism, and
Catholic dogma which is known as Scholasticism, a system of
philosophy culminating in theology which seemed to be the
final achievement of human reason when illuminated by divine
revelation. The later formulations of theology, both Catholic
and Protestant, are deeply indebted to the Schoolmen, especially to Thomas Aquinas. Moreover, the Catholic Church itself,
that majestic all-embracing synthesis of revelation, philosophical
speculation, ethics, and the institutions of the ministry, the
sacraments, the system of liturgical worship, the rules of the
religious orders, the formulated teachings of moral theology—
all this, as someone has said, is the most complete and perfect
fulfilment of the prophecy contained in Plato's *Republic* that
the world has ever seen. It does not derogate from the uniqueness of a Christian institution that it was foreshadowed in
pagan antiquity. Did not the Greek and Latin fathers declare
that the coming of Christ had been predicted by pagan poets
and seers, and especially by the various Sibyls?

Medieval mysticism likewise had antecedents in the ancient
world: in fact, from what source could it have been derived

---

[45] The Schoolmen became acquainted with the whole of Aristotle's *Organon*
after 1128. St Augustine and Simplicius, Boethius and Cassiodorus had studied the
"Categories" in their time; but in the Dark Ages the work was chiefly cherished
by Syrian and Arab scholars. The Latin scholars had the "old logic" of Aristotle;
but the "new logic" and the rest of his writings came to them via the Arabs after
the third decade of the twelfth century. See J. E. Sandys, *History of Classical
Scholarship*, VOL. I, Cambridge 1903, Chs. 28–30.

if not from the mystical strain in Greek religion?—certainly
not from the Hebrew or Jewish.[46] If one insists that it came
from the Orient, the reply is that the Orient had influenced
Greece at a very early age, and that by the fifth century (as we
see, e.g., in Orphism) this type of thought was practically
indigenous in Greece and in Magna Graecia (witness the
Pythagoreans). And the allegorical exegesis of the Scriptures,
for which the Middle Ages are famous, had come down from
Greek antiquity, by way of the Stoics, Philo of Alexandria,
Clement, Origen, and the biblical exegetes in the West.[47]
There was also a school which more strongly emphasised the
literal meaning of Scripture, with less attention to the allegorical; but this school was more influential in the East than
in the West. Its contacts with Judaism (e.g. around Antioch
and also in eastern Syria) account for its sane historical view
of the Old Testament. That it dropped into the background for
some centuries only made its re-emergence at the Reformation
the more remarkable. When John Colet returned from Italy
in 1496 and began lecturing at Oxford on the Epistles of St
Paul, he said that they must be studied just as one would
study the letters of Cicero, not with a preconceived system of
mystical or allegorical interpretation to which they could be
made to conform.[48] And that was the beginning of the English
Reformation.

Let us summarise. The survivals of the classical tradition in
Western religion are almost as marked as in Eastern, and are to
be seen both in liturgy and in theology, in thought as well as in
language, in ethics as well as in dogma. The early Christian
religion is like the Swiss Rhône, below Geneva, which combines
the blue waters of Lac Leman with the white waters of the
melting glaciers from the Arve, and the two currents flow
along side by side for a long way before they mingle. The
Graeco-Roman, or classical, inheritance was just as real and
effective as the Hebraic-Jewish, especially in the elaboration
of Christian theology. And this composite religion, speaking

[46] The later Jewish mysticism itself has to be explained, and not wholly from the
Old Testament or earlier Jewish antecedents. See Gershom G. Scholem, *Major
Trends in Jewish Mysticism*, Jerusalem 1941; 3rd revised edition, New York 1961.
[47] See R. M. Grant, *The Bible in the Church*, New York 1948; rev. edition 1953.
[48] The method is still sound. See Ch. VII.

historically, lies at the heart of Western culture, just as truly as Buddhism and Islam lie at the heart of the cultures they have influenced. Religion is not inherited as an extraneous thing, whether decorative or not, whether a burden or a support—it is "stuff o' the very stuff" of which life is made and by which life is shaped. In spite of the criticism of classical religion in its decadence, by ancient Christian apologists and theologians, the evidence for the use of Graeco-Roman philosophical ideas by the early Church is overwhelming. Moreover, it was Christianity that kept the classical tradition alive through the long dark age that followed the downfall of the Roman Empire, that brought it to a fresh revival and new fruition in the successive periods of renaissance which culminated in the fifteenth century, and that finally handed it on—or what was left of it—to the modern world. The debt is a mutual one: the classical tradition is obligated to Christianity, and vice versa. Later theological reactions against classical religious ideas, and even against the idea of human culture in general—as is conspicuously apparent in one very popular school of continental theology today—do not blot out the fact of the Church's debt to Greece and Rome, or the obvious historical continuity of Christianity as a whole with its own past, rooted in the ancient Hellenistic-Roman world. Theologians may ignore history and philosophy if they choose; they cannot destroy them. Many modern writers have pointed out our indebtedness to the Greeks in the realm of scientific and artistic ideas, for the concept of history, and other major ideas by which we live; but it should be pointed out that these ideas are also of significance for religion. The ideas of cosmological order, of law (both natural and human), of destiny, of moral standards governing men and nations—these classical ideas reinforce those set forth in the Bible and enshrined in the Jewish and the Christian faiths. Other ideas, such as the cyclical idea of history and its endless repetitions, of human nature as limited, not depraved, of folly and stupidity as related to sin—and to sinfulness—of the future state as that of the soul's immortality, not the resurrection of the body—these ideas have been influential. The Christian religion has modified them; yet it has not denied or abolished them. Except for modern science, which dates from the seventeenth century, the major cultural heritage of the

West has been derived from Greece and Rome; its religious inheritance is a combination of the classical tradition with the Hebrew, Jewish, and primitive Christian traditions. In one sentence, the classical tradition of religion and mysticism is now chiefly embodied in Christianity.

# Chapter II

## Greek Education and Religion

Hellenistic culture may be said to be concentrated in Hellenistic education. The school was the most characteristic institution in the Greek world, as the synagogue was the most characteristic in the Jewish world and the basilica, the forum, or the law-court was the most characteristic in the Roman. Not the Greek language only, which became the language of the civilised world, or trade, or art, or architecture, but education: this is what made Greece "the light" not only of Hellas but of the whole earth. Hellenistic religious history cannot be separated from Hellenistic culture as a whole, and that means it cannot be separated from education. True, there were religious cults and movements under the early Roman Empire which did not bear the Greek stamp, at least not conspicuously (though some of the Oriental cults had been adapted to Greek ritual and ideas); but these semi-hidden, subterranean movements were themselves not wholly characteristic of the age, in spite of views popular at the present time. The special emphasis in education was practical, and centred in oratory, the art of persuasion. Not only was this art—as "rhetoric" it embraced literature as well—the most assiduously pursued branch of learning under the successors to Alexander, but it became even more so under the Empire. Roman education was even more "practical" than Greek. It both centred and culminated in rhetoric, taught and exemplified by the *rhetores*, who were both rhetoricians and orators. A career in law and administration was open to men who mastered this art. Cicero was the great exemplar—this fact helps to account for the survival of most of his works, while those of his teacher Posidonius, the philosopher, have perished. The bright young coterie about Pliny the Younger were all interested in oratory, and the "old boys" coming back to the school were eager to know who were the most promising public speakers among the lads now finishing their course. The sound and sober principles of

Quintilian summed up several generations of superb skill in teaching the art, and his *Institutes* remained the standard textbook for sixteen centuries.

The influence of oratory on other branches of literature is most marked in the writing of history, which is frankly designed to persuade, Tacitus almost as frankly as Livy or the Augustan Histories. It was the vogue in the later decades of the first century for historians to be brought in to entertain the assembled guests at an afternoon party by reading from their latest chapters—though we must not forget the precedent set by Herodotus, who read his Histories at Olympia during the Games. Lucian's essay, *How to Write History*, is a caustic criticism of the lesser breed of history-writers in his time, who "fail to realise that the dividing line between real history and laudatory panegyric is no narrow isthmus but a great wall—as musicians say, they are two diapasons apart!" And he tells the story of Aristobulus, one of Alexander's encomiasts, who read the King a passage describing his combat with Porus, full of imaginary exploits and achievements: Alexander grabbed the book and threw it into the river—they were sailing down the Hydaspes at the time—and said, "Aristobulus, you deserve to be thrown in too for fighting single-handed for me and killing elephants with one javelin-throw!" Intelligent readers despised such drivel, so Lucian assumes, but they tolerated it. And even he himself recognised the opportunity which the writing of speeches afforded the historian: "If it is necessary to introduce someone making a speech, by all means let it be in character and suitable to the subject and as clear as possible. And then comes your chance to turn *rhetor* and show yourself a master of eloquence!" The speeches were evidently the main interest of many readers—from the master down, beginning with Thucydides, whose speeches are still viewed as the most magnificent parts of his work. Schoolboys in the Hellenistic age memorised these speeches. Among the papyri is a volume of Thucydides's speeches, culled out for study, obviously a pupil's textbook. Lucian also suggests that if mythical material comes to hand it must be used, but "sparingly: you yourself mustn't believe it altogether, but let your audience [your *hearers*, not your readers] decide whether it is true or not—so you will run no risk, not leaning to one side or the other!" Lucian's testimony—and criticism—is the more valuable in that he himself is knee-deep in the popular stream of literary composition, history included. No doubt many of our own contemporaries would echo his words: "The run of the mill artisans in the writing of history think they need no advice, any more than for eating and walking; there is nothing tricky about it; anyone can write history who takes whatever comes to him and puts it into words."[1] This was almost Juvenal's rule, *Quicquid agunt homines . . . farrago est libelli.*[2]

But it was an evil day, unnoticed but nevertheless ominous, when the aim of the historian became the mastery of an art designed to please or persuade rather than to set forth the fundamental realities of the past, the great tidal forces which mastered historical events and determined the fates of nations—as in Herodotus's account of the clash between East and West; or Thucydides's account of the suicidal war between Athens and Sparta; or Polybius's account of the rise of Rome, monitored by a powerful destiny which the Romans themselves only half understood. History in the hands of orators was in a dangerous way. And oratory, rhetoric, literature in the hands of "practical" men was equally under duress. It all began in the fifth century B.C. with the Sophists, who undertook to show young men how to get ahead in the world, regardless of traditional ethics, religion, political loyalty, or common sense. These were the "practical" men against whom Socrates and Plato inveighed all their lives—Socrates paying for his temerity by the forfeiture of his life and Plato eventually substituting an ideal state for the impossible political mess in Athens, Sparta, and Syracuse, now dominated by the post-war go-getters bred up by the Sophists. One regrets that a more favourable account cannot be given of Hellenistic education under the influence of rhetoric and oratory. But the facts are indisputable. And when we come to the New Testament, the clear cold evaluation and rejection of the "wisdom of this world," the debaters and clever tongue-twisters who made the worse appear the better reason, who appealed to philosophy only for argumentative aids and to the great teachers only in order to refute or justify their disregard for them, ignoring whatever failed to chime in

---

[1] Lucian, *How to Write History*, §§ 12, 58, 60.
[2] "Whatever men bring me becomes material for a book." *Satires*, I. 85 f.

with and support the orator's brief—the rejection of Hellenistic education by the Christians, at least at first, was inevitable.[3] It took the better part of a hundred years for the Church to get inside the pagan schools and begin transforming them: the Apologists were converts to Christianity from Greek philosophy, and the Catechetical School in Alexandria was an educational institution designed to lead up to Christian religious teaching by way of the Greek classics, arithmetic, music, and the usual "liberal arts" (arts suitable to the study of freemen, not slaves).

This was not an altogether new idea in education. Plato's Academy contained an altar to the Muses; so did Aristotle's Lyceum; in fact these two schools were organised as cults (θίασοι) of the Muses. The great Alexandrian Museum, the foremost centre of Hellenistic learning and research, got its name thus, as a μουσεῖον.[4] Religion and education were accordingly closely related in the earliest decades of the Hellenistic age, before sophistry and oratory and the cult of success changed everything. Accordingly, the literary sources for Greek religion, along with what is left of ancient Greek literature as a whole, were preserved by those who shared this ideal of education. The almost total extinction of the records of early Roman religion is probably due to the totally different idea of education fostered by the "practical" Romans. Among the Greeks the records were redolent of the soil of their beloved homeland: the cults were "cults of the Greek states," as Lewis Farnell entitled his great work. For in the classical age religion was an affair of the city, which had its own sacral history, its own rites, its own mythology; and all this remained true in the Hellenistic age, even though the old city-state had now lost its independence and was caught up into the larger political units, first of the empire of Alexander, then of the empires of his successors.[5] The mythologies of various cities and districts were now written

[3] On the influence of Hellenistic rhetoric and oratory upon the New Testament, see "Rhetoric and Oratory," § 3, in *The Interpreter's Dictionary of the Bible*, 1962. See also, now, *Early Christianity and Greek Paideia* by Werner Jaeger (Harvard Univ. Press 1961), a brief but profound account which carries the story down to Gregory of Nyssa, and supplements the author's great three-volume work on *Paideia: The Ideals of Greek Culture* (Oxford 1943–45).

[4] Strabo, *Geography*, XVII. 1. 8; C 794.

[5] See "Greek Religion in the Hellenistic-Roman Age," in *Anglican Theological Review*, XXXIV (1952), pp. 13 ff.

up by experts, not only by the atthidographers, who compiled the sacred history of Attica, but also by the professional mythographers, e.g. Apollodorus, who wrote large works on all areas of Hellenic mythology. We also find people who are interested in foreign mythologies and religions—for example Strabo, who was interested in the Persian religion, and Julius Caesar who has left us a fair account of the Druids—not to mention the enormous amount of information preserved by Herodotus. Along with these went the "interpreters" of the myths. A favourite interpretation in the Hellenistic age was to identify the figures in mythology with great men in the past (Euhemerism); another was to identify them with the constellations in the sky. In addition to these interpreters of the myths there were also writers who collected details of the marvellous (the paradoxographers); and writers who compiled collections of hymns, some of them very ancient (e.g. the *Homeric Hymns*), some of them more recent, some of them addressed to the gods, some to the heroes, some of them filled with deep religious thought and genuine faith, some of them shallow, verbose, and artificial. In a word, it was a great time for compilers and encyclopedists, that industrious and indispensable tribe which is still with us, to whom we owe so much of our (nevertheless incomplete) knowledge of the details of ancient religion.

Along with the authors, as sources for our knowledge of Hellenistic religions, there are the inscriptions, and, for certain areas (chiefly Egypt), the papyri. The inscriptions really shed a great flood of light upon the actual religious life of the times. As the one over the door leading to the Etruscan collection in the Museum at Florence tells us,

HIC MORTUI VIVUNT
PANDUNT ORACULA MUTI

They record the appointment of priests and other officials. They list the officers (or clergy) serving at various temples. They set forth the rules governing the admission and exclusion of worshippers. They describe the statues and other ornaments of the temples, and they list income and expenditure. They record the resolutions of town councils relating to the erection of sacred edifices or statues. All these and many more subjects were recorded on stone for all generations to read—so certainly that the architect of Pharos, the famous lighthouse off Alexandria, recorded his true sentiments in stone and covered it with gypsum on which he inscribed the name of the reigning monarch, fully confident that in time the gypsum would wear away and his message to posterity would stand revealed for ages to come: "Sostratus of Cnidus, son of Dexiphanes, to the Saviour Gods [Castor and Pollux], on behalf of those who sail the sea."[6] Religious inscriptions are as important for the history of Hellenistic religion as coins are for political history. Perhaps the most interesting of all the inscriptions are those found at Epidaurus, tablets recording the miraculous cures experienced by worshippers of Asclepius. A vast number of inscriptions have survived, and are among our most valuable records of Hellenistic religion.[7]

As we study the Hellenistic records of the surviving ancient cults in Greece, Asia Minor, and the Islands, their festivals, their temples, and the whole institutional side of religion which they reflect, we are struck by the direct continuity of Hellenistic religion with the past. Religion is always conservative—perhaps the most conservative force in human society—and changes only under immense, one might almost say geological, pressures or cosmic attractions. The mysteries, for example, continued as of old. New mysteries were added, it is true, but the most popular in the Hellenistic age were still the most ancient ones, those at Eleusis, at Andania and elsewhere in the Peloponnese, the widespread mysteries of Dionysus, and those of the Cabiri—the "Great Gods"—on the island of Samothrace. It was a long time before the Oriental mysteries began their westward sweep in full earnest—though the control of the eastern Aegean by the early Ptolemies gave the Egyptian rites a toe-hold in the

[6] Lucian, *History*, §62.
[7] The student will find lists and description of the great collections in the articles on Epigraphy, Greek and Latin, in the *Oxford Classical Dictionary*. Or, in more detail, in Wilhelm Larfeld's *Griechische Epigraphik*, 3rd edn., Munich 1914, and in J. E. Sandys, *Latin Epigraphy*, 2nd edn. rev. S. G. Campbell, 1927. The New Testament student should make early acquaintance with Wilhelm Dittenberger, *Sylloge inscriptionum graecarum*, 3rd edn., 4 vols. Berlin 1915 ff. and his *Orientis graeci inscriptiones selectae*, 2 vols. 1905; Hermann Dessau, *Inscriptiones latinae selectae*, 5 vols. Berlin 1892–1916. A magnificent modern introduction to the subject is A. G. Woodhead, *The Study of Greek Inscriptions*, Cambridge 1959. It has everything the beginner needs.

West and North. So too the ancient oracles, especially those at Delphi, Dodona, and at the shrine of Amon in the Libyan Desert: these ancient oracles continued to enjoy popular esteem and use, and so did several in parts of Asia Minor. In fact, it even looks as though a kind of revival of the oracles took place in the second century B.C., and then later, in the age of Plutarch (second century A.D.), a decline. In time collections, i.e. books, of oracles enjoyed wide circulation, among them the so-called *Sibylline Oracles*, presumably derived from the Sibyl of Cumae described by Virgil (*Aeneid*, VI), and the later so-called *Chaldean Oracles*. In the Greek world it is noteworthy that many of these collected oracles came from remote places. It was thought that there were seven, or perhaps nine—there were really ten—great Sibyls of the various nations, the Persian, Egyptian, and others. Michelangelo was to use this idea, and also the designer of the windows in the south transept of the thirteenth-century chapel of Jesus College, Cambridge, where the Chaldean Sibyl, the Persian, the Erythraean (in Ionia), the Cumaean and the others are duly pictured. The Sibyls are also found in the floor of the nave of Siena Cathedral. The whole conception goes back to the Hellenistic age. The Romans had a Sibyl close at hand, at Cumae on the Bay of Naples. Her oracles and traditions may have been Greek in origin, but the later use of them, and especially the story of the sale to King Numa, seem to be Etruscan.

In the second volume of his already famous *Geschichte der griechischen Religion*, Professor Martin Nilsson has raised the question how the Oriental religions came to be provided with mysteries, since originally they were only old nature cults, vegetation rites, or nationalistic worships. It is interesting that the Oriental religions were as a rule headed by a professional priesthood, devoted exclusively to the cultus and to propaganda for it, and that in a foreign environment the members of the cult formed a distinct and separate group. But even this is no explanation, since in their homeland these cults were by no means "mysteries," in the later sense, and in the Graeco-Roman world they conducted services of worship, open to all, and public processions. There must have been, as Nilsson insists, some added factor which accounts for the production of mysteries which were open only to the elect. This factor he finds in the age-old native Greek mysteries, which in the Hellenistic age had already taken on a new lease of life and were being zealously observed and promoted. From the beginning of the Hellenistic age they had even begun to produce sacred books.[8] Their influence is observable not only in the later Roman emperor-cult, but much earlier in the transplanting of the Greek mysteries to Egypt—the wide spread of the mysteries of Dionysus, for example, is clear from the decree of Ptolemy IV. It seems, therefore, "much more probable that the incentive and the occasion for the creation of mysteries lay in [the example of] the age-old Greek mysteries than in the cult-organisation of the worshippers of a common deity in a foreign land." As Professor Rostovtzeff also held, the Oriental religions were transformed into mysteries by Greeks or half-Greeks, not by Orientals, and they did this in imitation of the model seen in the Eleusinian and Orphic cults. The transformation took place in small groups of devotees, and was one of the products of the great intellectual, moral, and religious crisis of the second and first centuries B.C. As the writer of the *Epinomis* had said, "Whatever the Greeks take over from the barbarians, they make it more beautiful and bring it to perfection" (987*d*). But the converse was not always true!

The mysteries, accordingly, were the further development and refashioning of various cults of foreign deities which the Greeks took over and revamped under the influence of the then dominant religious ideas. They did not possess a common mystery "theology," as is often assumed by popular interpreters today. Such a theology was simply impossible, as must be obvious from their complete disparity and differentiation. What could a "theology" of Isis and one of Attis have in common? Or Isis and Mithras? Further, the theory does not take sufficient account of the divergence possible—and actually achieved—in the allegorical interpretations of the cults and their myths as setting forth deep cosmological truths. That they were influenced by popular ideas is clear: see how astrology attached itself to one and another of them. For one of their main purposes was to achieve for their votaries a blissful after-life. And their success resulted in no small measure from the emotional satisfaction their rites provided.

[8] On the translation of an Egyptian sacred book into Greek, see *Oxyrhynchus Papyri*, VOL. XI, no. 1381, translated in my *Hellenistic Religions*, pp. 124–7.

How does this explanation fit the facts? Such cults as those of Isis and certainly Sarapis were no doubt refashioned to suit the demands of the now-Hellenised Mediterranean world. And they were provided with mysteries *à la grecque* by Greeks themselves, no doubt. In the case of the cult of Sarapis we know who it was—the liturgiologist Timotheos of Athens, invited to Alexandria to supervise the new ritual. But does the theory account for the mysteries of the Persian Mithras and the Phrygian Great Mother and the Syrian Goddess? These Oriental cults barely touched the Greek world proper (Hellas) and passed by on their westward journey. The probability is that Mithras got his mysteries from Greeks in Mesopotamia, in Cappadocia, or in Cilicia, where his cult was planted during the Persian rule (538–331 B.C.) and came westward only after Pompey's war with the Cilician pirates (67–66 B.C.): at least this is a major date in the history of the expansion of Mithraism. The mysteries may have been the creation, as Nilsson thinks, of some unknown religious genius. On the other hand, Cumont believed that it was Hellenised magi who transformed the cult;[9] and this view is supported by M. J. Vermaseren.[10] In any event, the ultimate source of the transforming influence was Greek. But certainly the *taurobolium* was a late addition to Mithraism, perhaps in Anatolia where it originally belonged to the cult of the Great Mother. And as for *Magna Mater* herself, the probability is the same as for Mithras: where else, or when else, would she have acquired mysteries of the Greek type if not from Greeks in western Asia Minor or the Islands during the period between her arrival in Athens (where she had a shrine in the Agora) and her widespread cultus under the early Empire—or, let us say, between her arrival in Rome, where she was severely restricted, and no Roman was permitted to join the cult, and the first century A.D.? In her native Anatolia the cult seems to have relapsed into barbarism early in the Hellenistic age, due not to Greek influence but to the wild native votaries of her consort Attis.[11] The thesis is a most interesting and illuminating one, not popular in British or

[9] See J. Bidez and F. Cumont, *Les Mages hellénisés*, Paris 1938.
[10] See his article "Mithras," in the new edn. of *Die Religion in Geschichte und Gegenwart*, VOL. IV, Tübingen 1960.
[11] Nilsson, *Geschichte*, VOL. II, p. 616.

American circles, but greatly deserving the fullest examination.

Turning to the personal side of religion, which of late has received much fresh investigation, notably by Fr A.-J. Festugière in his Sather Lectures at the University of California,[12] it seems clear that after, say, about 250 B.C. the ordinary individual paid much more attention to religion than formerly. The individual's view of the world and his religious attitude toward life come to far fuller expression. And religion is now far more concerned with the individual and his personal needs. He is still somewhat "too superstitious," even by way of being "very religious" (Acts XVII. 22). Theophrastus's picture of him, the δεισιδαιμονέστερος (see the *Characters*, 16), is an unforgettable sketch from real life. But he was probably no more superstitious than his ancestors had been, at least not in the early Hellenistic age. Later on, with the growth of magic and necromancy and all the "black arts," people probably became far more superstitious; but, as we have seen, superstition was a revival or re-emphasis of something that had existed for many centuries, probably ever since primitive times.

There was also a far more widespread belief in Chance or Luck *(Τύχη)* who may be either a good character or a bad one, just as a person's luck may be good or bad. On the whole, Τύχη seems to be a virtuous and trustworthy goddess: Αγαθὴ Τύχη seems to be referred to rather oftener than her opposite number—or mood! There was also a vast increase in the belief in demons, so much so that Wilhelm Nestle and others refer to the "demonising of religion." We see the parallel in the New Testament and in ancient rabbinic traditions—demons were ubiquitous in the Near East; but so were they also in Greece, by now, and in the West, while Thessaly and Egypt had been the native heath for multitudes of them from time immemorial. Belief in demons had probably existed from far back in prehistory; only it had got brushed aside by the great poets, Homer, Pindar, the tragedians; in Hesiod and Plato they are on the whole benevolent beings, as they are in Plutarch, but far less common than in the folk-religion. If we could only explore some of the back alleys in Greek religion of the sixth and fifth centuries B.C., it might turn out that people believed in demons

---

[12] *Personal Religion among the Greeks*, Berkeley 1954. Professor Nock blazed the new trail with his book, *Conversion*, Oxford 1933.

then as much as ever, and almost as much as in the fourth and third.

Offsetting this belief in Chance was the growing conviction that all events have been predetermined by the stars—whose motions, conjunctions, angles of distance, emergence and obscuration were all-important for the system of thought known as astrology;[13] it even rated as a "science" in the Hellenistic age and later, and survived well beyond the Middle Ages and the Renaissance into the modern world, at least until the seventeenth century. Originating in Babylonia and reinforced by the experts in Egypt, in both of which countries careful observations of the stars had been made for many centuries, the full impact of this type of thought came to be felt in the West by the first or second century. How widely respected it was may be gathered from the fact that the chief ancient editor of Plato, Thrasyllus, was the chief astrologer of the Emperor Tiberius and his instructor in astrology. It was Thrasyllus who arranged the Platonic Dialogues in tetralogies, i.e. in the order in which they were to be read by students: it is still the order of Burnet's Oxford edition.

The rigidly fatalistic view of life which astrology encouraged led in turn to a device for escaping the clutches of Fate: there was an immense increase in the practice of magic, which is evidenced by the magical papyri and also by the *defixionum tabellae*—tablets of clay or lead pierced with nails or other sharp objects, in the hope that the person named on the tablet would meet a bitter fate before long as a result of this occult attack, supernaturally supported. But these were scarcely religious practices, and clearly they belonged in the twilight zone beyond the range of religious faith and practice. Many of the magical papyri are in an almost illiterate kind of writing, which indicates the cultural level on which they were popular.

Beliefs regarding the other world, especially Hades, received fuller expression in the fourth and third centuries than they had received in the classical age; but Erwin Rohde's great work, *Psyche*,[14] has enabled us to realise that such beliefs were indigenous in Greece and elsewhere, and had been universally

---

[13] See especially Franz Cumont's *Astrology and Religion among the Greeks and Romans*, New York 1912.

[14] E. Rohde, *Psyche: Seelencult und Unsterblichkeitsglaube der Griechen*, 8th edn. Tübingen 1925; English trans. by W. B. Hillis, London 1925.

recognised and understood for many centuries. We must be careful not to be thrown off balance by the predominance of certain emphases in the literature of the period, and jump to the conclusion that what is now dealt with more fully must have been wholly absent from the minds of men long before. After all, literature does not reflect the totality of human thought and feeling in any epoch, but only the spot-lighted area of the special interests of the educated.

What characterises the religion of the Hellenistic age in general is chiefly a "new emphasis" moving in the direction of things occult. More attention was now paid to the mysterious backgrounds of man's life and to the miraculous—or at least supernormal—means of maintaining contact with the supernatural. There seems to be also a renewed conviction of what a Hebrew or early Christian would have called the "terrors" of the Lord. There was more emphasis on what is dim and grim in the backgrounds of man's life, and consequently more attention was paid to ways and means of meeting this situation. But instead of being something entirely new in the history of Greek religion, this emphasis likewise was probably a revival of what was old or even "primitive" in it (except for astrology). Looking backward, we can see what happened. The beautiful, quite rational, highly poetic, somewhat philosophical view of religion, so widely influential in the classical age, was created under the influence of the poets, Homer, Pindar, and the others down to Sophocles. The Homeric pantheon, with its relatively purified mythology—no cap of darkness, no thyestean banquets, no cannibalism—cast an increasingly powerful spell over the educated for several centuries, and left behind it the most perfect body of poetry ever written. But the day came when the Olympian hegemony began to weaken, and old myths, superstitions, even gods began to emerge once more from the shadows into which they had fled from the bright noonday of Homer's all too human Olympic society. It was "the end of an era" for the Olympians. Professor Gilbert Murray's phrase, the "failure of nerve," which was designed to explain what happened, is quoted by everyone, with or without its proper context.[15]

---

[15] See his *Five Stages of Greek Religion*, new rev. edn., New York 1925. This striking book is now in a paperback edition.

As an explanation of the fourth century *débâcle*, it assumes that the Olympian faith was too good to be true and that hence people could no longer go on believing it. Belief in the special protection of the Greeks as against the Persians, yes: yet Zeus was clearly impartial, as Homer insisted, and if he favoured one side against the other, *cherchez la femme*. Belief in the protection of Delphi by Apollo, or Aegina by the sleeping heroes buried there, yes; but their patriotic leadership had come to be questioned, in the case of Apollo, or had simply not been evident in the later war between Athens and Sparta as it had been in the repulse of the Persians. By the fourth century divine patriotism was as dead as it had been in Jerusalem after 586. Something better was required than local gods as *defensores patriae*. The Supreme God had more on his mind than the exploits of a band of raiders who rode into the grainfields of Attica and set them afire; but worse, he did not even seem to notice the outbreak of plague between the Long Walls or the diabolical and treacherous treatment of the people on Melos. This is not "failure of nerve" but stark realism cutting down a narrow patriotic religion. And surely the revival of superstition, occultism, belief in Chance or Fate or magic has parallels enough in the history of religions to suggest something else by way of explanation. The end of the Peloponnesian War brought a vast and overwhelming disillusionment and along with it a moral decline—as Thucydides makes perfectly plain.[16] Josephus has something of the same to say of defeated Judea in A.D. 70.[17] The revival of crass superstition and occultism, once banished by the poets, was like the return of "the deep tangled wildwood," which creeps back across what were once cultivated fields on now-abandoned farms, somewhere off the beaten track in New Hampshire or Connecticut. And the theory has the support of more recent writers on Greek religion than Dr Murray: e.g. Wilhelm Nestle in his *History of Greek Piety*, W. F. Otto in his book on *the Gods of Greece*, now translated by Professor Moses Hadas, and Martin Nilsson in his *History of Greek Religion*.

---

[16] Book III. 82 f. Plato's *Republic* begins with the problems raised by the very views set forth, according to Thucydides, by the Athenian imperialists and the mob they led. Evidently these views were still held in the fourth century.

[17] *Jewish War*, esp. Books V–VII *passim*.

One may venture to summarise Nilsson's views briefly as follows:[18] The Hellenistic age was an age of transition. This was what endangered its transmission of the old creative powers. Its earlier period was not a religious period, but was oriented in the direction of scientific and technical progress, very much like the latter years of the nineteenth century. And so, in place of religion, there grew up a belief in Fate, in the form either of accident (Chance) or of causality, and along with it a scientific explanation of the origin and course of the world's existence. The so-called supreme deity of philosophy, even when he was called God or Zeus, was only a scientific principle, no real God. It is easy to see how astrology could be so successful in such a period—and also how, when people turned once more to religion, astrology itself could make the same transition. It is also easy to see how the door was opened for the entrance of the Oriental deities with their mystery rites, a phenomenon not limited to the Greek world but universal in the Mediterranean basin and even farther north and west.

The general characteristics of Greek religion in the Roman period (from 31 B.C. to the fourth or fifth century A.D.) are more or less the same as those of the preceding period.[19] The Greek cults continued to be popular and widely patronised. The ancient mysteries of Demeter, Dionysus, the Cabiri, the Curetes, and other private mysteries continued to be honoured and observed. In place of the ancient cults of the Olympian deities, somewhat more worship was now paid to the Saviour Gods, especially Asclepius. The political domination of religion, observable under Alexander's successors and the later Hellenistic kings, led on to the imperial cult, the worship of Roma and the emperor, at first in the East and finally throughout the West. The traditional Roman religion survived in fragments: its almost total collapse had been the consequence of its collision with Greek culture in the third and second centuries B.C. What survived—or revived—was greatly altered.

[18] *Anglican Theological Review*, XXXIV (1952), p. 19.
[19] The Roman period is the subject of Part II of Nilsson's second volume. See also now Professor Kurt Latte's *Römische Religionsgeschichte*, Munich 1960. It takes the place of Georg Wissowa's famous *Religion und Kultus der Römer* in the Handbuch der Klassischen Altertumswissenschaft (2nd edn. 1912), for many years out of print.

We hear a great deal more about oracles, astrology, the worship of the Sun, miracles, prodigies, wonder-workers, magic and magicians, occultism in general, and about what Nestle, Nilsson, and others have called the "demonising" of religion.[20] There is also a widespread and growing emphasis upon beliefs about the dead and the underworld, although these also were survivals from the distant past, rather than something new. There is an increasing interest in religion among literary men, and a general tendency in the direction of monotheism and a high religious morality. This may be seen in the collection of oracles, especially the Jewish additions to the Sibylline Oracles; from the inscriptions, especially the famous one at Philadelphia dedicating a house to the worship of powerful and highly ethical gods;[21] from various authors, for example Seneca, Epictetus, Plutarch; and from such anonymous but deeply religious writings as those contained in the Hermetic corpus.

Finally, the climax of the whole development is reached in Hermetism—which Nilsson views as a pagan form of Gnosis— and Gnosticism, where the great problems of cosmology, anthropology (the nature of the world and the nature of man), and eschatology (the destiny of the world and of man) are dealt with.[22] It was a type of religion largely centred in the self of the devotee, whose salvation was effected by the imparting of secret knowledge. This knowledge usually concerned the nature of the soul and its destiny (at least its potential destiny) as the "pearl of great price" lost and hidden in the dark dungeon of the physical universe—the damp sub-cellar of dead matter at the very bottom of the ladder of existence. Redemption consists in the soul becoming aware of itself and beginning once more its ascent to the realm of light and of life and of true eternal being. Sometimes the message is conveyed by a messenger, who comes to awaken the lost; sometimes the words themselves echo in the ears of the drowsy soul and it awakens and says, "I will arise and go to my Father." The basic presupposition of the whole system—or congeries of systems that make up Gnosticism —is dualism: light versus darkness, being versus non-being,

[20] See Wilhelm Nestle, *Griechische Religiosität*, VOL. III, ch. VII; M. P. Nilsson, *Greek Piety*, Oxford 1948, pp. 170 ff.

[21] See my *Hellenistic Religions*, pp. 28–30; A. D. Nock, *Conversion*, pp. 216 f.

[22] See the titles listed under Hermetism and Gnosticism in the bibliography at the end of this volume.

truth versus falsehood. This was a principle that characterised more than one ancient system both before and during and also after the Hellenistic-Roman age. It was found in ancient Persia, and perhaps also in Babylon: it was expounded by Marcion and by Mani, and it persisted long after the end of the Graeco-Roman age. It came to life again in more than one sect and movement in the Middle Ages, sometimes within the borders of organised Christianity.

Thus the religion of the latter part of antiquity was immensely complicated and contained many contradictions, and it can be understood only by approaching it from different angles. One of the most important of the shaping forces was the new view of the world provided by Greek science, the new geocentric astronomy—new, that is, with Hipparchus (c. 190–126 B.C.) though anticipated by Heraclides (c. 360 B.C.), a disciple of Plato, and earlier still by Eudoxus (c. 408–355 B.C.). The heliocentric view of Aristarchus of Samos (c. 310–230 B.C.) had been rejected as too complicated; the geocentric view was apparently simpler, as based on direct observation, and it was eagerly seized by the Ptolemaic theorists and also capitalised by the astrologers and others interested in locating the realm of the gods or the forces governing human life in the sphere of the fixed stars: the planets did much to alter the scheme of human life, and the region below the moon was the source of constant daemonic interference. In this system of astronomy, the earth was conceived as floating free in space, surrounded by the seven—or eight—concentric spheres which rotate constantly about it, always in perfect harmony and obedient to eternal laws, the swiftest of the spheres being the outermost, that of the fixed stars, which make one complete revolution about the earth every twenty-four hours, the slower being those of the planets, the sun, and the moon; while the lowest or innermost or central sphere is that of the earth itself, stationary in the middle of the system. This geocentric astronomy required a complete re-thinking of the concepts of Olympus, the realm of the gods, and of Hades, the subterranean abode of the dead, and of the relations between the super-lunary and sub-lunary spheres: it was generally agreed that the realm below the moon was the abode of daemons and restless spirits, while only pure souls and spirits of gods and heroes could live in the celestial sphere above that of the moon. It was not simply that the old world, narrow and confining, had to give way to a much larger one: the old world really was quite spacious, and one could easily get lost in it, as even Odysseus, that man of many devices, had found to his sorrow; what was different was that the new world-view required a total reorientation *vis-à-vis* the external universe, and that it distinctly favoured a transcendental view of God or the gods. There was no other place for them but beyond the utmost realm of starry space—unless, forsooth, one was content to identify them with the fixed stars, and their lieutenants with the swift-moving "wanderers," the planets in the spheres closer to the earth. This is precisely what the astrologers did, with the result that men found themselves "cabin'd, cribb'd, confin'd" within a realm of relentless law which controlled all events in time and space, the rise and fall of nations and equally the destinies of individual men and women, born into this world under some particular constellation or conjunction of stars and planets. There existed a fine "sympathy" between heaven and earth, so that what was done here was felt there (as in Faber's hymn!), and what was effected there had its repercussions here. All was the result of a perfect system of mechanical law. In George Meredith's words ("Lucifer in Starlight"),

> Around the ancient track marched, rank on rank,
> The army of unalterable law.

Hilaire Belloc's lines in "The Prophet Lost in the Hills at Evening" express perfectly the aspiration and the despair of many a soul in the later Hellenistic age:

> Strong God, which made the topmost stars
>   To circulate and keep their course;
> Remember me, whom all the bars
>   Of sense and dreadful fate enforce.

The result, for religion, of this new scientific world-view was an increasing emphasis upon transcendence, upon universal law, upon astrology, and also upon mysticism and even—as we have said—upon occultism; for how else could men come in contact with these transcendent astral or super-astral deities ("the elemental spirits of the universe," Gal. IV. 3) except by the

inner pathway of renunciation, asceticism, the observance of a
rigid rule of life, and the cultivation of inner forces enabling
one to lay hold upon the divine powers superior to external
nature. The intellectual exposition of this view is clearly to be
seen in Hermetism, Gnosticism, and in Neoplatonism. And
the practical application of it is to be seen in the growing
asceticism and world-flight of the later Hellenistic-Roman period
—in asceticism and also in various magic rites, including the
theurgy of Iamblichus and the later Neoplatonists: rites that
were designed to bring down the very gods into visibility and
approachability by their devotees. But such rites could only be
successful when undertaken by the pure in heart, as a pagan
priest told an Egyptian abbot.[23] It was asceticism, "prayer
and fasting," that made the miracle possible and the rite
effective.

Another consequence of the new scientific geocentrism was
that the supreme deity became so transcendent that he required
a mediator, a second god (δεύτερος θεός, the term used of
Christ by Justin Martyr in the second century), chosen or
created to function as the agent of the supreme deity in his
relation to the world.[24] This μεσίτης is found in Philo (the
Logos), in Gnosticism (the chain of aeons stretching between the
One and the world of matter, or, in some systems, the Gnostic
"Redeemer"), in the Hermetic writings (the Logos, or Tat, or
Hermes Trismegistus himself), and in the New Testament (where
the doctrine of the Logos is also found). The doctrine is found in
Paul and John and is implied in Hebrews, but with this difference, viz. that the Christian Logos can and does become man,
incarnate; i.e. he takes upon himself human flesh (in biblical
language this means human nature) and lives a perfectly
human life—a doctrine which eventually became the very
heart of the classic Christology of the Catholic Church.

A still further consequence of the new world-view was the
temporary popularity (especially in the third century A.D.) of
Sun-worship, encouraged by the Syrian emperors (see p. 19)
—though its real roots are probably much older than the Greek

---

[23] See Nilsson, *Geschichte*, VOL. II, p. 686 n. Cf. Mark IX. 29 (A.V.); II Esdras
XIV. 37–48.
[24] See M. P. Nilsson, "Nähe und Distanz von der Gottheit," in *Opuscula Selecta*,
VOL. III, Lund 1960, pp. 11–26.

science of the early Hellenistic age, even as its full expression came far later than the astronomy of the fourth century B.C. Sun-worship was very ancient in the East, and one may suspect that it was adapted to the geocentric system—with some difficulty—under the Severi in order, in the first place, to provide a tangible (at least a visible) universal deity to match the new universal citizenship in the empire (Caracalla made all free men citizens of Rome in A.D. 211), and secondly to symbolise, perhaps to sanction, the universal lordship of the emperor on earth. Certainly the new emphasis had consequences for theology, i.e. for speculative religion; it even influenced Mithraism, indeed it had already influenced it for a long time. Mithras was not only the friend of the Sun-god from of old; he in a sense now *became* the Sun-god, for many of his worshippers in the Roman Empire. In this he resembled Apollo, and other old deities, who were sometimes identified with the Sun.

Although there was no "theology of the mysteries," there was a widespread and growing mysticism in many circles. This mysticism was far more important for the history of religion from the first century onward than the "mystery religions." The question arises, What was the source of this widespread mysticism? Professor Nilsson has considered the various possible sources, Egypt, Asia Minor, Greece, and favours the latter two. Much Egyptian mysticism was read into the rites, the myths, even the hieroglyphic symbols inscribed on temples and stelae. But in the Archaic age, Greece had been full of strange figures, prophets, wise men, wonder-workers, oracle-mongers, healers, gods in disguise; and it also showed a tendency in the direction of what later became "mysticism" in thought— direct apprehension of reality by other than rational steps and expressible only in part and by symbol or gesture or hint; that is, a tremendous development of the feeling element in religion, which may after all be a survival from the earliest stages in religious history. As Dean Inge held, with Pascal, "the heart has its reasons"—and the heart is "biologically older than the brain." This early or incipient "mysticism," which later survived in Orphism and Pythagoreanism, may possibly have been derived from the Minoan-Mycenaen age, then covered over for a time by the Homeric veneer of rationality and by the cold inquiries of the philosophers, but reviving as soon as human need broke through the thin covering of well-thought-out theories of gods and men, the divine and the human, reality and appearance. And now once more, in the Hellenistic age, even among the educated, the same process is repeated: the age-old yearning for divine power-to-help, for divine revelation, for the uncovering of the future, for assurance of a blissful and satisfying life to come, beyond the grave—all this is so strong in the Hellenistic age, when the individual has been cut loose from his moorings and is adrift upon the open sea in a vast new world, that the age-old practices and beliefs revive once more, not only now in Greece but everywhere, wherever the Greek language and Greek thought have penetrated the inhabited earth. But Greece was always closely related to Asia Minor; in fact, Ionia was one of the oldest strongholds of Greek thought, and the relations between the peoples of the hinterland, especially Phrygia, and the Greeks of the western fringe along the coast were closer in the Hellenistic age than ever before. No wonder if ideas of sin, confession and forgiveness, ecstasy, and priesthood were absorbed once more from this fertile ancient source of religious movements.

There were three great outstanding characteristics of the new pagan religion which was emerging toward the end of antiquity. These were monotheism, the belief in supernatural power, and an antipathy for matter. The structure as a whole was what we call syncretism, a vast, complex, heterogeneous mixture of religion, superstitition, morals, idealism, psychopathology, theology, philosophy, mysticism, self-interest, chicanery—an utterly human, in many ways far too human, mixture of religion and everything else that attracted and interested the human mind. Belief in demons (*daemons*, not necessarily evil spirits) and in magic and occultism generally was everywhere on the increase. Magic especially held a great place in the lives of men, as much in Babylonia as in Egypt, while the belief in demons was especially dominant in the Orient; the most famous magicians were the Egyptians and the Babylonians; and as for Persia the fact that the Persian priests, the *magi*, gave their name to the practice shows in what esteem it was held among them, or at least in what esteem Persian magicians were held in the West. The Babylonian doctrine that the stars are gods, with the consequence that each of them (i.e. the planets) received the name of a Greek god, was accepted by the Greeks and Romans and provided the scientific basis for the cosmic system assumed by astrology and for the causal sequence of Fate (Εἱμαρμένη). Finally, the doctrine of the mediator, the Logos, found in more than one system of thought or religion, met the need for a bridge between the transcendent deity and this world of men and things, between the purely celestial spirit and the world of matter, and for an agent in the carrying out of divine purposes in this lower realm. How all this set the stage for the appearance and development of Hellenistic Judaism, especially as seen in Philo, and for the early expansion of Christianity, especially after the first century, is quite obvious. And by the end of the second century or the beginning of the third, as Simone Pétrement has said, it is true that "there were really three religions: the Christianity of the Church, Gnosticism, and Neoplatonism (or paganism); but it is no exaggeration [to say] that among these three there was only one theology."[25] This *mélange* of cults and creeds in later antiquity was like a gold-bearing stream, whose rich sands the Church in due time took over and sifted and panned, preserving whatever was precious and permanent. In its liturgy, its hymnary, its devotions, even in its theology and its moral teaching, as in its vestments and its ministry, may still be found survivals from this long-past age of Hellenism.

It is now obvious what the consequences for education must have been—and were—in the religious and political *milieu* of the Hellenistic world under the early Roman Empire.

> For what avail the plough or sail,
> Or land or life, if freedom fail?

The revival of occultism, the westward-moving flood of Oriental "mystery" cults, the rising tide of astrology and magic, the growing belief in Fate or Chance (or both), the absence of experimental methods in science, the triumph of oratory and rhetoric over all other disciplines—this was not at all a favourable background for free, progressive, far-reaching education. Hence despite the growth of literacy, or the superb achieve-

[25] *Le Dualisme chez Platon*, Paris 1947, p. 132.

ments of Greek geometers and mathematicians, or the industrious and long continued pursuit of jurisprudence, together with the wide dissemination of popular philosophy, the creative urge had begun to die away and could not be restored. Education is something which must be renewed or replenished in every generation, like a lamp with its daily supply of oil. And it does not thrive where the religious unity of a people has been destroyed or its moral standards have weakened or have disappeared. This was just as true in the ancient world as it is in the modern.

# Chapter III

## Syncretism in Philosophy and Religion

When the Church crossed the borders of Palestine and entered the broad Graeco-Roman world of Hellenism, it became necessary to restate the gospel in a language (Greek) whose background was philosophy, not law. Hence the importance of Greek philosophy in the background of the New Testament, and the "influence of Greek ideas" upon early Christianity—the subject of Edwin Hatch's classic Hibbert Lectures. Philosophy was very old, in the Greek world, and it had been influencing Greek thought as a whole for many centuries, so widely and deeply that it was virtually indigenous by the first two centuries of our era. The contrast between ancient Greek philosophy and modern European, British, and American in their influence upon popular thought, especially religious thought, is very marked. Whereas ancient philosophy was taught, discussed, and debated in the market-place, modern philosophy, often wrapped in a sombre garb of obscure and impenetrable terminology—each philosopher inventing his own vocabulary—is limited in its influence to the select few among the educated who can understand and appreciate it. The pooling of influence, the exchange of terminology, the mutual attraction and the modification of one school of ancient philosophy by another is a conspicuous feature of the early Roman period: something our modern philosophies have not yet achieved—though some philosophers would doubtless call such syncretism a loss. For all our likeness to the age of Roman Hellenism, conspicuous on many fronts, this is a feature which marks us off as decidedly different.

The hallmark of the Hellenistic age was "syncretism." This term is a modern one, as applied to the mixture of cultures, religions, and philosophies which took place in the period from Alexander to Augustus, and even later. Originally συγκρητισμός meant the political union of towns for purposes of common trade, worship, or defence—like the Decapolis in Palestine, or the Hanse towns in northern Europe in the fifteenth century, or the amphictyons ("neighbours") in ancient Greece.[1] As referring to the mixture or pooling of cultures, the term is now widely used to cover such varied phenomena as early Buddhist sculpture in India, which shows the influence of Greek models; or the *interpretatio romana* by which Greek and barbarian gods and their rites were identified with Roman ones; or even eclecticism in philosophy, whereby the cosmology of Plato, the ethics of Aristotle, and the political ideals of the Stoics could be combined in one system, taking whatever was best in all the ancient schools.

Such eclecticism was a natural correlate to the universalism of the age. The national spirit—and national pride—was dying out everywhere; men were "citizens of the world," as the Stoics affirmed, and one god, one cult, seemed no better than another. Religious toleration was the presupposition of syncretism. In fact, the chief recommendation of the various deities, in the past, had been their avowed championship of their own people —an essential feature in the complex situation assumed by Homer, leading to consequences sometimes humorous, often tragic. Gradually it had dawned upon men that instead of national deities there was only one family of gods who ruled heaven and earth—or, indeed, as some suspected, only one divine being supreme over all gods and men, daemons and powers of nature. Parallel to the emerging world government, whose first stage was the four great Hellenistic monarchies which arose soon after the death of Alexander and the division of his empire; whose second stage was the chaos of the "age of agony," as Arnold Toynbee calls it (this term also is modern); whose third stage was the Augustan "restoration of the Republic" and the later absolute monarchy of the Caesars—parallel to this final development was the conception of one supreme invisible dynasty in heaven, which in time became the conception of one supreme heavenly monarch. Macrobius, about A.D. 400, drew the final inference: as there is one emperor on earth, so there must be one—and only one—ruler in heaven. And vice versa! Even the Christian creed used such language: "We believe in *one* God . . . in *one* Lord Jesus Christ . . . in *one*

---

[1] See Paul Wendland, *Hellenistisch-römische Kultur*, Tübingen 1907. Index s.v. Synkretismos, and ch. VII. So Plutarch explained it: *On Brotherly Love*, 490b.

[Holy] Catholic Apostolic Church . . . in *one* Baptism for the remission of sins." Thus the so-called Nicene Creed expanded the Pauline formula: "One body and one Spirit, . . . one hope, . . . one Lord, one faith, one baptism, one God and Father of us all, who is above all and through all and in all" (Eph. IV. 4 f.). This creed comes from the same period, the fourth century.

The part played by the philosophers in this development of thought was neither paramount nor decisive, yet it could by no means be ignored. Their influence was far-reaching, and they anticipated some of the "new directions" which religious and political thought was destined to take. The old, primitive (i.e. prehistoric) ideas of the gods; the naïve, primitive cosmologies of various peoples; the ethical conceptions and imperatives sanctioned by the earlier religious views (for example, the sacredness of oaths, the inviolability of suppliants, the duty of tendance to the departed, the rights and duties of the members of a clan, a tribe, a family)—all these still survived; they were criticised and revised by the philosophers, but they were never wholly rejected. In cosmology, for example, as we have seen, the revolutionary views of Aristarchus of Samos, who demonstrated that the sun, not the earth, is the centre of the solar system, failed to gain popular support, and even scientists and philosophers clung to the old geocentrism, though it was generally admitted that the earth was round. We must be careful not to trace later developments as if they were either derived wholly from the philosophers or arose automatically as a result of progress. The truth is that then, as always, there was an interplay between new ideas and old, between radical insights and conservative loyalties, and the history of philosophy was a slow lumbering progress in the direction of what eventually emerged —the eclecticism of the third, fourth, and fifth centuries, after which new forces entered the field and fresh "new directions" came about, chiefly ecclesiastical or—somewhat later—metaphysical.

Plato (427–347 B.C.) belongs at the very beginning of the Hellenistic age. His conception of God was really part and parcel of his conception of the soul, which is the principle of activity,

change, and motion—the principle which bridges the gap between timeless, changeless being and actual change and becoming in the universe. But the soul creates by contemplating
the eternal Forms, with which it tries to bring the world into
conformity, as fully as this is possible (there is always a "margin
of error" or of failure throughout the physical universe). As
Theophrastus summed up Plato's view, "Not even God can
bring all things to perfection, but only within the limits of possibility"—a far cry from the biblical idea that "with God all
things are possible" (Mk. x. 27, xiv. 36; Lk. xviii. 27; Mt. xix.
26). In the words of Professor Field, "The soul is always . . .
striving to overcome the limitations of the medium in which it
works, [and so,] in Plato's metaphor, to 'persuade necessity'.
But it can never do this completely or absolutely, and there
necessarily remains an irreducible element of imperfection in
the material universe."[2]

The soul of the individual, like the world-soul, makes progress and rises to higher levels as it too contemplates the eternal
Forms, chiefly the Form (or Idea) of the Good, and sees all
things in true mathematical proportion and harmony. One may
question whether Plato thought the World-Soul, or even the
Demiurge (the Creator), or the Idea of the Good, to be a
divine person; the answer is, probably, that the question is too
modern, and never arose for him. (The ancient world was not
interested in personality, at least not before late classical days,
certainly not in the early Hellenistic age. And it was not really
much interested in persons, or in scientific psychology, until
after the time of Aristotle.[3]) Plato speaks sometimes of God,
sometimes of the gods, sometimes of "the divine" or "the deity"
(τὸ θεῖον)—like an eighteenth-century French rationalist.
Hence he pictures God himself contemplating the Forms: for
goodness is good, not because God decrees or wills it, but because it is "there"—one might almost say, because it existed
before God did. It is like the lure of mountaineering to the
climber: the mountain is "there," and he must climb it; so
goodness exists, and God must love it, pursue it, enforce it,

---

[2] G. C. Field, *The Philosophy of Plato*, Oxford 1949, p. 144.
[3] J. R. Illingworth in his Bampton Lectures, 1894, on *Personality Human and
Divine* (long a textbook in Anglican seminaries) attributed the chief influence to
St Augustine.

create it. The poet's phrase, "eternal form," is even more profoundly true in Plato's thought: Reality is prior to God, Being
exists before God—just as, in Homer, *Moira* stands back of the
gods and compels even them to conform. But of course God and
Being are identical, at least for most of us; and it is perhaps only
a modern distinction in thought upon which we are insisting,
in the case of Plato's theology.

The later theory of *two* world-souls, and even of a lower,
"evil" world-soul, is a perversion and caricature of Plato's
thought, and should not be attributed to him. In spite of
Eduard Zeller[4] and the plain language of Book X of the *Laws*
(896*e*), modern interpreters tend to discount Plato's final
theory of an evil world-soul. What he said in the *Laws* was a
kind of *jeu d'esprit*, a fanciful aside: "We must not suppose that
there are less than two [souls which inhabit and order all things
that move, including the heavens]—one the author of good, the
other its opposite." For one thing, this statement is not an
essential part of his argument, which is that the divine self-
moving source of all motion is "soul"; nor does he elaborate the
suggestion further—in fact, he proceeds at once to describe
"soul" as directing all things in heaven, earth, and sea, "a goddess, when truly receiving the divine mind she disciplines all
things rightly for their happiness, but when she [singular] is the
companion of folly, she does the contrary," for "it is soul which
controls heaven and earth" [not two souls]. Finally, Plato does
not explain what it is he referred to by this cosmic "folly,"
whether comets, meteors, or various unaccountable planetary
aberrations (897*d*) which the system of spheres in the Eudoxan
astronomy left unexplained: at least he is talking about the
celestial motions in the passage as a whole. Eudoxus used the
pattern of a "horse-fetter" or "figure eight" to describe the
orbits of the planets (the "wanderers") in his geocentric system
of spherical astronomy—an explanation rendered unnecessary
by Copernicus; unless perchance we sometime discover the
orbit of our entire solar and planetary system in its motion
through space. We may therefore dismiss the view that Plato in
his old age fell victim to a mood of pessimism which spread from

---

[4] Part II, Div. I (i.e. VOL. II) of his *Philosophie der Griechen* deals with Plato. Or
see his *Grundriss der Geschichte der griechischen Philosophie*, §40 f. Both works have been
translated into English.

his politics to his physics and engulfed his bold and balanced spirit in a cloud of gloom; for he was only tossing out one of the possibilities in the case—a possibility which may have been suggested by the popular Iranian dualism of the day, but which, taken seriously by later thinkers, all the way down to the Gnostics and the later Neoplatonists, was fraught with tragic consequences, for religion as much as for philosophy.

Nevertheless, there was a hierarchy of divine beings between the supreme One and the lowly Many; and beneath the divine hierarchy stood the daemonic, the spirits who serve as messengers between the gods and men, bearing human prayers aloft, returning with divine blessings, oracles, messages.[5] All these deserved to be worshipped. Plato finally identified (so it seems) this heavenly hierarchy with the heavenly bodies, which, according to the astronomy of Eudoxus, governed the celestial spheres. One of the most majestic descriptions in Plato is the procession of the heavenly gods, led by the Sun—a description which was surely derived from observation, not fantasy, for we also have seen it with our own eyes not long ago, at twilight on five successive days in July, 11th to 15th, in the year 1959. The new moon and the visible nearer planets were marching steadily westward in line behind the setting sun. The other planets were also in line, but visible only with a telescope.[6] The phenomenon is recurrent at long intervals. The period of Saturn's orbit is $29\frac{1}{2}$ years, Jupiter's almost 12, Mars's $1\frac{9}{10}$. The swift inner orbits of Mercury and Venus, like governors on an old-fashioned Corliss stationary engine (so they appear in diagrams of the Ptolemaic planetary system!), take 3 months and $7\frac{1}{2}$ months respectively. Choosing any observable 120° arc of Saturn's orbit, which it would require approximately ten years to traverse, Jupiter would cross this only once, taking almost four years for the transit; Mars would cross it five times; Mercury and Venus would be visible, near the sun, at frequent intervals, the former forty-one times, the latter sixteen. If the "procession of the heavenly gods" took place once in thirty years, it would have been rarely enough to impress all viewers and to become a sacred legend, handed on from father to son. But it really took place far more rarely; the exact positions just described

---

[5] See the *Symposium*, 202e–203a.
[6] For Plato's figure, see the *Phaedrus*, 246e.

are repeated only once in almost 658 years. Allowing somewhat
roomier spaces, what the old astrologers called "houses", say
30° for each planet ($=\pm15°$), the spectacle would have been
observable somewhat more frequently. In fact, the year Plato
was born (427 B.C.) the planets Saturn and Jupiter were thus
visible—Mars being appropriately absent!—a conjunction of
the kind Johannes Kepler proposed as the explanation of the
Star of Bethlehem. And it was repeated in 387 B.C., the year
Plato was forty.

We may wonder how it was possible that Plato's theology, so
vague, so impersonal, so theoretical, can have influenced later
religious thought, especially Christian, as it has. Benjamin
Jowett, his Victorian translator, had an explanation.[7] It was
"due partly to a misunderstanding. . . . In the supposed depths
of [the *Timaeus*] the Neoplatonists found hidden meanings and
connexions with the Jewish and Christian Scriptures, and out of
them they elicited doctrines quite at variance with the spirit of
Plato." More recent interpreters are somewhat more favourable
to these Neoplatonists; but the low level of scholarship reflected
in much of the patristic interpretation of holy Scripture is fully
equalled by much of the philosophical interpretation of Plato.
Plotinus, the master, was the great exception.

But we must not overlook the advantages (at least for ancient
thought) which Plato's conception of God offered: No one can
say to his Maker, "What doest thou?" (Job IX. 12) or, "Why did
you not make a better universe?" or, "Did you not plant the
Garden and provide it with a tree of evil and a serpent?" The
problem of evil does not arise for Plato—not, certainly, in this
shape. God is doing the best He can. If we are to "become as
like God as possible" (μάλιστα ἄν), then God himself is doing
the same with the world, making it as good as possible. "God
desired that all things should be good and nothing bad, so far
as this was attainable" (κατὰ δύναμιν).[8] That it is not a better
world is no fault of God, but of the intractable material out of
which it is made—or rather, the intractable element that runs
through all existence, material, psychic, even spiritual. Only

---

[7] See his introduction to the *Timaeus*, in *The Dialogues of Plato*, new edn. Oxford
1953, VOL. III, p. 631.

[8] *Timaeus* 29e, 30a. For the latter phrase, see Aristotle, *Eudemian Ethics*, 1243b,
and II Cor. VIII. 3. See also *Phaedo* 83b, *Laws* VIII. 835e.

the eternal Forms are perfect, changeless, imperishable; it is the earthly reflections or copies which are imperfect, not the originals. Eternal Reality is good, and chiefly good because it *is*, because it exists, because it is ever good and supremely desirable. Without that permanent anchorage in the invisible (cf. Heb. vi. 19 f.), the universe would of course be nothing but "hells beneath hells, in horror descending." *Why* the Forms exist is a question as meaningless as it is impossible to answer: they simply *are*. And the way to them is the *via contemplativa* —which is not the way most beloved by us moderns, namely religious "experience." Nor is there any "Beatific Vision" for Plato. It is not the Vision of God that represents the end and goal of the individual soul's long journey, but the vision of the Forms, eternal Reality, which God himself contemplates.

Plato, in brief, stood where every ancient Greek stood, from Homer down: the gods themselves are *inside* the universe. The overarching Reality, which is both ultimate and therefore initial and also everlasting, embraces all: gods, daemons, heroes, ghosts and spirits of the dead, and living men. It embraces all that is; and this must include all lower existences, animals, trees, mountains and seas, and the vast deeps beneath. Plato, like other ancient Greeks, was not interested in either private "personality" or in personal "salvation." As he says in the *Laws* (x. 903), "The parts exist for the whole, and the whole for the parts." It must be admitted that some of our Christian saints have shared this view: nothing *really* matters but the final achievement of the purposes of God—

> Not with the hope of gaining aught,
> Not seeking a reward,
> But as thyself hast lovèd me,
> O ever-loving Lord!

(The new Christian element of feeling in this hymn does not wholly obliterate its fundamental philosophical presupposition.) And there have been some who were prepared to be sent to hell, for ever, if it so pleased God or added to his glory or served his wise if inscrutable purposes. This also may be a faint and distant echo of Platonism, though it is more likely to stem from the Bible. For God can save "by many or by few" (1 Sam. xiv. 6), or he may indeed decide not to save us at all, his purposes requiring our defeat or extinction, since we are mere expendables (see Judith VIII. 11–17). *Soli deo gloria*, not merely *ad maiorem dei gloriam*—this is the motto of the highest sanctity. Plato might not have recognised it; nevertheless, he laid the ground for such a conception by his insistence upon the central importance of the invisible world: for him as for St Paul "the things that are seen are transient, but the things that are unseen are eternal" (II Cor. IV. 18). And the true end of life is not activity but the contemplation of Eternal Reality.

Modern study of the philosophy of Aristotle (384–322 B.C.) has made more sharp and clear the agreements and the differences between him and his master Plato. The notion that he completely rejected Plato's teaching and began his research and speculation *de novo* is mistaken, as is also the view that he only elaborated Plato's teaching. The great work by Werner Jaeger[9] has demonstrated the dependence of Aristotle during his early years, and his independence after his removal to Assos, following the death of Plato in 347. From Assos he went to Lesbos, where he became head of his own school, and later to Macedonia, where he became the teacher of King Philip's son Alexander. By the time he returned to Athens, probably in 336, his intellectual independence was fully established. But the fundamental principles of his philosophy were still Platonic, despite his growing interest in science, observation, and factual knowledge. His cosmology was still the Eudoxan astronomy assumed by Plato, with its hollow spheres composed of *aether*, an element which cannot be destroyed or transmuted into other elements, invisible, impalpable, but unchanging and unyielding. The earth is still the centre of the solar system and of the universe as a whole, which is spherical, finite, and eternal. All things move in six directions, up, down, right, left, forwards, backwards; but there is also an element which moves only in circles or in rotation, and—like a gyroscope—cannot be forced from its natural course. Since this motion is irreversible, it cannot lead to collapse or decay and is therefore indestructible.[10] Further, the life-principle, the ψυχή or "soul" (also "mind" in some

[9] *Aristotle: Fundamentals of the History of His Development*, first published in Berlin by Weidmann in 1923; Eng. trans. by Richard Robinson, 2nd edn. Oxford 1948.
[10] See D. J. Allan, *The Philosophy of Aristotle*, Oxford 1952, p. 50.

connexions) animates and controls all growth and becoming, in the universe and in human bodies. Soul is therefore *prior* to body, as in Plato's thought, and the real *raison d'être* of the body.

> For soule is forme, and doth the body make.

Moreover, God is still the supreme being or "Prime Mover" who steadily contemplates the eternal Forms ("Ideas") and makes things in conformity with their unchanging patterns. But more: He is the *unmoved* Mover, who creates by thought, not by act or deed (Plato had already rejected the "mason and carpenter" view of creation); and since he is supreme and his own thought is creative, his contemplation centres upon himself, i.e. his thought, his perfect mind. (This sounds absurd: but it was an inescapable inference from the axioms and the arguments which preceded it; and it is no worse than the less logical but more imaginative declaration of an ancient rabbi that God studies Torah several hours a day!) The creation of the universe and its maintenance are the result of a universal tendency toward God, drawn by the ineluctable attraction of divine power and wisdom. It is not force that rules, but attraction (ὄρεξις). As Dante long afterwards explained the view, combining it with Scholastic theology, it is

> Love that moves the sun in heaven, and all the stars.[11]

The Ideas or Forms are no longer "eternal in the heavens," apart from God; nor are they really "thoughts in the mind of God," as later Platonists tended to view them; instead, "the purposiveness and order of the world are now simply ascribed to Nature, which is not a personal force, but an all-pervading aspiration toward form and actuality, blind, but for that very reason more accurate than any deliberate pursuit of an end."[12] We are now well on the way toward the modern scientific outlook, divorced from theology. But Aristotle is still a pronounced theist. God is above and apart from the material world of change (which means "change and decay," as in the Christian hymn). This immaterial First Cause is both substantial and devoid of potentiality—all God's potentialities are realised,

---

[11] Dante, *Paradiso*, XXXIII. 145: *l'amor che move il sole e l'altre stelle*. This famous last line concludes the *Paradiso* and is the climax of the whole *Divina Commedia*.
[12] Allan, *Philosophy of Aristotle*, p. 114.

we might say. He is engaged in ceaseless activity, and yet is at perfect rest. As for the secondary gods, they exist outside the last, ethereal sphere, that of the fixed stars: somewhat as in Epicurus's system, where all the gods live far removed from us, in the "interstellar spaces." As for the animation of the planets (or their spheres) by souls, Aristotle is somewhat averse to the view: the movement of the universe is not a complex system of planetary and other motions, cyclical and epicyclical, like a mechanical planetarium (this instrument had already been invented in the ancient world), but is the result of a single, unitary motion reflecting the desire (ὄρεξις) of universal nature to imitate the eternal activity of God. That is, Aristotle "ascribes the movement of the universe to the love of the imperfect creation for God *as its perfection*." So Edward Caird summed up the view, and added an apt reference to the words of St Paul:

The creation waits with eager longing for the revealing of the sons of God; for the creation was subjected to futility, not of its own will but by the will of him who subjected it in hope; because the creation itself will be set free from its bondage to decay and obtain the glorious liberty of the children of God. We know that the whole creation has been groaning in travail together until now; and not only the creation, but we ourselves, who have the first fruits of the Spirit, groan inwardly as we wait for adoption as sons, the redemption of our bodies (Rom. VIII. 19–23).

No one will assume that Paul is expounding Aristotle, or that the two views are identical; but they certainly have something in common, as well as much that is distinct and heterogeneous, for example Paul's eschatology.[13]

The importance of this conception of God and of the world for later thought is clear and obvious. Thinkers as different as Philo of Alexandria, Clement, Augustine, the Schoolmen, the medieval Arabian philosophers, the poet Dante—all reflect the influence of Aristotle, whose conception was in some ways quite superior to the more poetic, less rigidly intellectual view of his master. Even in the New Testament, where we should scarcely expect it, there are traces of his influence: e.g. Jn. v. 17, "My Father is working still, and I am working," where the language is framed to offset the idea of a divine sabbath rest (Gen. II. 2) following the six days of creation (we must remember that the

[13] See Edward Caird, *The Evolution of Theology in the Greek Philosophers*, Glasgow 1903, VOL. II, p. 29.

Incarnate *Logos*, who is speaking, is the one "through whom all things were made," Jn. i. 3). God is eternally active—yet unmoved. He is separate from the world. He grants freedom of the will to human beings—without it no moral judgment would be possible. Man is to achieve the greatest possible likeness to God *(ὁμοίωσις θεῷ κατὰ τὸ δυνατόν)*—Plato had used this phrase in *Theaetetus* 176*b* and elsewhere. Man is to "serve and contemplate God"[14]—a phrase which reminds us of both the Westminster Catechism: "Man's chief end is to glorify God and enjoy Him for ever"; and Milton's Sonnet on His Blindness: "They also serve who only stand and wait." ("Stand" was the very word Plato had used.) The essentially contemplative element in religion is not lacking from the New Testament: "Blessed are the pure in heart, for they shall see God" (Mt. v. 8). The background of this idea is the repeated denial, in both the Old Testament and the New, that man has ever seen God (e.g. Ex. XXIII. 23; Jn. i. 18; 1 Jn. IV. 12). There is, moreover, the testimony to a theistic view which may be found in the *consensus gentium* (e.g. *De Caelo*, II. 1). These few examples suffice to show that Aristotle and the New Testament are not as far apart as many interpreters suppose.[15]

The words "Unmoved Mover" are the traditional rendering of the Greek τι δ οὐ κινούμενον κινεῖ (*Metaphysics*, XII. 1072*a*)[16] or τὸ πρῶτον κινοῦν ἀκίνητον αὐτό (IV. 1012*b*)—Plato had used a similar phrase, τὰς δὲ πέντε κινήσεις ἀκίνητον καὶ ἑστός (Tim. 40*b*), the five motions which "are always at rest and never move." Aristotle does not say ἀκίνητος κινητής, which would be the literal Greek for our term: the words are too personal—Aristotle is talking about *motion* and its unmoved, unmoving *source*. Our popular modern idea is a caricature of his real meaning. Nevertheless the words were so taken, and they sounded very cold, especially when combined with Epicurean or Stoic ἀπάθεια and ἀταραξία: eternal "peace of mind," free-

---

[14] Cf. *Nicomachean Ethics*, 1177*b*, where ἀθανατίζειν means "following God." See Nilsson, *Opusc. Sel.*, VOL. III, p. 23.

[15] Nor should we forget the language of the Epistle of James, which is one of the most thoroughly "Hellenistic" writings in the New Testament. In Jas. i. 17f. God is "the Father of lights, with whom there is no variation or shadow due to change. Of his own will he brought us forth by the word of truth that we should be a kind of first fruits of his creatures."

[16] "Something which without moving or being moved is nevertheless the cause of motion."

dom from irritation, passion, frustration, or desire. In reality the conception was still, like Plato's, poetic and anthropomorphic: not "unmoved" in the sense of cold and indifferent or "unfeeling," but in the sense of depending upon no prior cause of motion; and God is not a "mover" but the *cause* of motion. We might paraphrase this in more popular terms: God is the unruffled, undisturbed centre of attraction of the whole universe. Poetry requires poetry for its exposition—and so does philosophy. The line in Tennyson's *Locksley Hall* (line 24) sets it off perfectly, if no doubt unconsciously:

> The current of my being sets to thee.

Or Oliver Wendell Holmes's hymn may be compared. God is the

> Lord of all being, throned afar,
> [Whose] glory flames from sun and star;
> Centre and soul of every sphere—
> Yet to each loving heart how near!

He is

> Lord of all life, below, above,
> [His] light is truth, [his] warmth is love . . .
> Grant us thy truth to make us free
> And kindling hearts that burn for thee,
> Till all thy living altars claim
> One holy light, one heavenly flame!

Only, for Aristotle, God is the one who is universally loved, not the lover of all. This is somewhat different. We have no assurance that Aristotle would have appreciated this hymn, or Plato either, though both were more religious than some of their modern interpreters would have us suppose. Nevertheless, the conception of God in his relation to his creatures and to the whole universe is one which has influenced Jewish and Christian and Islamic mysticism from an early time, as the works of many poets and theologians clearly show. It is an intellectual concept, which leaves the crude myths of creation in all the old religions far behind; for mysticism is not a religion of feeling, as many writers now assume, but a religion of hard thinking, of thought reaching out beyond its own utmost limits in order to catch a view of the Eternal.

We must not, of course, assume that the philosophies of Plato and Aristotle determined the general religious outlook or world-view of all later generations: most men and women are religious, but very few are philosophers. Nevertheless, these two philosophies remained in the intellectual background of the Hellenistic world like two great mountain massifs—like the twin mountains, Eternity and Trinity, on the lower Saguenay in Canada. Later schools of philosophy, including the most popular ones, were influenced by Plato and Aristotle; and so it has continued ever since, even to the present day. These more popular Hellenistic schools, chiefly the Cynic, Stoic, and Epicurean, were more concerned with human conduct, i.e. with ethics, and less with metaphysics than were either the Academics or the Peripatetics, the schools founded by Plato and Aristotle. The political and social experience of Greece and the Near East in the latter part of the fifth century, which witnessed the final agonies of the Peloponnesian War; and in the fourth and the third, with their social and political chaos, which lasted in fact until the coming of the Romans as a world power (they destroyed both Carthage and Corinth in 146 B.C.)—this experience led men to suspect that the world was governed, not by God or gods but either by capricious Fortune, Τύχη, or by inescapable Necessity, 'Ανάγκη, in whose hands the individual was simply helpless. The older philosophical schools might continue to debate the questions of epistemology (whether or not we really know what we think we know), or the organisation of scientific knowledge; but men generally cried out for guidance in their attempt to live in the midst of political and social chaos. The new schools had the answer. The Sceptics, founded by Pyrrho (365–275 B.C.), may be dismissed at once—all they did was criticise the presuppositions or the conclusions of other philosophers. According to them, there was no answer to the human problem: at best, you can only accept your fate. But the Cynics, founded by Diogenes (?412–323 B.C.), held that the answer was very simple: man is a product of nature and lives within it; he is healthiest and happiest when in tune with nature; therefore let him get rid of all the artificial conventions of society—including houses, clothes, and baths—and become once more what nature meant him to be. Diogenes lived the simple life in an empty tub;[17] his followers railed at kings and their courts, and at all who wore purple and fine linen and fared sumptuously every day. Their motto, which they passed on to the Stoics, was *Sequi naturam*, Follow nature. But they often turned out, as we might have expected, to be merely crude and vulgar, like the "beatniks" of today. As Voltaire said of Rousseau, who advocated a similar reversion to nature, "Such teaching makes us want to creep on all fours." But a better view is possible. As Sir Richard Burton counselled in the *Kasidah*:

> Do what thy manhood bids thee do,
> From none but self expect applause;
> He noblest lives and noblest dies
> Who makes and keeps his self-made laws.

And this is really Stoic.

A cultivated and creditable and far more influential philosophy was the Stoic, founded by Zeno of Kitium (?330–260 B.C.), a Phoenician or Cypriot who had come to Athens as a trader and remained to study and finally (*c.* 300) to teach philosophy. He had a noble line of successors: Cleanthes (?305–230 B.C.) whose *Hymn to Zeus* is one of the finest survivals of ancient Greek religion; Chrysippus (?280–207) and his two disciples, Zeno of Tarsus and Diogenes of Seleucia ("the Babylonian"), who came to Rome in 155 B.C.; and the still later and more famous Roman Stoics, Seneca (4 B.C.–A.D. 65), Epictetus (A.D. 50–138), and the Emperor Marcus Aurelius (A.D. 121–180). And there were many others who expounded, promoted, systematised and clarified the teaching of this school, teaching which embraced logic, physics, politics, and theology; but their main contribution was to ethics. Life "according to nature,"

---

[17] See the anecdote in Lucian's *How to Write History*, §3. When it was reported that Philip was on his way all Corinth was stirred and busy with preparations, getting weapons ready, reinforcing the walls, shoring up battlements, and doing other useful things. Diogenes looked on at this vast activity and, having nothing else to do—no one had asked him to take a hand—he girded up his philosopher's cloak and rolled his crock, in which he happened to be living, up and down Cornel Hill. One of his friends asked, "What are you doing that for, Diogenes?" and he replied, "I'm rolling my crock so no one will think me the only man idle among all these busy workers."

the term taken over from the Cynics, meant life in accordance with a divinely planned and supervised scheme of things in which man had a part to play, just as important as that of the gods. Each man was an actor, and must play his assigned role, not departing from the stage before the signal was given, and recognising from the outset his severe limitations: some things are within his power, others are not, and there is no sense in repining or sulking or in trying to assume more responsibilities than one has already been given. Here is Aristotle's "golden mean" stated in new terms; and also his and Plato's theory that gods and men form one society. No matter what the surrounding conditions, one may—and must—"play up," and "play the man." Thus and thus only can a man maintain his freedom, however circumscribed, in a totalitarian world: the small area of what is really within one's power—perhaps only that of his thoughts (as Boethius found in prison)—was enough to enable him to bear up, and like Atlas support the burden of a world of responsibility, of tragedy, or of evil.

The Stoics' cosmology was the traditional system of concentric spheres—Cleanthes, alas, had joined the majority in rejecting the Aristarchan heliocentric astronomy. The soul is an efflux from the fiery *aether* which inspires and guides the stars. God is the divine Force, Power, *Logos*, Mind in all phenomena. This is a kind of pantheism, in which divine *logos* or reason "runs through all things everlastingly," as Cleanthes said,[18] the *logos* or wisdom by which God "knows to make evil good, the crooked straight," and achieve ends which seem utterly impossible because of human folly, sin, or blind frustration. God can bring good out of evil; he also is a redeemer God, like the God described in the Old Testament. The universe continues to exist by a cyclical repetition of all things: in the course of infinite time, all possible worlds will be tried out, and the flowing tides of life and energy will necessarily produce successive systems, each rising and falling, burned out and burned up, like satellites returning into the atmosphere, and then renewed again, thus producing repeated wars at Troy, with many successive heroes like Achilles, poets like Homer, teachers like Socrates.

What has been shall be, as before!

[18] See the translation of his Hymn to Zeus in my *Hellenistic Religions*, pp. 152–4.

They also contributed to the reinterpretation of the old myths and tales of the gods and heroes by the use of allegory—thus salvaging for religious instruction and edification many stories that were essentially false or degrading. Plato's rejection of the poets and their tales had been too sweeping: rightly interpreted, the myths held noble lessons to be unfolded by the allegorist.

But the Stoics went still further. Posidonius (135–51 B.C.) made room in the system for divination and astrology—on the theory that since things on earth are like things in heaven, i.e. in the heavens, and since the weaker must be controlled by the stronger, therefore heavenly events must always influence earthly. If you could only understand the meaning of the stars in their courses, you could foretell events destined to come to pass upon earth. Hence the wide-open door to astrological "science," so-called, through which weak and prying minds have ever since wandered into a realm of illusion and fantasy. But this unfortunate development in later Stoicism must not blind us to the real merits of the philosophy, or its importance in the lives of many of the noblest figures in Roman history, men who achieved independence of mind even under political tyranny, persecution, or martyrdom. Epictetus, for example, never tired of quoting the saying of Socrates: "Anytus and Melitus may bind my leg, but Zeus himself cannot fetter my will." And in his own life he demonstrated its truth. Born a slave, he was lamed in childhood by a brutal master, but he never let this handicap break his spirit or destroy his equanimity. His epitaph was preserved by St John Chrysostom:

> Slave, poor as Irus, halting as I trod,
> I, Epictetus, was the friend of God.

Of somewhat less extensive influence but equally a symptom of the determination to find a ποῦ στῶ, a *modus vivendi*, i.e. standing room, if nothing more, in a hostile universe, was the philosophy of Epicurus (341–270 B.C.). This has often been described, in ancient times as well as in modern, as pure hedonism, the pursuit of pleasure, and an attempt to find a philosophic excuse for such a view and its pursuit. But Epicurus's problem was the same as that of the others: how to be inwardly free in a chaotic totalitarian world. His answer was, first of all get rid of superstition: the gods are not interested in human affairs, and take no thought about justice, personal or social—the view of Adeimantus in Plato's *Republic* (II. 362*d*—367*e*). You have your own life to live: the gods are far away, perhaps in some remote realm in the skies; therefore trample under foot the threat of Tartarus, the terrors of Acheron, and the legend of Minos and Rhadamanthus with their final subterranean court! (I suspect that if any of us had lived then, we too might have been inclined to welcome such a message.) The good life *can* be lived, albeit quietly; therefore λάθε βιώσας, "Live quietly." Pain can be endured. Epicurus himself, a school-teacher, suffered the recurrent agonies of gall-stone all his life. The goal of ἡδονή, as he described it, was not pleasure, but *happiness*: and "the teaching," as his followers called it, told how one could achieve happiness here and now, whatever the outward conditions one had to face. As a later Epicurean, Diogenes of Oenoanda (*c.* A.D. 200), taught, according to a brief "tetractys" setting forth his doctrine:

> There is nothing to fear in God;
> There is nothing to feel in death;
> Evil can be endured;
> Good can be achieved.[19]

It would be interesting to speculate over a question: What would St Paul have made of this summary? "Nothing to fear in God"—of course not, for God commends his love for us in the life, the death, and the resurrection of his Son, Christ our Lord. "Nothing to feel in death"—of course not, for death is swallowed up in victory. Who shall separate us from the love of God which is in Christ Jesus our Lord? "Evil can be endured"—of course it can, for I reckon the sufferings of this present time to be as nothing in comparison with the glory that shall be revealed. "Good can be achieved"—certainly, for in fact God works all things together for good to them that love him.[20] It is along this line that one begins to see what the Greek Church fathers meant by the *praeparatio evangelica*, the divine preparation for the coming of Christ, in Hebrew prophecy, in Roman law, and also in Greek philosophy.

[19] Cf. Gilbert Murray, *Five Stages of Greek Religion*, Oxford 1925, pp. 204f.
[20] See Rom. v. 8, VIII. 32; I Cor. xv. 54; Rom. VIII. 38f., 18, 28.

As we now recognise, traces and echoes of all the Greek philosophies are to be found in the New Testament—not only Platonism, Aristotelianism, Stoicism (these we might have expected, since the New Testament came out of the Greek-speaking eastern Mediterranean world during the ten decades between A.D. 50 and 150), but also Cynicism and Epicureanism, and the criticisms levelled against these schools by their rivals. As Christianity advanced in the Graeco-Roman world, and as more and more converts were made among the better educated, it was inevitable that the prevailing philosophy or philosophies should influence at least the language of apologists and theologians. Such important concepts as that of the *Logos* in which (or "by whom") all things "hold together" (cf. Col. I. 17, τὰ πάντα ἐν αὐτῷ συνέστηκεν: the word *logos* is not used here, but the idea is present; συνίστημι=*con-sistere*); or the conception of the Primal Being, superior to the *Dēmiourgos* or Creator (Heb. XI. 10) and yet the Παντοκράτωρ (II Cor. VI. 18, from the Septuagint), the All-powerful All-ruler to whom all things in the universe bow and obey; the eternal God "who only has immortality" *(ἀθανασία)*, as the one and only source of life, including life after death—who "dwells in unapproachable light, whom no man has ever seen or can see" (I Tim. VI. 16, a combination of biblical ideas with Greek philosophical); the φιλανθρωπία, "the goodness and loving kindness of God our Saviour," i.e. his "love for man" which "appeared" (or "was manifested," ἐπεφάνη) in Christ (Ti. III. 4)—this language is obviously tinged with meanings derived from the classical schools of philosophy. But popular Cynicism, in the philosophical sense, is also to be found. "Sufficient unto the day is the evil thereof" (Mt. VI. 34, A.V.), or, rather, as in the R.S.V., "Let the day's own trouble be sufficient for the day"—i.e. Don't borrow tomorrow's trouble today—this is a Cynic maxim. "Let what you say be simply 'Yes' or 'No'; anything more than this comes from evil" (Mt. V. 36)—i.e. it partakes of the evil in the world, for it presupposes the probability of a large percentage of lying and misrepresentation in all human speech. To translate this as "from the evil one" (R.S.V. mg) is possible, but unnecessary.

Even Epicureanism is reflected—and rejected: "Let us eat and drink, for tomorrow we die" (I Cor. XV. 32; Is. XXII. 13) sounds like a caricature of Epicureanism. The world was full of criticism and caricature of Epicurus's teaching—though there was nothing quite so vitriolic as the modern tag, "the swine in Epicurus's sty"—an unworthy line of a worthy poet. But the nobler sort, men like Virgil, for example, knew these to be only libels, of which there were many. Epicurus's ancient biographer listed these attacks and added, "These calumnies are insane"— μεμήνασι δ' οὗτοι.[21] The fact that pain, defeat, injustice, maddening disappointment or frustration *can* be overcome and trodden underfoot is clearly affirmed throughout the New Testament, not least in the story of Jesus' arrest, trial, and crucifixion: it was also the teaching of Epicurus. And there are other examples which can readily be found in the New Testament, e.g. Paul's statement, "I consider that the sufferings of this present time are not worth comparing with the glory that is to be revealed to us" (Rom. VIII. 18).

There were still other schools and types of philosophical thought which ought to be considered. There was, for example, an underground stream of Platonism, emerging in Neo-Pythagoreanism and in such writings as the *De Mundo*, wrongly ascribed to Aristotle, or the famous lecture of Plato *On the Good* (to which Aristotle was once thought to have referred, but which is no longer extant—even Aristotle's own treatise on this subject has survived only in fragments). This was the Platonism which inspired Philo and the Alexandrian fathers; which influenced Paul and the author of Hebrews, and perhaps also the author of the Fourth Gospel; and which eventually emerged in full force on the surface in the philosophy of Plotinus and the Neoplatonists. This hidden school or tradition of Platonism, whose doctrines were wholly distinct from the teaching and tradition of the official Academy, was a life-giving stream flowing down through the centuries. It is presupposed by St Augustine and by the medieval Schoolmen, by Richard Hooker and the Cambridge Platonists, and by many others. It has influenced Christian theology for eighteen centuries—probably for nineteen, i.e. from Paul to the present day.

Moreover, there was still another type of philosophy—if we can call it that—in the first and second centuries, coming out of the borders of Judaism side by side with Christianity, and tak-

---

[21] *Vita*, §9.

ing on the darker hues of popular speculation in the Hellenistic-Roman world. I mean Gnosticism, the theory which presupposes that the evil in the world is inherent in its very nature,
or at least is derived from some cosmic or pre-cosmic misfortune or collapse which had involved the Demiurge and all his
works. It also shares the speculations about an evil World-Soul
which, as we have seen, rested upon an *ex parte* interpretation
of a phrase used in Plato's latest writings, the *Laws* and the
*Timaeus*. This dark theory is also reflected in the New Testament: "The whole world lieth in the evil one" (1 Jn. v. 19, A.V.),
or, as in the R.S.V., "is in the power of the evil one"—we cannot quite translate it "is under the dominion of evil," though
this seems to be implied. Man's only hope of salvation lies in
*escape* from the dismal dungeon of matter, of endless generation
or "becoming,"[22] of false opinion in lieu of the truth, of helpless entombment in the flesh, this dying life, this "body of
death" (Rom. VII. 24), this unbreakable chain of sex and pro-
creation (Jas. III. 6), this slavery to the senses. But how can he
escape unless someone sets him free? And how can he even
know his peril, while he lies drugged and impotent at the bottom of this foul, stifling dungeon of matter—unless someone
tells him of it, and bids him rise and mount upwards toward the
light? What he needs to learn is the fact that he *is* in prison (like
the cave-dwellers in Plato's *Republic*, Bk. VII), and that there is a
way out. He needs to discover—or be told—what his own true
nature really is, and the possibility of his release and return to
the higher realm, his "true native land" (as in St Thomas's
hymn), and what his final destiny can be: all this is γνῶσις,
"knowledge"; it is a body of information, and it is also a message of salvation.

The sources of the Gnostic world-view and philosophy are
various. They include Greek Orphism and Pythagoreanism,
Mazdaean dualism, Jewish apocalyptic (which collapsed with
the two unsuccessful wars against Rome in A.D. 66–70 and 132–
35), Egyptian mystery-lore, popular Hellenistic astrology and
numerology and the occult pseudo-sciences allied to magic,
along with the crass "spirituality" of mediums, quacks, and
religious adventurers. For Gnosis, like Christianity, like all
religions, had various levels; some high, some low, and many

[22] Another echo of Plato. Cf. *Timaeus*, 29d.

intermediate. But in general its world-renouncing principle of escape and abnegation, its total disillusionment with the things of this world, and its insistence that safety lies only in flight, helped to set the total scene for the rise and spread of the early Christian Church. This feature also has echoes in the New Testament. For example, in Jn. xvii. 15 Christ's "high-priestly" prayer contains the words: "I do not pray that thou shouldst take them out of the world, but that thou shouldst keep them from the evil one"—who is not the jolly old devil of popular European folklore or even the malicious "accuser of our brethren" in the days of persecution, but the vast, world-embracing principle of evil, the cosmic power that now holds the universe in subjection (as in 1 Jn. v. 19), but whose power is doomed and will eventually be destroyed. The language is quasi-Gnostic; the petition is completely non-Gnostic, even anti-Gnostic.

It is for this reason, no doubt, that Rudolf Bultmann concludes the Introduction to his *Theology of the New Testament* with an account of Gnostic *motifs*, the principles underlying a religious philosophy which soon became all but ubiquitous and could be found in every quarter of the civilised world. It was certainly one of the most important elements in the background of the early Church and its developing theology. As the Church emerged upon the scene, in the Graeco-Roman world of the first century, perhaps even before it had left the motherland of Palestine on its far-flung mission and began its steady advance northward and westward, the Apostles had come in contact with this strange type of religious thought—so very un-Hebraic, un-Jewish, un-Semitic. The picture of early Church evangelism preserved in the Clementine Recognitions and Homilies is undoubtedly late; but very probably, as Hans-Joachim Schoeps maintains,[23] there are older, traditional elements in these fanciful works. The probability of conflict with Gnostics is supported by some of the oldest material in the New Testament, such as the story of Simon Magus in Acts viii. 4–25. And the possibility of real influence may be seen in the incorporation of what at least looks very much like a Gnostic hymn in Mt. xi. 25–30; Lk. x. 21–2. There is also Gnostic material in John—especially in John. Bultmann's main source, the *Redequelle*, from which the author of John drew his discourse material, was, according

[23] In his *Urgemeinde, Judenchristentum, Gnosis*, Tübingen 1956, and other works.

to Bultmann, a Gnostic poem (see his Commentary, *passim*). On the other hand there is the all but total rejection of Gnosticism in the letters of Paul, and its open disavowal in the Johannine epistles. The final struggle with Gnosis came in the second century, with a tapering off in the third and fourth; the course of the conflict may be traced in the writings of Irenaeus, Tertullian, Hippolytus, and Epiphanius. Modern discovery has enriched our knowledge of this movement, which threatened to engulf the early Church. The surviving literature of Gnosticism, now enlarged by the discovery of a whole Gnostic library at Nag-Hammadi in Egypt, makes it clear that the Church's victory was indispensable for the further progress of the gospel and the survival of historical Christianity.[24]

The definition of Gnosticism which Paul Wendland gave in his *Hellenistisch-römische Kultur*[25] is still suggestive: it was "the theology of syncretism." The vast pooling of religions and philosophies in the early Roman Empire resulted in conflict as well as coherence. Along with the widespread practices of astrology and magic, the belief in Fate or Destiny, in dualism, in the dichotomy of the spiritual world and the material, and the superiority of the former over the latter, in oracles and divination, in "signs and wonders" and in the possibility of foretelling the future, in theurgy and all the varied lore of occultism and spiritualism, in ghosts and demons and in second sight, in daemonic possession—this whole vast realm of *Aberglaube*, which, once swept back for a time by Greek rationalism, was now once more infiltrating the whole world of religious belief and practice—*this* was the syncretism to which Gnosis undertook to provide the key, the systematic explanation, and the solution. There was, in fact, no one system of Gnosis, but many —as many systems of Gnosis as there were Gnostic teachers. This made the Church's task both harder and easier: harder, in that the Gnostic thesis took protean forms; easier, in that the Church's front was far more united than that of the Gnostics.

Still another example of syncretism may be seen in the spread of the so-called "mystery" religions, which sometimes seemed

[24] See R. M. Grant, *Gnosticism and Early Christianity*, New York and London 1959; *Gnosticism: A Sourcebook of Heretical Writings from the Early Christian Period*, New York and London 1961. [25] Tübingen 1907, 2nd edn. 1912.

to imply certain philosophical presuppositions.[26] Fifty years ago it was commonly believed that the Oriental "mysteries" supplanted the traditional cults of Greece and Rome; that in fact the abandonment of the traditional cults had created a religious "vacuum" into which the new Eastern rites flowed without hindrance, during the opening years of the early Roman Empire. And it was believed that a profoundly spiritual "mystery theology" was shared by these Eastern cults, and that it was propagated by them in more or less uniform terms. One scholar even held that he had identified a Mithraic "liturgy" among the Egyptian papyri; and it was common belief that one and all these "mystery" rites conferred immortality upon their adherents, chiefly through such sacramental rites as baptism and a common sacred meal. From this view it was only a short step to the assumption that here was the source from which the early Church derived its "sacramentalism," its theology of divine incarnation and human regeneration, its observance of a seven-day week beginning with a "Sun" day, its central idea of a dying-rising Saviour, its graded ministry to which admission was granted by initiation and consecration, its notion of a cleansing, revivifying, life-renewing bath of blood— all these were "borrowings" from the Eastern cults. Traces or echoes of this theory can still be found in novels and in book reviews—especially reviews by writers whose equipment for discussing religion is chiefly "literary" or journalistic rather than expert acquaintance with the subject. For the experts know—and tell us—that the theory was grossly exaggerated; that three-fourths of its foundation was mere hypothesis, like the "floating foundations" of heavy buildings which rest upon soft clay; that there was no such thing as a mystery "theology," shared one and all by the Oriental cults; that the so-called Mithras liturgy was neither Mithraic nor a liturgy, but a document which belongs among the voluminous magical papyri; that the main period of *floruit* of the mystery religions was not the first century but the second and third—much too late to have provided Christianity with sacraments, ministry, or the fundamental doctrines of salvation, regeneration, or the death and

[26] The best introductory work in this field is still Franz Cumont's *Les Religions orientales dans le paganisme romain*, Paris 1904, 4th edn. 1929; English trans. of 2nd edn. by Grant Showerman, Chicago 1911. It has recently been reprinted as a paperback.

resurrection of a divine Saviour; that, in simple fact, as the early Church fathers and apologists held, some of the "mystery" features and terms were really borrowed from Christianity, not the reverse; that the fascinating formula, *taurobolio criobolioque in aeternum renatus* ("reborn unto eternity in the bath of bull's blood and in that of a ram") is found—as we have already seen[27] —in only one inscription, and that from the late fourth century, a time when the "pagan reaction" was doing its best to copy and take over the more appealing elements in Christianity—a sacred book, baptismal regeneration, holy communion, even a blessed Trinity; and that in reality the taurobolium (which was common to two of the cults, first that of Cybele and later that of Mithras) was only a kind of life-renewal or restoration of juvenile vitality undertaken every twenty years; and that on the whole the Oriental mysteries were only ancient—indeed primitive—vegetation rites freshly refurbished and "humanised" for export to the West. The model on which they were repatterned was that of the ancient Greek cult of Demeter, which had long been interpreted as guaranteeing a blessed immortality in the life to come and as effecting an improvement in character here and now.

The real significance of the mysteries was not their "evocation" of Christianity, "the last and greatest of the mystery cults," as a recent writer has affirmed, or even their preparation for the gospel—they came too late for that. Their real significance and importance lie in their manifestation of the widespread human longing for personal religion and for the satisfaction of deeper needs than the civic cults or the traditional round of old agricultural and military festivals could provide. Not immortality, but a *blessed* immortality—this is what the mysteries offered, as a rule. Anyone could look forward to some kind of life after death in the dark realm under the earth, but this was no more inviting in the first three centuries than it had

---

[27] See above, Ch. I and Ch. II, pp. 18, 38ff. The *taurobolium*, as the word suggests, goes back to the bull-hunt in ancient Anatolia. Presumably the wild bulls were brought down with ropes, six or eight feet long, with two or three lead balls attached to their ends (two balls at the ends of a single rope, or three at the ends of two ropes tied together in T form). To this day the *gauchos* in the Argentine use *bolas* in a similar way. But in the third and fourth centuries A.D. the old Anatolian custom had been forgotten and the word now meant the bath of physical and moral regeneration in the bull's blood.

been in the days of Homer (*Odyssey*, XI. 488–91). What men craved was reunion with their departed friends and families, their loved ones—see the funerary monuments, and also many of the inscriptions—and, especially, with the divine, benevolent, kindly spirits whom men had once known here on earth: the "good" gods, the heroic, self-sacrificing men and women who had been their passing manifestation, the gods who had once been men, according to the widely-held view of Euhemerus, or who had in one way or another shared the vicissitudes, the misfortunes, even death, with the rank and file of mankind. What the people of Lystra said of Paul and Barnabas was also said by these devotees of the mysteries: "The gods have come down to us in the likeness of men!" (Acts XIV. 11). As a consequence, these particular gods understood men's needs and their hunger for life, for "more abundant life, whereof our nerves are scant"; above all, their craving for divine sympathy, patience, a divine readiness to listen and understand. This is precisely what the author of the Epistle to the Hebrews recognised in "our great High Priest who has passed through the heavens, Jesus the Son of God," who bears with him for ever "a feeling for our infirmities" and "can deal gently with the ignorant and wayward, since he himself is beset with weakness" (Heb. IV. 14 f., v. 2). Once more, it is the *psychological* significance of the mysteries, as a vast and portentous phenomenon in Hellenistic-Roman religion, that should engage our attention, not the mere question of borrowings or of derivations by one cult from another. What they unite to testify is not to any "mystery theology," but to the world-wide hunger for a deeper, more personal experience of religion, which was still centred in its double goal of cleansing and power. As Martin Nilsson has shown, at the beginning of his great *History of Greek Religion*,[28] this two-fold quest, for cleansing and power, had characterised Mediterranean religion from its remotest prehistoric stages. Only, in the period of Roman Hellenism, the purification and the power which men now craved was often more spiritual and moral than physical.

This was the world of the early Gentile churches. It was the world in which all early Gentile Christians had been reared, the world whose language the Church had to learn and whose

[28] *Geschichte der griechischen Religion*, VOL. I, pp. 41–3, etc. See above, pp. 4f.

ideas it had to comprehend if it was to engage in missionary propaganda and proclaim its "gospel for all mankind," the world which inevitably influenced—as well as was influenced by —the swiftly-spreading message of the Christian missionaries and evangelists. The result was a *Christian* syncretism, a type of belief and teaching somewhat different from the old Galilean gospel of "the Twelve" or of "the apostles and elders" in Jerusalem or of "the churches of Christ in Judea." In brief, the circle became an ellipse, with two foci: to the old original centre, the Jewish Law and the Old Testament revelation which had now been completed and fulfilled by Jesus' messianic teaching, life, death, and resurrection, was now added another, the rational understanding of the world and of human life and its true ethos as set forth in language moulded or created by Greek philosophy, language which included such terms as λόγος, ἦθος, σωφροσύνη, ψυχή, ἀθανασία, δημιουργός. For a time the two sets of terms, the Hebraic and the Greek, were used simultaneously, but distinctly; then more and more interchangeably; until in the end the two melted into each other and a Christian theological vocabulary was produced. Even before the New Testament period the Greek terms had begun to take on a Hebraic tinge in some circles—especially among the Jews of Alexandria, whose Greek translation of the Old Testament was the Bible of the early Gentile churches, and whose religious and philosophical writings (especially those of Philo) were destined to exert an immense and far-reaching influence not only upon Christian biblical interpretation but also upon Christian theology, including Christology—one might even say *especially* Christology. The two currents flowed along side by side in the New Testament; but by the end of the second century they were becoming indistinguishable; by the fourth and fifth it could be held that the Christian terminology applied to the Old Testament as fully as to the New, and that one consistent system of doctrine underlay the whole of revelation, from Moses to the Apostle John, from the Creation story in Genesis to the description of the future Consummation at the end of the Apocalypse. Thus the "emergence" of early Christian doctrine was conditioned from its very beginning by a twofold inheritance, the Greek-speaking Judaism of the Western Diaspora and the eclectic popular philosophy inherited from the Greek schools.

# Chapter IV

# Hellenism under the Early Roman Empire

Everyone knows, by now, that there are no "breaks" in human history. It is all one continuous stream of events. Even such catastrophic events as the fall of Nineveh, of Babylon, of Jerusalem, of Rome, Constantinople, Paris, Berlin, are only markers or milestones: what went before led up to these inescapable crises, what followed after them worked out the fateful consequences, sometimes very slowly. It took Rome 150 years to fall; it took ten centuries for the final consequences to be worked out—if, indeed, they have ever been fully worked out even now. Nevertheless, as everyone knows, there is a difference between ancient history and modern, between the Dark Ages and the Middle Ages, between the long dim periods of slow human emergence and of nascent civilisation, followed by the more or less static age of the Old Oriental empires— Egypt, Assyria, Babylon, Persia—and then the ages that succeeded them, when the centre of gravity swung westward. And so the question is a natural one: When did modern history begin? There have been many answers: it began with Christopher Columbus, or with the Renaissance in Italy, or with Marco Polo and the Venetian trade routes to the East, or with Charlemagne and the Holy Roman Empire. A good case can be made for the view of Thomas Arnold of Rugby[1] that modern history began with the rise of the Athenian sea empire in the time of Pericles; or, better, with the eastward thrust of Greek civilisation a century later, under Alexander.

The Hellenistic age marked the end of the long period of the Old Oriental empires, with a powerful westward shift in political and cultural domination and in the range of world trade. The bazaars of the East did not disappear; but their goods now found larger markets in the West than ever before.

[1] See A. P. Stanley, *Life of Thomas Arnold*, London 1844, VOL. I, p. 180. Arnold was made professor of Modern History at Oxford in 1841, and delivered his inaugural lecture on 2 December.

New markets and manufactures opened up, especially in Asia Minor, whose goods henceforth reached not only the old Greek colonies and settlements in Italy, Gaul, and North Africa, but also the newer ones throughout the Near and Middle East. Human culture or civilisation follows the routes of trade far more often and more successfully than it does the pathways of armies. But in this case the two routes were the same: Alexander's conquest of the Persian Empire followed age-old routes of trade and travel, and in turn the trade routes of the later centuries continued to be those of antiquity which had been the routes taken by Alexander and his armies.

The Hellenistic age opened with an attempt to achieve world empire, an attempt which succeeded momentarily and then suddenly failed, when Alexander died at Babylon in 323 B.C. But in the end it partly succeeded; for the three (really four) main divisions of Alexander's empire were sufficiently similar, in their pattern of control and in their possession of a common culture, to approximate to the Graeco-Oriental world empire which the conqueror had foreseen. Egypt, together with the rest of north-eastern Africa (Libya and Cyrenaica) and also Palestine and southern Syria and the island of Cyprus, went to Ptolemy and his successors; Syria, southern Asia Minor, Mesopotamia, and the whole of Persia and the Middle East as far as India, were held by Seleucus and his successors, reigning from Antioch; Macedonia went first to Cassander but was seized in 298 B.C. by Demetrius the son of Antigonus, who founded the Antigonid dynasty; in addition there were a number of small independent states, such as Pergamum, Rhodes, Delos, and the territories of the Aetolian and Achaean Leagues in Greece.

The long and chequered history of the "Successors" to Alexander was eventually brought to a close by the eastward advance of Rome. Antiochus III of Syria was defeated at the battle of Magnesia in 189 B.C.; Corinth was conquered and destroyed in 146 B.C.; the kingdom of Pergamum was bequeathed to the Roman people by its last king, Attalus III, who died in 133 B.C.; Pompey the Great conquered Mithridates, cleared the eastern Mediterranean of pirates, driving them into the mountains of Cilicia, and took over Syria in 64 B.C., annexing Palestine the following year; Egypt was

seized by Augustus when the coalition of Antony and Cleopatra collapsed in 31 B.C.; Trajan, who extended the borders
of the Empire to their greatest limits, added Armenia and
Mesopotamia in A.D. 115. But here Rome halted in its eastward
advance, and Trajan's boundaries were soon relinquished by
Hadrian in 117; he recognised the impossibility of defending
such far-flung frontiers without natural boundaries of seas,
rivers, or mountains. A sandy desert is no boundary at all.
But by this time the world's centre of culture, trade, and
political administration had been shifted far to the West, to
Rome, which an early Church father once described as "at the
utmost bounds of the West" (1 Clement v. 7).

The history of these five centuries, from Alexander's conquest of the Near and Middle East to the imperial Roman
conquest and pacification of both East and West—the period
from 330 B.C. to A.D. 170—is the history of the Hellenisation
of the whole civilised world, from the western borders of India
to the Straits of Gibraltar, and from the upper Nile Valley as
far as Nubia, from Arabia and the Sahara to the damp forests
of Britain, Gaul, Germany, Dacia, the valley of the Danube and
the broad plains north and west of the Black Sea. Even beyond
these frontiers Roman traders had carried Hellenism, at least
its articles of trade, as Sir Mortimer Wheeler has shown in his
fascinating *Rome Beyond the Imperial Frontiers* (1954; now available as a paperback). The rise of Rome had brought new
factors into play and had set new forces at work throughout the
whole οἰκουμένη, i.e. that part of the known world where men
lived in houses, as contrasted with the wild nomads wandering
freely beyond the frontiers. Hence the Hellenistic age must
either be limited to the period from 331 to 31 B.C., after which
the Roman age followed; or, better, from the point of view of
the history of culture, it must be divided in two parts, viz.,
Earlier or Alexandrian Hellenism (331–31 B.C.) and Later or
Roman (30 B.C. to the fall of Rome)—though Jean Seznec and
others are quite right in tracing the full course of Hellenism
down to the Italian Renaissance and even later. It was this
period of Later or Roman Hellenism which formed the background of the New Testament and the rise of Christianity.
And it was Roman Hellenism which formed the climax of the
whole long cultural and religious development of the ancient

world, the second stage in the rise of the modern world which eventually took its place.

At its widest extent, the Roman Empire embraced a territory of approximately 1,600,000 square miles; the figure is Edward Gibbon's, in the *Decline and Fall of the Roman Empire*. With this figure one may compare the present area of the United States, now over 3,600,000 square miles, or the Russian Soviet Republic, now over 2,600,000 square miles. The territory of the Roman Empire, which surrounded the Mediterranean Sea on the north, east, and south, included the whole of Italy and the thirty-six provinces. Most of this vast region was fertile, though parts of it were already threatened with depopulation, chiefly as the consequence of war, slavery, and pre-scientific agriculture. Adolf Deissmann's famous map, "The World of the Apostle Paul,"[2] shaded the areas where the olive was cultivated —a very good index to density of population and also, appropriately in a Hellenised world, marking the centres of higher civilisation—was not the olive sacred to Athena? The total population of the Roman Empire, in the first or second century, has been variously estimated at from twenty-five to one hundred million. The generally accepted estimate is now that of the German historian Karl Julius Beloch, who favoured an intermediate figure of 54,000,000. This would be an average of just under 34 persons per square mile; but, as in the modern world, even in densely populated countries, the average was not often found, and there were some areas of extreme over-population, especially in the great cities, Rome, Alexandria, Antioch; there were also areas where the population was very sparse, and some where it was declining, even in the relatively prosperous first century.[3]

It is unfortunate that our information about the boundaries and the population of the Empire is so scanty and speculative.

[2] Published in his *Paulus*, Tübingen 1911.

[3] Professor Michael Grant in his recent book, *The World of Rome*, London 1960, estimates the population of the empire under Augustus at between seventy and ninety millions, with from thirty to fifty in Europe, the same number or fewer in Asia, and something under twenty millions in Africa (p. 30). The average for the United States is now (1960 census) 50·4 per sq. mile and ranges from 800·2 in New Jersey, 798·7 in Rhode Island, and 650·1 in Massachusetts to 3·4 in Wyoming, 2·6 in New Mexico, and 0·4 in Alaska. There were similar contrasts in density of population in the ancient world.

The first-century data are no longer available—it is not improbable that earlier archives containing such data were destroyed in the fire at Rome in the days of Nero. The Emperor Augustus, for one, had required meticulous book-keeping, census, and land records. But the frontiers fluctuated through the decades both before and after his time. Military strategy was usually the decisive factor in deciding the boundaries—as under Vespasian, Trajan, and Hadrian. But the information from the frontier was not always accurate: few emperors sat facing the foe along the Danube, as Marcus Aurelius did when writing his *Meditations*. Nor was a well-thought-out plan ever adopted and consistently pursued. It is most regrettable, from the point of view of the later history of Europe, that Roman army intelligence was not more efficient, and that the plan, partly carried out later on by Marcus Aurelius, to shorten the northern frontier by following the line of the Carpathian mountains and the Vistula river, was not adopted and reinforced. This would have shortened the frontier by 1500 miles, and might have enabled the Empire to hold back the Huns and Vandals. Had Rome been granted two more centuries of civilising control in northern Europe, and had it done for Germany what it did for Gaul and Britain, the future of the Continent would have been far happier. But Roman information about northern and central Europe was unbelievably bad. For example, Julius Caesar's invasion fleet was almost wholly destroyed by storm as it anchored off Dover; six miles to the east lay the safely sheltered harbour behind the Isle of Thanet. The great catastrophe in A.D. 9 when Varus and his three legions were destroyed in the Teutoburg forest, like the terrible defeat of Crassus at Carrhae, was the tragic result of inadequate information plus over-confidence and amateur strategy.

The older and more settled provinces, e.g. Sicily and Asia, were under the administrative control of the Senate, and hence were called "senatorial" provinces. On the other hand, those which still required military occupation were under the control of the emperor, and hence were called "imperial" provinces. Here the emperor was represented by military and civilian authorities, legates, procurators, governors. Egypt was under the absolute control of the emperor: even a Roman senator could not visit Egypt without the emperor's permission, for it

had been the base from which Antony and Cleopatra had undertaken to split the empire and make themselves autocrats of the
East. Palestine, before the revolt of A.D. 66, was attached to the
Province of Syria, under the control of the emperor's legate at
Antioch; but the direct administration, the collection of taxes,
and the policing of the country were the responsibility of the
procurator, resident at Caesarea on the coast—one of these
officials was Pontius Pilate, whose term of office ran from A.D.
26 to 36. The procurator's armed forces were comparatively
few in number, and were composed of auxiliaries, i.e. local or
native troops. Jews were exempt from military service, and
hence the recruits were neighbouring Gentiles—a fact which
helps to explain the intense antagonism between the Jews and
their Roman rulers, whose army of occupation was made up of
aliens, the hereditary enemies of Israel. The garrison in
Jerusalem was probably only one cohort strong, i.e. about 500
to 600 men, together with a small unit of cavalry (Acts XXIII.
23); but even this mediocre force was enough to irritate the
sensibilities of the Jewish populace, for Jerusalem was a sacred
city, and the presence of idolaters and "unclean" persons in the
very precincts of the Temple was abhorrent to all the devout.
Moreover, behind this token force in the Castle of Antonia
beside the Temple, or in the praetorium (Herod's palace) on
the west side of the Old City, and also behind the garrisons in
Sebastē and Caesarea, were the legionary camps up the coast,
all the way from Ptolemais to Antioch, with thousands of
veteran soldiers in reserve. In the time of Augustus these
legions had been three in number; in that of Tiberius there
were four, one of them the Legio VI Ferrata, another the
Legio X Fretensis, and the other two probably the Legio III
Gallica, which had fought under Mark Antony against the
Parthians, and the Legio XII Fulminata. Each of these legions
was composed of ten cohorts or sixty centuries, i.e. between
5000 and 6000 men, trained, disciplined, thoroughly seasoned
troops, against whom it was madness to undertake a war—
as King Agrippa II warned the people of Jerusalem.[4]

The political history of Palestine, from the coming of Rome
in the person of Pompey in 63 B.C. to the second fall of Jerusalem in A.D. 135, and even later, down to Byzantine times,

[4] Josephus, *Jewish War*, II. xvi. 4=§§345–401.

was conditioned by two constant factors. First was the Roman
requirement of an unbroken eastern frontier against the
Parthians, the Nabataeans, and other nomads in the Arabian
desert—for once, at the very beginning of Herod's reign (in
40 B.C.), the Parthians had invaded Palestine and plundered
Jerusalem. The long frontier line from the Black Sea to the Red,
approximately 800 miles, could not be left with its middle and
southern sectors wide open to the desert, an inviting open gate-
way to the swift-riding mounted archers and terrorists who had
repeatedly swarmed across from the Tigris–Euphrates valley
or down from the mountains farther east. Sound Roman
strategy demanded that this open sector be closed and firmly
held. The other factor was the basic principle of the Jewish
religion, viz. the divine theocracy founded upon God's Covenant with Israel and his authoritative Law. "No king but God"
was not only the slogan of the Zealots: it was also the presupposition of a petition in the *Shemoneh Esreh*, the central prayer in
the Jewish synagogue service:

> Blow the great trumpet for our deliverance,
> And raise up the banner for the gathering of our dispersed.
>> *Blessed art thou, O Lord, who gatherest the dispersed*
>> *of thy people Israel!*

> Restore our judges as in former days
> And our counsellors as at the beginning,
> And be thou alone Ruler over us.
>> *Blessed art thou, O Lord, who lovest judgment!*

"Be thou alone Ruler over us"—this was the prayer of the whole
Jewish people, from the days of the restoration following the
Exile to the end of ancient history and beyond. It was the
prayer which throbbed at the heart of the whole eschatological,
messianic, apocalyptic movement—or movements—from the
time of the author of Daniel and the long twenty-five-year Mac-
cabaean War of Independence to the final crushing blow under
Hadrian (i.e. from about 165 B.C. to A.D. 135), and even later.
It is still the hope of the religious-minded among the Zionists.
Israel must be free to worship God in Israel's own way—or
rather, in God's own prescribed way, founded upon his self-revelation to Moses and the prophets—without let or hindrance by any
external earthly power, whether imperial or daemonic, human,

bestial, or satanic. In fact, the conception of the theocracy was very old. The early historical tradition in the Old Testament represents Samuel as protesting against the popular demand for an earthly (i.e. a human) king, and reluctantly anointing Saul (see 1 Sam. VIII–XVI). The Deuteronomic editors do not hesitate to represent the monarchy as a grudging concession on the part of Yahweh the God of Israel.

We can scarcely imagine two more sharply, diametrically opposed principles, from two more completely alien outlooks upon the world, upon human life and its purpose and meaning, than the military view of the Romans and the religious view of the Jews. Out of such strange, irreconcilable discord evolves the human tragedy, in age succeeding age. Neither side understands the other—like the Sepoys and the British at the time of the Great Indian Mutiny a century ago. Neither side will make, or can make, any concession, for their basic presuppositions all rest upon deep-laid, mutually exclusive foundations; the one is a cult of patriotism and power, the other is a heroic martyr loyalty to divine revelation and a simple trust in the certainty of God's protection.

The Roman theory assumed that an imperial province would in time become a senatorial one, administered as a rule by an ex-consul or an ex-praetor with the title of proconsul, holding office for one year; such provinces required no military establishment save for the defence of their own frontiers. Here Roman citizens were settled, traders, merchants, manufacturers —like the firm of leather-workers headed by Paul's friends Aquila and Priscilla, operating (as many scholars now think) with a main house in Ephesus and a branch in Corinth, and perhaps with other branches elsewhere. These senatorial provinces were the mainstays of the Empire, and were no longer viewed as military outposts, liable to insurrection or invasion. At least, after the wars of Mithridates in Asia Minor and the Civil War launched by Antony and Cleopatra, there was no major disturbance in the East until the Jewish War in A.D. 66. Judea, of course, never became a senatorial province, but was always under military domination.

Throughout this vast world empire, one common language was everywhere in use. Even those who spoke it only occasionally and not very well, probably understood more of it than they could repeat. The widely scattered inscriptions in this Koine (i.e. common) Greek, throughout the whole Mediterranean basin, prove its general use and understanding. There was also, under the Roman occupation, a common and still-growing body of law, a system of legal procedure, and the generally accepted principles of justice and equity, all bearing the Roman stamp.[5] Even though Rome as a rule undertook to preserve, guarantee, and administer local law and custom in the occupied countries, an inevitable process of levelling and inter-penetration was already at work in the first century. Out of it eventually emerged the great legal system of the Code, the Digest, and the learned Commentaries of later teachers and jurists; but it was the emphasis of the Roman Stoics (e.g. of Seneca in the days of Nero) upon the *ius gentium*, the "law of nations," with its universally recognised principles of right and wrong, which was one of the earliest consequences of the Roman conquest of the Mediterranean world. It was also one of the finest, one of the most lasting fruits of Roman Hellenism. It is obviously presupposed, gratefully, throughout most of the New Testament. So important was the achievement of the *pax romana* that certain early Church fathers claimed a divine purpose behind the contemporaneous reign of Caesar Augustus and the coming of Christ. It is not impossible that St Luke also shared this view: note how he correlates events in the Gospel history with contemporary events in the Empire (see Lk. II. 1–7, III. 1).

Of course Caesar's monarchy was absolute—as Ulrich Kahrstedt insists at the very beginning of his brilliant sketch of the civilisation of the early Empire.[6] Under a just and benevolent emperor, the blessings of peace and prosperity were sure to be more or less universal. But under a tyrant or a madman, the results were inevitably tragic. It was fortunate for the early Christian Church that the first and second centuries were on the whole an era of peace and good will: Augustus, Tiberius, Claudius, Vespasian, Titus were better than average rulers. The reigns of Nero and Domitian and the anarchy of the "year of the three emperors" were interludes which did not set back

---

[5] See the three volumes of *Fontes Iuris Romani Antejustiniani*, new edn., especially VOL. I, ed. Salvator Riccobono. Florence 1941.

[6] *Kulturgeschichte der römischen Kaiserzeit*, new edn. Bern 1958.

permanently the rising tide of benevolent despotism, nor shatter the Roman peace. Highly placed individuals suffered the ill will of their absolute lords—as did similar unfortunates in the reigns of Henry VIII, Mary Tudor, and other more recent monarchs. But the strong upward, forward thrust of the Roman world toward the high level of social stability, peace and prosperity, and general good will achieved in the second century under the benevolent rule of the Antonines, was steady and continuous.

Fifty years ago it was commonly assumed that oppressive social, economic, and political conditions in the first century had given rise to a widespread revolt which eventually "sublimated" itself in Christianity, a religion which promised a compensation in the glorious "Age to Come" for the intolerable evils of the present. The Marxists pushed this theory with great vigour, and many "socially minded" Christians also shared it, more or less. But we know now that the social conditions under the early Empire were very different from those of the last two centuries before its establishment, and that especially from the time of Vespasian to that of Marcus Aurelius the Mediterranean world was increasingly prosperous. As Kahrstedt says, the Empire "bloomed" like a garden, up to the very eve of the economic collapse at the end of the second century— like a luxuriant garden which reaches the height of its splendour just before the frosts begin. This is his summary at the end of a two-hundred-page survey of the political, social, industrial, and economic conditions of the early Empire.[7] The Marxist theory is completely mistaken. Nevertheless it is often reflected in current books, articles, book reviews, novels, and even sermons by men who should know better. The "peace on earth" proclaimed by the angels at Christ's nativity was already in process of realisation under Augustus, and along with peace went a widespread and growing prosperity. It was certainly no false temporising or pretended loyalty that led Paul to write, at the end of Romans: "Let every person be subject to the governing

[7] This conclusion is confirmed and supported by the extensive researches of Michael Rostovtzeff, in his *Social and Economic History of the Hellenistic World*, 3 vols., Oxford 1941, and *Social and Economic History of the Roman Empire*, new edn., 2 vols., Oxford 1957. See also *Economic Survey of Ancient Rome*, ed. Tenney Frank, 5 vols., Baltimore 1933–40, and other modern works (see titles listed in the bibliography at the end of this volume, I, §F, Economic Conditions).

authorities. For there is no authority except from God, and those that exist have been instituted by God. . . . Pay all of them their dues, taxes to whom taxes are due, revenue to whom revenue is due, respect to whom respect is due, honour to whom honour is due" (Rom. XIII. 1–7). Nor was it mere prudential compromise that led Jesus to say, "Render to Caesar the things that are Caesar's" (Mk. XII. 17), for Jesus was an anti-revolutionist, an anti-Zealot, and he left revolutions in the hands of God. Nor was the dictum in 1 Peter an early example of political compromise or erastianism: "Be subject for the Lord's sake to every human institution, whether it be to the emperor as supreme, or to governors as sent by him to punish those who do wrong and to praise those who do right. . . . Honor all men. Love the brotherhood. Fear God. Honour the emperor" (1 Pet. II. 13–17). Except for local outbreaks—as under Nero in the city of Rome in A.D. 64 (see Tacitus, *Annals*, xv. 44); or in Bithynia during the Younger Pliny's governorship (see his *Letters*, x. 96 f.); or, far earlier, during Paul's missionary journeys in Asia Minor and Greece (see Acts XIII. 50, XIV. 2, 5, 19, XVI. 19, 22, XVII. 5, 13, XVIII. 12, etc.)—the Christians were unmolested; the Empire itself did not persecute the Christians. In fact, it is a difficult question to answer: When, and why, did the persecutions begin?[8]

The generally favourable condition of the Empire during the first two centuries goes far to explain why the early Church did not undertake a programme of social and political reform, such as freeing the slaves and establishing a democratic régime throughout the Mediterranean world. Quite apart from its eschatological expectation of the New Age "wherein dwelleth righteousness," which naturally forbade any movement in the direction of revolt, such a programme would only have resulted in the prompt suppression of the Christian Church everywhere and at once. And it explains why the early Christian ethics, like the teaching of Jesus himself, had, in Joseph Klausner's words, "nothing to say to the judge on the bench." "Man, who made me a judge or divider over you?" (Lk. XII. 14; cf. Ex. II. 14) might have been asked by any Christian in the first three or four generations. It also explains the somewhat one-sided orientation of Christian ethics to the present day: unquestioning

[8] See the appendix, *Religio Licita*.

obedience to the civil and military authorities, observance of the law, the prompt and uncomplaining payment of taxes, humility and patience in the face of injustice and oppression—all this we find in the New Testament and in the Church Catechism, but little or nothing about the duties of governors and kings or magistrates and law-*makers*, or the responsibilities of political appointees and representatives, of employers and employed, of teachers, entertainers, doctors and nurses, buyers and sellers, borrowers and lenders. On the whole, the early Church took over a body of agreed ethics, partly scribal (based on the Old Testament), partly popular Hellenistic (based on the teaching of the philosophers, especially the Stoics), and wove together a combination of these, using the New Testament (chiefly the teaching of Jesus and Paul) as the dominant pattern, but revising, re-emphasising, reorientating, adapting, and modifying as it went along. Compare, for example, the ethics found in the Didache and the Apostolic Fathers with those of the New Testament; or the *De officiis ministrorum* of St Ambrose with the *De officiis* of Cicero on which it is based; such studies will show how the Church proceeded. Or study Clement of Alexandria's writings; or examine the Christian recension of such a Jewish work as The Testaments of the Twelve Patriarchs.

Hence it is futile to appeal to the New Testament—or the Old—for a pattern of government today. This was the mistake of our Puritan ancestors, and of the seventeenth-century Scots Church Assembly, the Fifth Monarchy men, the Massachusetts Bay Colony, and even the "social gospellers" early in the present century. It had also been the mistake of the Lollards and of other medieval groups and sects which took the gospel for a political programme. In fact, *no* pattern from the past can be used now. Democracy was a total failure in Greece, as was the Republic in Rome, and theocracy in Judea. Greek democracy led to endless political atomism, disunity, and internecine mutual rivalries: it scarcely survived the Peloponnesian War— in fact it scarcely survived the life of Pericles. Roman autocracy was a military rule, whose finest period of administrative balance soon led to the fatal plunge down a deep precipice at the end of the reign of Marcus Aurelius; the reign of his son Commodus began the swift *descensus averno*. Roman republican- ism had been a good form of government, in certain periods and in rare places, under just and able administrators, and it was the envy of other nations; but the good governors were offset by the bad, by such men as Verres in Sicily and the governor whom the emperor sent back to his post: "You have robbed the people; now go back and live among them!" Moreover, it was, in most places, a government of armed force controlled by a distant emperor or Senate. (In theory, the early Empire was a "restored" Republic.) Hence, to return to the problem of today, our great venture of faith here in the West has no precedent or pattern derived from the ancient world, no structural outline set forth in the Bible, no theocratic legislation thundered forth from Sinai, no simple though profound exposition in the Sermon on the Mount. What Sir John Seeley called "Christ's legislation"[9] was not an outline of ideal politics. In America, our fathers went forth in faith, like the patriarchs of old, not knowing whither they went, but seeking a city whose Builder and Maker is God—not a city in heaven but one upon earth, to which they trusted God to guide them. We can study and learn much from the political dreams of such ancient thinkers as Plato, Aristotle, and the Stoics; and we can also discover the deep principles of personal ethics set forth in the Gospels and in the New Testament epistles (but scarcely in the Apocalypse); and these we can take as our "guide for life." But we must learn as we go along, and profit by our own experience, and recover from our mistakes, and still "follow the gleam" on the distant horizon. For our dream of representative, democratic government is no copy of anything to be found anywhere else in human history. It is, *sui generis,* the latest and boldest experiment in human government. Yet its mistakes can be recognised, checked, and corrected by principles set forth in the Scriptures; and its "vision on the mount" is certainly derived from those who were inspired not only by late eighteenth-century French radicalism but by the revelation of God's purpose and man's destiny set forth in the Jewish and Christian Sacred Book. This new approach to the New Testament on the political and ethical level is only one result—but a most important result—of its study in the light of the contemporary ancient Hellenistic-Roman world.

[9] See his famous *Ecce Homo.* London 1866.

But it was not only a common language, a system of law and government, and a world-wide network of trade and commerce that tended to unite and solidify the ancient Mediterranean *orbis terrarum*; other factors were the spread of philosophy and the progress of religious syncretism—these also must be examined. We should not overestimate the influence of philosophy; and yet its wide dissemination among the educated and the quasi-educated in all countries bordering on the great Inland Sea was a marked feature of the Hellenistic age, no less in its Roman phase than in its Alexandrian. As we have seen, the leading schools were now the Stoic and the Epicurean, both of which undertook to show men how to be happy and inwardly free, despite the tyranny of bad rulers, fate, chance, and all other misfortune. The schools of Plato and Aristotle were more academic and less popular in their appeal. But eventually their tenets reached the common level, where they were reflected in such movements as Neo-Pythagoreanism, Eclecticism, and eventually Neoplatonism (which, let us add, was somewhat above the "common level"). The direct influence of philosophy upon the New Testament is perceptible only in certain rare passages, as for example the Platonism of Paul in II Cor. IV. 18. But the indirect influence of philosophy was greater, especially by way of Alexandrian Judaism, as seen in the Book of Wisdom and in the writings of Philo. In the New Testament, the Epistle to the Hebrews is profoundly influenced by this Alexandrian type of Platonism, while the Gospel of John betrays to some extent the influence of popular Hellenistic philosophy, combined with much else, including an incipient Gnosticism and a biblical exegesis moving in that direction.

The pooling of religions, and also their resulting "conflict," described by T. R. Glover in his famous *Conflict of Religions in the Early Roman Empire*[10]—though we might prefer to call it "rivalry"—goes back a long way. As early as Greek travel and trade with Egypt and the East, an *interpretatio graeca* identified the gods of various foreign peoples with those of the Greeks: Amōn-Rē in Egypt was really Zeus; Artemis and Apollo were worshipped under other names in Scythia, the Crimea, and elsewhere in the North, which they visited annually. When the Romans identified the Greek gods—and others—with their

[10] London 1907.

own (Zeus, Bel, Amōn-Rē, and other supreme gods becoming Jupiter, and so on), this *interpretatio romana* was only a step removed from a universal polytheism, unified and subordinated to the gods of Rome, who had first proved themselves superior to all others by the Roman conquest of the Mediterranean world, and then were identified with them in a systematic mythology. The Stoics added their contribution by rationalising all gods, and identifying them with the processes of nature: for example, Zeus is "life," from ζάω; Hera is "air," from ἀήρ; Mercury is Hermes, the interpreter, from ἑρμηνεύειν; and so on. One of the most beautiful examples of this syncretism is the so-called Hymn to Isis found in Apuleius's *Metamorphoses*, XI. 5. It is not really a hymn, but an account of an epiphany, in which the goddess addresses her penitent votary:

Behold, Lucius, I have come, moved by your prayers! I, nature's mother, mistress of all the elements, earliest offspring of the ages, mightiest of the divine powers, Queen of the Dead, chief of them that dwell in the heavens, in whose features are combined those of all the gods and goddesses. By my nod I rule the shining heights of heaven, the wholesome winds of the sea, and the mournful silences of the underworld. The whole earth honours my sole deity [*numen unicum*] under various forms, with varied rites, and by many names. There the Phrygians, firstborn of men, call me the Mother of the Gods, she who dwells in Pessinus; there the Athenians, sprung from their own soil, know me as Cecropian Minerva; there the sea-girt Cyprians call me Paphian Venus; the Cretans, who are archers, call me Diana Dictynna [of the hunter's net]; the Sicilians, with their three languages, call me Stygian Proserpina; the Eleusinians, the ancient goddess Ceres. Others call me Juno, others Bellona, others Hecate, while still others call me the Rhamnusian. But those on whom shine the first rays of the Sun God as daily he springs to new birth, the Arii and the Ethiopians, and the Egyptians mighty in ancient lore, honouring me with my own peculiar rites, call me by my true name, *Isis the Queen*.[11]

Behind this movement of identification of deities was a kind of monotheism—or at least of henotheism—which Paul Wendland recognised as already in process of development in the third century B.C., and which reached its culmination in Solar Monotheism (see pp. 19, 49 f). Its political consequences, when combined with the absolute monarchy of the Caesars, now became obvious, and were ominous and fateful for the Christians. As there was but one supreme god in heaven, *Sol invictus*, the Unconquerable Sun, with many subordinates, so

[11] See my *Hellenistic Religions*, p. 138. The Rhamnusian goddess was Nemesis

there was, and could be, only one supreme ruler on earth, with countless subordinates, including all the peoples of the empire. (Caracalla, in 211, as we have said, made all freemen, everywhere, citizens of Rome.) And the bearing of all this upon emperor-worship is clear, though emperor-worship had its beginnings long before, in the early Hellenistic age, under the Ptolemies and Seleucids.

It was little wonder that in the Province of Asia, whose prosperity and Roman investments Cicero had described in his oration on the Manilian Law over sixty years earlier (in 66 B.C.), the grateful cities should decree divine honours to Augustus and establish a political-religious cult in his honour, and that they should alter the calendar to make the year begin on his birthday (23 September). Thus an inscription found at Halicarnassus in western Asia Minor, and dated some time after 2 B.C., reads as follows:

Since the eternal and deathless nature of the universe has perfected its immense benefits to mankind by granting us as a supreme benefit, for our happiness and welfare, Caesar Augustus, Father of his own Fatherland divine Rome, Zeus Paternal, and Saviour of the whole human race, in whom Providence has not only fulfilled but even surpassed the prayers of all men: land and sea are at peace, cities flourish under the reign of law in mutual harmony and prosperity; each is at the very acme of fortune and abounding wealth; all mankind is filled with glad hope for the future and with contentment over the present; [it is therefore fitting to honour the god] with public games and with statues, with sacrifices and with hymns.[12]

In striking contrast with the East, emperor-worship was for a long time not established in the West, and living emperors made—or accepted—no claim to divinity. Only the dead emperors, their predecessors, their ancestors, were deified, following the example of the deification of Julius Caesar. This explains why the collision between early Christianity and emperor-worship began in the East, not the West. The figure of the "beast rising out of the sea" in Rev. XIII. 1, with ten horns and seven heads, is generally recognised to be the Roman imperial cult: "Men worshipped the dragon, for he had given his authority to the beast, and they worshipped the beast, saying 'Who is like the beast, and who can fight against it?'" (vs. 4).

[12] *Ancient Roman Religion*, p. 174. See also the inscription from Priene, dated 9 B.C., on pp. 173 f. Its language reminds us of the Gospel of Luke, e.g. εὐεργέται, εὐαγγέλιον, Σωτήρ.

The other "beast," which "rose out of the earth" (vs. 11), is explained as Nero, or perhaps Domitian (vs. 18), since either name can be totalled numerically to either 666 or 616 (the latter is Irenaeus's variant reading). The following chapters (xiv–xx) are a thinly-veiled prediction of the coming conflict between the tiny Church and the universal, all-powerful Empire of Rome—a conflict destined to end at the Last Judgment with a final victory for the saints and martyrs over their persecutors.

How did the Church come to find itself in opposition to Rome? How did the gracious, benevolent *pax romana* come to exclude Christians from its protection? These are questions which greatly concern both the early Church historian and the New Testament exegete. Certainly the friendly and apprecia- tive attitude toward the Empire found in Paul, 1 Peter, the Gospels, and elsewhere in the New Testament is not reflected in the Apocalypse of John—or in any other apocalypse. Moreover, the administration of the *pax romana* had passed through various levels of responsibility since the days of Augustus: mad Caligula and Nero, and even Claudius, had contributed to the disruption of the peace. Men who believed in no god at all could readily claim themselves to be divine, and they either sought or accepted divine honours from their subjects.

It has often been pointed out that the persecution of the Christians was unnecessary; the "pinch of incense" was only a trifling symbol of political allegiance, and to refuse it was like a modern citizen refusing to salute the flag. But it has not so often been pointed out that the administration of this symbolic bit of patriotic ritual, with its implied oath of allegiance, was fre- quently in the hands of stupid, blundering army sergeants and police officers and local magistrates for whom the acknowledg- ment of Christ as heavenly King meant only treason and a threat of revolution. Speaking very generally, the Roman ad- ministration, while usually just and fair, was sometimes colos- sally stupid, literal-minded, materialistic, and unimaginative. In matters of religion, the ancient Roman was still profoundly legalistic, sceptical, superstitious, and wholly lacking in imagi- nation. As Professor Jean Bayet has reminded us,[13] psycho- logical considerations are indispensable for the understanding of

---

[13] In his recent *Histoire politique et psychologique de la religion romaine*. Paris 1957.

ancient Roman religion.[14] This is equally true of both its tolerance of some non-Roman cults and its total exclusion and antagonism for others, especially for Christianity.

These then are some of the more important factors in the Hellenistic background of the New Testament. The traditional emphasis upon a unified world government and its resulting world peace; upon a universal language (Greek), understood everywhere throughout the Empire; upon good roads and safe travel in almost all countries; upon freedom from molestation or attack by bandits, slave-raiders, or foreign invaders—all these factors are true and important. But deeper than all, in their significance, both positive and negative, were the spiritual conditions. The old religions were dying, but not dead: this called for a faith of a truer, firmer kind which could support men in life and death, in prosperity and adversity, under peaceful rulers and under tyrants. There were new religions abroad, responding to an aroused sense of moral impotence, futility, political frustration, and the universal dominion of Fate or Destiny. These new cults promised much, but not enough; and their promises were often better than their performance. Here was the opportunity for another and truer answer to men's hopes and aspirations, a religion "with power," able to make good what it promised, and promising even more than men had ever dared to hope.

> What no eye has seen, nor ear heard,
> nor [has] the heart of man conceived,
> what God has prepared for those who love him—

all this "God has revealed to us through the Spirit" (1 Cor. II. 9 f.).

[14] See also now Professor Kurt Latte's *Römische Religionsgeschichte*, esp. ch. III.

# Chapter V

# The Jewish Bible in the Graeco-Roman World

It is a popular modern idea that the New Testament was the Bible of the early Church—and some persons would like to make it the sole collection of sacred Scripture in the Church today. But the idea is quite mistaken. The Church already had a Bible, the Greek Old Testament, before any of the New Testament books were written. This Bible contained the Hebrew scriptures, which began to be translated into Greek as early as the third century before Christ, i.e. very early in the Hellenistic age; and the translation and collection of sacred books to form this Bible, the so-called Septuagint, was still continuing in the first century of the Christian era. Some of the added works— the so-called Apocrypha, fourteen books found in the Greek Old Testament but not in the Hebrew—were translated from Hebrew into Greek; others were composed in the latter language, presumably at Alexandria. To this still-growing collection of sacred writings of the Greek-speaking Jewish synagogue in the Western Diaspora, the early Christians added their own books as they came gradually and steadily into use at the services of public worship. In fact, some of the early Christian writings which were not included among the twenty-seven canonical New Testament books, when the Canon was finally determined, had been added to the Septuagint in several of the larger and more luxurious manuscripts (e.g. I–II. Clement, the Shepherd of Hermas, the Epistle of Barnabas); and so were some of the favourite Jewish books which eventually failed to be received into the Canon—for example, the beautiful collection known as the Psalms of Solomon.

As a consequence of the collection and circulation of the Jewish Bible, not only were there many proselytes to Judaism but also many "God-fearers" in the Graeco-Roman world, men and women who had been attracted to Judaism but never became full members of the Jewish community, devout persons whose knowledge of the Old Testament could be assumed by the early Christian apostles and evangelists. It is not difficult to imagine the appeal of this exotic collection of religious literature to many a Gentile reader—either through hearing it read in the synagogue or, better, by reading it for himself, perhaps in a copy borrowed from some Jewish friend. As a factor in the Hellenistic background of the New Testament, this Greek translation of the Old Testament had an importance which can scarcely be exaggerated. As we shall see, it not only prepared the way for the propagation of Christian ideas and teachings, but was of paramount importance in the earliest formulation of Christian doctrine.

One of the most interesting, most beautiful of nineteenth-century historical novels is Walter Pater's *Marius the Epicurean*, published in 1885. Somewhat slow-moving, at least for the taste of our hectic times, it still repays the careful reader; many will find themselves carried along by its simple plot and the liquid eloquence of its style. Experts in liturgical history have criticised Pater's mingling of later sources with early, the fourth century with the second; but the general representation is good and unforgettable. It is the story of a young Italian who lived in the days of Marcus Aurelius, an account of his literary education and tastes, of his contacts with philosophy, and of his eventual discovery of the Christian Church. By the Christian faith he was at once intellectually captivated and spiritually released.

It might be interesting, if it were possible, to follow Pater's example but go back a hundred years, to the first century, and picture in imagination what an intelligent, well-read Greek or Roman youth would have made of the Hebrew scriptures, coming upon them for the first time. These books were now widely disseminated over the Western world. Let us suppose he had happened upon the Book of Genesis, the "book of beginnings"—the beginnings of the world, of human life, of civilisation and the arts, of culture and religion. Like many another, he would have been charmed and fascinated by it—a book whose style, subject-matter, and the vast background of those things which it simply took for granted entirely differed from the literature he was reading at school. And yet there were not a few common elements, shared by the Hebrew Bible with the

Greek and Latin classics. Surely these would impress him, even upon a first reading. And then the secret of the difference would begin to grow clear: it was a difference in religious outlook and conviction. Here was a faith, portrayed even in the most archaic of legends and traditions, which differed completely from the religious views of the rest of the world, at least for all but a few philosophers and people who had studied the ancient religions. Here was the story of the Flood—only the man's name was Noah, not Deucalion. Here were lists of genealogies, not of the gods, as in Hesiod, but of men—tribal history, obviously, and much of it merely patronymic, for the ancestors took their names from their descendants. Here were migrations—of which Greek history was also full, for from the eighth century before Christ Hellas had sent out its colonies to the far corners of the southern and western Mediterranean and to the shores of the great Euxine Sea in the north. Here were wars and battles, the enslavement of captives, polygamy and family feuds, even as in the ancient legends of Greece and Italy. Abraham, Isaac, and Jacob matched Thucles who settled in Sicily, and the Arcadian Evander, who was described by Virgil as an early pioneer settler in the hills of Rome long before the founding of the city, not to mention Aeneas who discovered him there. Melchizedek, the priest king of Salem—were there not mysterious figures like him in early Greek and Italian history, or prehistory? Even child-sacrifice, like the offering of Iphigeneia, is here: Abraham's offering of Isaac. Only, the story tells how God interposed, and a ram caught in a thicket was substituted for the boy. So were the dolls thrown each year from the bridge over the Tiber— substitutes for the men who were sacrificed there in the days of old. At least this view has been popular in the modern world, and may have been known in the ancient.[1]

"Much of this is like what we have read in our own history and mythology," he would say; "but how differently it is told, how exotic, with what a strange atmosphere of wonder, awe, and mystery!" Even Abraham, the most fully described figure in the book, is like an ancient magician or devotee of divination—like the *Wundermänner* of early times, the cleansers, the sacrificers, the occult expounders of portents, the men who lived *en rapport* with the invisible world. Abraham divides his

[1] But see now the appendix to Kurt Latte's *Römische Religionsgeschichte*, 1960.

sacrifice in two portions, and then, "as the sun was going down, a deep sleep fell on Abram; and lo, a dread and great darkness fell upon him"; and "when the sun had gone down and it was dark, behold, a smoking fire pot and a flaming torch passed between these pieces," and God spoke to him and promised to him and to his descendants the whole of Canaan and Syria, "from the river of Egypt to the great river, the river Euphrates" (Gen. xv. 7–21). What a vision! How occult! What profound supernaturalism! The deep, powerful undertow in that ebbing tide of all first-century religion, throughout the whole Mediterranean world, was a current of occultism and of attempts to touch and control this realm of the supernatural. And how the promise of earthly inheritance, in fact of world influence if not of world rule, touched the heart of a Roman reader! In his beloved Virgil were the lines:

> Thou, O Roman, remember—such arts be *thine*!—
> To rule the nations by thy power,
> Crown peace with ordered law,
> And spare the weak but crush the proud!
>
> (*Aeneid* vi. 851–3)

Here was a similar dream—but on the other side; and, though echoed through almost all the sacred books of the Hebrews, it was one destined never to be realised, as current events in Palestine, even now under the Roman procurator, clearly indicated. Rome ruled the earth, or most of it; Rome would rule the whole, before long, and for ever. What a pity the Hebrew dream stood opposed to the Roman plan; for, in combination, the two might have been not only invincible but could have been realised all the sooner! But what stood in the way was the Hebrew religion: a nationalistic cult firmly fixed and attached to pure and exclusive monotheism.

And yet what lovely archaic nuances of thought the old book reflected! Clearly this was one of the works of that ancient wisdom of which philosophers and historians had spoken: Herodotus and Plato under the spell of Egypt; Strabo influenced by the names of Zamolxis and the Chaldaeans; even the divine Julius, in his *Commentaries*, fascinated by the barbarous Druids. Perhaps Euhemerus was right: here Yahweh, the *Kyrios*, is "a man of war" who "kills and makes alive"—

were not all the ancient gods once men on earth? But again the difference! For Yahweh, the Hebrew Lord, is loving to his own people, with a "steadfast love" which endures through all vicissitudes, and even persists and triumphs despite their own disloyalty, disobedience, or defection from his "ways." Where else are such features portrayed, in any of the ancient gods? Where else is such loyalty displayed?—even though it be on the earliest level, where religion is only the regulation of a *quid pro quo*: "Protect me on my journey into this foreign land, alien and dangerous, and upon my return I will worship you forever." Like the common prayer of the ancient Roman, *Do ut des*, "I offer you this, so that you in turn will give me that," so it is here: only, it is not long before men realise that everything belongs to God, good and evil alike, and therefore sacrifice is only a token of submission, or an acknowledgment of dependence, or an attempt at reparation or renewal of broken friendship and good will.

No doubt the most impressive, most unforgettable passage in the whole of this Book of Beginnings, for our young first-century reader, was the opening chapter. The best literary critic of the day, "Longinus," as he was ever afterwards to be known, had said that of all the literature known to him the opening words of the Hebrew scriptures were the sublimest: "In the beginning, God created the heaven and the earth. . . . And God said, *Let there be light*, and there was light." Surely this story reminds us of others—is it Oriental, Babylonian, Greek? But no, none tells it in this fashion, with one God, supreme above the primeval chaos, creating the universe "by the word of his mouth"! And there are other differences, if one examines the Greek translation more carefully: "In the beginning" (some scholars say that the Hebrew original means "When God began to create")—this is more than a title, though the Jews called the book *Bereshith*, "In the beginning," and still call it by that name. Many ancient books were known by their opening words, the first that one saw upon opening the scroll on which they were written. But this opening seemed more than a title, as our young reader noted, for it was definitely part of a sentence: "In the beginning, when God created the heavens and the earth, the earth [really the universe, the 'all'] was without form, and void [i.e. it was totally empty: for God created everything *ex nihilo*], and darkness was upon the face of the deep [the infinitely deep, abysmal waters of the primeval chaos]; and the Spirit—or the Wind—of God was moving over the face of the waters." Was this the Phoenician tale of the cosmic egg, or its Orphic version, with a warm spirit "brooding" over the waters like a hen or a bird upon its nest? But no, that is scarcely the idea. Or was it the philosophers' Demiurge, like an engineer laying a dam? No. Or the theory of Thales, who made water the original of all things, so that, as Heraclitus said, "All things flow" and eventually return to the watery substance from which they emerged? But no; this is not a philosophical theory at all, but a poet's dream, by someone like Hesiod or the Orphic hymn-writers! And how strange it is that the divine Wind should blow over the waters, as if to impregnate them with life—the Greek translation suggests this, for the verb ἐπεφέρετο ἐπάνω means "was brought upon," or "lay upon," like a bull upon a heifer—though the Hebrew *m'rakepheth* means "hovering over" or "brooding over." (The even more vivid ἐφήλατο used in 1 Sam. x. 6, xi. 6, xvi. 13 (LXX), meaning "leaped upon," is used of inspiration, the "seizure" of the ancient *nabi* which characterised or accompanied his prophesying; it was a kind of daemonic phenomenon, as in Acts xix. 16.) But for the Greeks and Romans, the god of the sea was Poseidon, and his symbol was a horse, a stallion who fructified the land, not the waters; in the Roman equation, he was Neptune, god of all waters, whether on land or sea. True, he impregnated mares; but not the bonny brooks or the rushing streams or swift Lynceus or smooth-flowing Liris or the tawny Tiber: these streams had, or were, their own gods. How strange, and how different, and how utterly sublime this Hebrew tale of a divine Spirit, a God whose breath or wind *is* spirit, and who creates by fiat, by simple word of command!

And the story of the successive days of creation: how much it resembles what some of our own scientists have imagined the course of development must have been, by which nature came to be what it now is! And of course it resembled the teaching of the divine Plato, who held that the world was created *good* (see *Timaeus* 30*a, b*; Gen. i. 31); only, according to Plato, soul was created before body (*Timaeus* 34*b, c*), not body before soul (Gen. ii. 7—a view destined to prevail in later Christian thought and to rule out all ideas of pre-existence). Yet the climax of all creation is man, as Protagoras held: "Man is the measure of all things." But, again, note the difference: for man is what he is only "under God," though he be made in God's image and likeness; for when he disobeys he brings upon himself utter disaster, as the very next story relates, man's expulsion from the Garden of Eden. The account reminds us of Hesiod's golden race, succeeded by generations ever less worthy and more unblessed; this was a vision of the past which the modern poets, Horace and Virgil, had recently repeated. Yet here—this is the strange feature—God does not abandon his creation, and even in the tale of the Flood provides for a faithful remnant to keep alive the flame of faith and obedience, and provide the fresh beginnings of a new society. Truly this is a precious book, one to be pondered and kept safe and re-read deeply and continually, until one gets to the heart of its meaning!

So it was, we may imagine, that hundreds of "God-fearers" in the Graeco-Roman world of the first century discovered the Jewish Bible, in the Greek translation, and found themselves irresistibly drawn to the Jewish synagogue with its noble ethics, its spiritual conception of the supreme Being, its positive revelation of God's requirements, and its deeply ingrained eschatology, its conviction of a divine purpose running through all of life and a definite goal toward which history is moving. These were the people among whom the early Christian missionaries and evangelists worked, and who became their strongest adherents. Some had been members of the synagogue, but many had not: their greatest deterrent was undoubtedly the requirement of circumcision, which to Greeks and Romans seemed a barbarous rite of mutilation—man's body was not meant to be injured or damaged or desecrated but preserved, and circumcision reminded them of Oriental barbarians, with huge metal rings hanging from their punctured ears, or dark Africans from the distant jungle with sticks penetrating their nostrils. The Christians of course required only baptism, not circumcision, and their food-laws were of the simplest; Sunday took the place of Sabbath, and the Temple sacrifices were of no account—the theological explanation was that Christ's death was the atoning sacrifice which had brought to an end all animal offerings, but another real reason was that animal sacrifice belonged to a cult now antiquated "and about to pass away" (Heb. VIII. 13) among the Jews, and also—if later—among the Greeks and Romans. As a matter of fact, in the year 70 the Temple at Jerusalem was totally destroyed and the system of animal sacrifice came to a complete end for all Jews.

These features help to explain the strong appeal which the Hebrew scriptures made to many religious minds in the Graeco-Roman world of the first century, an appeal echoed on almost every page of the New Testament—which is, let us never forget, a collection of writings in ancient *Greek*, not in Hebrew or English or German. For the knowledge which the New Testament takes for granted on the part of its readers, their familiarity with the Jewish Bible, the Greek Old Testament, is apparent everywhere. It requires but little imagination to make real to ourselves what must have been the initial impact of the sacred scriptures upon the minds of serious "seekers after truth," who were also "seekers after God," throughout the whole vast world of Hellenistic culture under the early Roman Empire.

There were many other features which must have impressed the first-century pagan reader of the Old Testament: the creation of woman after that of man (Gen. I. 27; cf. II. 24), an idea found also in one of Plato's myths, where the originally rotund uni-sexual creature was divided in two (*Symposium* 190); or the wrestling of a man with an angel—or perhaps with a divine being (Gen. XXXII. 23); the conception of sin as defilement or pollution (Deut. XXI. 1–9, XXXII. 43; II Sam. XXI. 1–14), an idea written deep in the Greek tragedies and in Homer;[2] the belief in the significance of dreams (Gen. XL. 1–XLI. 36), including simultaneous dreams, related to each other but experienced by different persons—an idea also found in the New Testament (Acts X. 1–33); belief in the significance of the stars—though not belief in astrology; a reference to the outstanding skill of the magicians in Egypt (Exod. VII. 11); the practice of divination (Jg. VI. 36–8); the social condition of the Egyptians, who were slaves of Pharaoh (Gen. XLVII. 19; Greeks and Romans were never slaves to any man!); the divine skill and power which brings good out of evil (Gen. L. 20), a truth also celebrated in Cleanthes' *Hymn to Zeus*:

[2] See my *How to Read the Bible*, pp. 49–54. See also Ch. VI, below.

Thou knowest to make the crooked straight,
Prune all excess, give order to the orderless;
For unto thee the unloved still is lovely—
And thus in one all things are harmonised,
The evil with the good, that so one Word
Should be in all things everlastingly.

But doubtless he would be shocked by some things, such as the
rule governing the sale or gift of food to resident aliens and
foreigners: meat from an animal that has been found dead may
be sold or given away to Gentiles, but not to Hebrews, who
are a "holy" people and therefore must not eat carrion (Deut.
xiv. 21); or Miriam's leprosy (Num. xii. 1–15); or the intolerable harshness of the judgment upon a boy who gathered
sticks for fuel on the Sabbath (Num. xv. 32–6). These passages
struck a false note in the ethical standards of the sacred writings
—and there was no historical criticism at hand to explain that
these were survivals of very "primitive" conceptions. Only
some kind of allegorical interpretation could "bend their point."

Still another feature in the Jewish Bible must have greatly
impressed a Gentile reader, if he read beyond the Book of
Genesis. In many passages in the Pentateuch, especially in
Deut. vii, the Israelites were ordered to exterminate the people
of Canaan, on the pretext that the land belonged to the Hebrews
by divine promise, and that the older inhabitants were idolaters
whose debasing cults polluted the soil. Hebrew religion was
just as intolerant as Roman, which forbade any foreign worship
within the *pomerium*—the furrow surrounding the most sacred
area of the early City. But how unlike it was to ancient *Greek*
religion! Further, though Rome had conquered all of Italy and
much of the rest of the world, the pretext, as a rule, had been
political or social, not religious, and only rarely was the extermination of the enemy total; such wholesale destruction,
slaughter, or enslavement as at Carthage or Numantia had
been rare and then only after extreme provocation. At least, the
later rationalisation in each case, the Hebrew and the Roman,
was different: in the hour of victory, logic or rationality rarely
tempers the retaliation meted out by conquerors. But perhaps
the intelligent Gentile reader may have guessed that the picture
drawn in the Pentateuch, especially in Deuteronomy, was a far

later afterthought, and in truth an example of "wishful think-ing." The author was really thinking, though not saying, "This is the way our ancestors *ought* to have treated the Canaanites, and thus have prevented their religion from corrupting the religion of the sacred Covenant with their idolatry and their degrading fertility magic." For this is just what happened, as later books of the Old Testament testify. The pioneers ought therefore to have made an end, once and for all, of the pagans and their cults; but alas, they did not! Even so, the first-century reader could scarcely have been spared a shock as he read what the good God of the Hebrew fathers, the faithful and true and only God, had bidden these invading nomads, pouring in from the wilderness, to do to the settled agriculturists who occupied the coveted "land flowing with milk and honey." So frank an excuse for invasion and extermination of a whole population was something new and unheard-of in the literature of the West. (See Deut. VIII. 7–10, 18–20, IX. 4–5.)

The glory of Israel is its sacred Law, as Paul had testified (Rom. III. 1–2). This Law, or "Torah," was often understood to include all divine revelation, in Law and Prophets alike—for Torah really meant, or was understood to mean, the *teaching*. But the tragedy of Israel is that its sacred Law includes these savage rules for the extermination of the old inhabitants of Canaan, who were to be put to the sword by the invading land-hungry nomads from the desert. Even the Book of Deuter-onomy, with all its liberal and humane legislation, prescribes such orgies of devastation and mass murder—which, as a matter of fact, were never carried out,[3] but for which Israel has been held responsible through the centuries, whenever the sword has been turned against the descendants of Abraham. The problem, alas, is the same in all religions, their inability to revise their sacred scriptures.

On a general view, our first-century youth would undoubt-edly have been impressed with the "primitive" culture re-flected in the Pentateuch and the early historical books: "primitivism" was the vogue among many of the best minds of the age, in Italy and elsewhere. Virgil had praised country

---

[3] Like the battle plans in the Dead Sea Scrolls, "The War of the Sons of Light Against the Sons of Darkness."

life in ancient Italy, and had idealised the ways of the ancestors of the Latin peoples. Tacitus was to anticipate Rousseau
with his sublimated, fanciful picture of the "noble savage," the
ancient German, Celt, and Briton. And it was clear that the
Old Testament, especially the Pentateuch, reflected a transitional culture, from nomadic to pastoral and then to bucolic
and finally to agricultural, but never to urban, until long after
the legendary "conquest" under Joshua. The blessings upon
the good earth, the land of Palestine, the very sacrifices prescribed in the Law codes, especially in the Priestly Code and
in Deuteronomy and Leviticus, presupposed an agricultural or
a nomadic way of life—or rather a combination of the two, the
transition from one to the other involving a long period of
overlapping and interpenetration. The sacrifices were offered,
at first, only upon the occasion of rare feasts, at which God
(Yahweh) was recognised as present to receive his share. But
in time other motives came into play, and "whole burnt offerings," sin and guilt offerings, sacrifices of atonement, i.e.
propitiation and reconciliation with God, were offered to him,
and the priests' share was the best of what was left after God
had been offered the choicer parts of the slain victim—very
different from the later Greek practice, when the gods received
only the inedible parts, though accompanied by the delectable
aroma of the roasting meat. Many Greek sacrifices were
ἄγευστοι—"untasted"—by men. Bloody offerings, of which nothing was eaten, were σφάγια—"slaughterings"—such as offerings
to the dead or sacrifices offered before a battle. It was only
the old sacred meal which stressed communion with the gods.
Such dinners (δεῖπνα) were presented to them, i.e. given in
their honour, and their gracious presence and sharing in the
feast was taken for granted, unless contrary "signs" proved
their absence or disapproval. But a time came when the fat
and bones were burned on the altar, along with some good
portions of the flesh. Satirists and sceptics ridiculed this decep-
tion practised on the gods, who thus received the inedible or
waste parts. The hides were saved and sold, and so, often, was
much of the meat: the practice is described in the inscriptions
(see, e.g., my *Hellenistic Religions*, pp. 8, 32), and is presupposed
in the letter of Paul to the Corinthians where he discusses the
problem of eating "food that has been offered to idols" (1 Cor. 8).

It was clearly obvious that the Hebrew provision for the sacrificer's portion was really "priestcraft," like the Greek; as various Roman poets had pointed out, such discrimination tended to lower religion to the level of crude magic, the cult being performed without rhyme or reason but solely because it worked and was effective *ex opere operato*, provided only the ritual was perfectly carried out. This our Roman lad could understand, for it was basic to the whole of traditional Roman religion; but he may have understood it all too well, and if influenced by philosophy he probably saw through it all, and looked for something more substantial and true in religion than primitive rites of animal sacrifice.

All the ancient religions enjoined and practised sacrifice; the priests were in effect butchers of domestic animals. In Italy, conspicuously, the overwhelming and predominant element in religion was sacrifice. And in Greece it was the same. Near the ancient temple sites at Olympia and elsewhere, there still survive huge mounds of solidified blood, ashes, and bones from the burnt sacrifice of animals through many generations. The Jewish Temple in Jerusalem must also have resembled a busy abbatoir most of the time; and Jesus' bold act of "cleansing the temple" may have been a prophetic protest against this debasement of divine worship, rather than against the priestly "graft" in selling animals for sacrifice or the casual profanation of the sacred shrine by people carrying burdens (Mk. XI. 16).

There were also passages in the Old Testament, even in Genesis—perhaps especially in Genesis—which bore a religious meaning only if allegorised, whether the original meaning had been allegorical or not: presumably it was *not*, in most cases. No wonder the eminent Jewish scholar, Philo of Alexandria, had recently undertaken to allegorise all the ancient tales, myths, legends, and laws, and to find spiritual or moral lessons in even the most barren or revolting "primitive" narratives. Just so the Stoics had begun allegorising the Greek myths; the Roman Stoic teacher Cornutus had recently published an *Outline of Greek Theology*, which was a model of this kind of interpretation.[4] And before long other minds would be pondering these same Jewish scriptures, looking for light on the mystery

[4] *Theologiae Graecae Compendium*, ed. C. Lang, Berlin 1881.

of evil, its origin and propagation, the strange, dark, alien strain that runs throughout this "good" universe (Gen. i. 31), corrupting it, distorting human minds and wills, frustrating the purpose of the Supreme God, and producing sin, vice, mortality, the whole "evil tendency" in man and its fatal consequences for the race. These Gnostic thinkers read far more into the Greek translation of the Hebrew scriptures than could be found there by ordinary impartial readers: but so have many others, down the centuries, proclaiming as secret divine revelation the dim reflexion, as in an ancient metal mirror, of their own cloudy speculations.

It was this Greek Old Testament which became one of the three most important creative factors in the emergence of early Christian doctrine. The other two were the tradition of Jesus' life and teaching, his death and resurrection; and the living, on-going experience of the Church itself as the Spirit-filled, Spirit-guided body of the Remnant, waiting for the Parousia and the Day of Judgment. These three sources provided a group of creative ideas which were poured at white heat into the matrix of Greek religious and philosophical language and thought during the first and second centuries. It is to the gospel that we now turn.

Some there are who tell us that the gospel of Jesus was completely overlaid with Hellenistic ideas, especially philosophical, or that the real founder of Christianity was Paul. Others say that there was no change, since Jesus had envisaged the whole development of the Church, and set forth *in nuce* the doctrine which the apostles and their followers, the "apostolic men" as Eusebius called them, were to elaborate. Neither of these views is correct. If we are to see the course of historical and theological development in true perspective we must take into account once more the *total* background of early Christianity, with its broad horizons in the complex society of the Graeco-Roman age, its religious and philosophical ideas and its customs, its social, economic, and political conditions; with its closer background in Judaism, especially the Greek-speaking Judaism of the Western Diaspora, and above all its sacred book, now translated into Greek; and with its foreground the little groups of believers found in the chief cities about the

Mediterranean, and *their* background. Among them were many who had become Christians before, or at least apart from, the missionary preaching of Paul in the forties and fifties. As Wilhelm Bousset and others rightly saw, a generation ago, the early Gentile churches were the most important of all in the onward march of Christianity, numerically and intellectually, during the first two centuries. If ever there was a "bridge" church in the whole course of Christian history, it was this early Gentile Church—which, as we shall see, was not created by Paul, but was presupposed, shared, and honoured by Paul. There were many who were "in Christ before" him (Rom. XVI. 7).

Much of the modern difficulty in tracing the expansion of primitive Christianity and the development of its doctrine is due to a mistaken assumption that the process was directly forward, in a straight line, from *a* to *b* to *c* to *d*: from Jesus to Paul (or Peter or James) to John to Ignatius of Antioch to Irenaeus and the other fathers. But the movement was not rectilinear; it was circular, like the expanding concentric rings spread by a submerged fountain. The variety in early Christian organisation and ministry, even in doctrine, cannot be denied or disregarded. This variety was inevitable. But it was a variety sprung from the impact of a powerful new faith coming into contact with new conditions, requiring to be formulated in new terms, with reference to new problems; and this faith was by no means the creation of the conditions it now faced in the wide world of Roman Hellenism—though the theory still finds its advocates in the field of popular journalism. Nor was the doctrinal development a mere restatement of Jesus' teaching— a view which some conservative ecclesiastical writers continue to reiterate. The first and second generation of Christians were fully aware of this—as the Gospel of John repeatedly recognises (for example, in XVI. 12–15). The remainder of this volume is concerned with the exploration of this phenomenon.

# Chapter VI

## The Gospel in the Early Gentile Churches

A new world had begun for Palestine and the rest of western Asia in the fourth century before Christ. The conquest of the Persian Empire and of all western Asia to the Indus River by Alexander of Macedon had brought to that part of the civilised world—and to many barbarian tribes—a knowledge of the Greek language, and with it a totally new outlook and orientation. It was, of course, the same old world with a new orientation; as we have seen (p. 81), there are no "breaks" in the continuity of history. As Goethe said, "Mankind is always advancing; man remains ever the same." Man has been much the same ever since the rise of civilisation, i.e. since the dawn of recorded history. But in the fourth century before Christ new forces were released in the world, new interests seized upon or allured the minds of men, new horizons appeared out of the mists of the surrounding seas. Nations that had slumbered for centuries suddenly became aware of great issues and possibilities.[1] Universal trade and travel soon followed. Men began to philosophise, to wonder about the meaning of life, to examine what is the right kind of life for men to live, and even what is the *best* kind of life, both for the private individual and for the state. What is man? What is this world we live in? What about the gods—are they many or few, or even only one? Does man live beyond death? How can one be sure? How can one obtain some guarantee of happiness beyond death? These and dozens of other questions entered men's minds, and demanded answers.[2]

For the whole world, as we have seen, had now become Greek. Only scattered pockets of non-Greek culture, language, and religion survived here and there. The fourth century was

[1] The very same thing is happening today in Asia and Africa.

[2] That they were questions of popular interest is clear from such fictitious narratives as the third and fourth century "Clementine" *Homilies* and *Recognitions*, in which, however, Professor Schoeps finds considerably older material. See his *Urgemeinde, Judenchristentum, Gnosis*, Tübingen 1956.

the beginning of the long "Hellenistic age" which lasted from Alexander the Great (some would say from a generation earlier) to the conquest of the Western world and of western Asia by Rome; in fact, it lasted longer still, for the conquering Romans were themselves conquered by Greek culture, art, and philosophy. "Captive Greece captivated her captor." This culture lasted on into the Middle Ages and later; the Renaissance in Italy was essentially a revival of Greek learning. Much that is best in Western civilisation is still marked by its Greek origin. Where the world has revolted against Hellenism, in art, learning, philosophy, it has tended to lapse into barbarism.

This was the world into which Christ was born, the world of Hellenised western Asiatic civilisation—not on the distant frontiers of the ancient world, but near its centre. For Syria on the one hand and Egypt on the other were among the foremost examples of Hellenisation—and tiny Palestine lay right between the two, open to both, traversed by roads from both, subject first to one and then the other for three centuries before the coming of the Romans, who opened the gates still wider to influences from both the North and the South. The remains of ancient Graeco-Roman cities, with their Hellenistic architecture and sculpture, are found in both Syria and Egypt, and in Palestine as well; the inscriptions, the books produced there, the thousands of papyrus letters and other documents, written in Greek, which have been found buried in the dry sands of Egypt—all this evidence proves how highly Hellenised that part of the world was, especially after the second century before Christ. The ancient Church fathers viewed all this as part of the divine preparation for the Gospel, for the coming of Christ and the spread of Christianity. The *praeparatio evangelica* included Jewish religion, both the sacred Law and the divine revelation through the inspired prophets, Greek philosophy, especially Socrates and Plato, and Roman law, with its principles of inflexible justice and its deep sense of equity. The idea is surely a true one, and should be borne in mind by every student of holy Scripture and of early Church history. It was the universal spread of the Greek language—Greek was spoken even in Rome (at least by the foreign multitude) for several centuries—which made it possible to proclaim the message of the gospel

throughout the entire Mediterranean world. (The apostles were
sent "into all the world," to preach "to all the nations": see
Mt. xxviii. 19; Mk. xiii. 10; Acts i. 8.) The spread of Hellenistic civilisation, the building of good roads, the suppression
of piracy on the high seas by the Romans, the dissemination of
learning, the opening of schools, the study of literature and art,
poetry, drama, history, philosophy—in brief, the spread of
education was all a part of this divine plan, God's true
"plan of the ages." Everyone could read—or very nearly
everyone; most men could write. Even day-labourers in the
dockyards and on the quays and in the grain warehouses
knew Greek and could converse in the language of Homer,
Plato, Aristotle—even though they did not often converse *like*
them.

But the great advantage was not only that a common language existed, and common ideas. There were also positive
gains in religious thought. The world was moving away from
the barbarous primitive cults which had survived from prehistoric times, and from the crude ideas and rites that clustered
about them.[3] There was a genuine movement in the direction
of monotheism, the belief in one God and one only. There were
ideas of divine providence, of a mediator between God and the
world, of grace and help to meet man's need, of the divine
response to prayer, of the divine demand of righteousness, all of
which prepared men for the gospel, either by making them
more conscious of their need or by familiarising them with the
ideas. On the one hand the teaching of the philosophers guided
men's minds in this direction, on the other the experience of
men and women in various cults and rites, especially the
mysteries, enabled them to grasp better the "deep things of
God." This does not mean that everyone was initiated, or that
the mystery cults were like sacraments conveying life and
immortality; but it means that the ideas of renewal, of a fresh
start in life, of a cleansing of the soul, were widespread and "in
the air." These ideas helped to prepare men for the Christian
rite of baptism, when it appeared. All this *praeparatio evangelica*

[3] How recently central Europe was barbarian everyone knows; how recently
it was savage is clear from the evidences of cannibalism there *c.* 2000 B.C., and
from the survival of such cults as that of Woden; see the still valuable little book
by H. M. Chadwick, *The Cult of Othin: An Essay on the Ancient Religion of the North*,
Cambridge 1899.

is of profound significance for the student of the New Testament and helps to make its background more real to him.[4]

For this reason, the New Testament student ought to know Greek literature—all of it—and he should "steep his mind" in it, year in, year out. As a noble Renaissance scholar said, "One can never get too much Greek."[5] The meaning of the words in the New Testament is partly derived from the common or *Koine* Greek spoken throughout the Roman Empire in the first century, and partly from the inherited literature of the classical age, the fifth and fourth centuries before Christ. It was also influenced by the use made of Greek by the translators of the Old Testament, from about 250 B.C. onwards, and by the Graeco-Jewish writers, especially in Alexandria. One can find these meanings listed in the lexicon, chiefly the great lexicon of Preuschen and Bauer, now translated and revised by Professors Arndt and Gingrich (1956), and in Kittel's *Theologisches Wörterbuch zum Neuen Testament*, of which a few articles have been translated into English. But I am speaking about something even more important, and lying beneath the philological history and analysis of language: I mean the ideas. There are certain religious ideas found in Greek literature which are simply indispensable for the interpretation of the New Testament as well as the Old. Of course they really are there, in the Bible—but the ordinary reader is not likely to see them when he reads only the Bible without the parallel literature of Greece, casting bright shafts of lateral light from a distance. Once more we are reminded of the observation, "There are only two religions whose history is adequately documented, the ancient Hebrew and the ancient Greek."[6] They illustrate each other repeatedly.

One of these important ideas to which I now refer again is that of sin as pollution, i.e. something which needs not simply to be forgiven and forgotten but actually removed. This was the meaning of ancient rites which undertook to take away sins, purge them, remove their miasma, the poison-cloud which settled down upon a city, a nation, a family, as the result of

---

[4] See A. D. Nock, *Conversion, passim*.

[5] A sentiment echoed by Dr Johnson: "Sir, Greek is like lace; . . . one cannot get too much of it!" Today we must substitute something for "lace"—perhaps gold, which, however, cannot now be hoarded.

[6] See p. 9.

sin. Such a sin could be unwitting or inherited, as in the case of
Oedipus; but it was nevertheless real. And its reality was as
clearly recognised in the New Testament as in the Old. Sin can
be handled, not by some book-keeping arrangement, with
credit enough to offset the debit; it must be met by positive
counter-activities, as an antibiotic counters a virus or an anti-
dote a poison. We do not just say, "Oh, I'm sorry; please
overlook it!" Reparation, restoration, renewed health and
wholeness are required. There must be a real and positive righteousness to take the place of the positive sins and the positive
sinfulness. It is this profound sense of the reality of sin and the
necessity for active and concrete steps to remove it that the New
Testament shares with Greek religious thought, seen especially
in Aeschylus and Sophocles but really present everywhere in
ancient Greek literature. A friend who heard me expound this
theme remarked, "But we all recognise the sin of pollution, i.e.
filthy conduct, words, thoughts." He had entirely missed the
point: it is sin *as* pollution; that is to say, sin *is* a pollution; it
contaminates, it infects; and as the remedy for this, cleansing is
absolutely indispensable. If once we really get this point of
view, and share the religious outlook of the ancient world somewhat more fully, we will begin to see why the New Testament
makes so much of holy baptism, of the holy supper, of the holy
estate of matrimony, of holy living and holy dying, of the totally
new orientation of human life which came to pass through the
Incarnation, what modern theologians call "the new being in
Christ." This is modern language, but the thought is very old,
certainly as old as St Paul, whose epistles—which are the earliest
surviving Christian writings—fill the whole New Testament
with its ringing proclamation.

As a matter of fact, the profound realism of ancient religious
thought, shared by both the Hebrew and the Greek, the ancient
Jew and the early Christian, and reflected throughout the
sacred writings, is drawn from another world than our modern
subjectivism and legalism. We live on the hither side of the
Middle Ages, of Scholasticism, of the Lutheran Reformation
and of Calvinism, of modern individualism and political liberty
(something totally different from the ancient conception of the
state, the city, or the family); moreover, we also live on this side
of Romanticism with its glorification of the peculiarities of the

private individual with his specific "personality," something for which the ancient Greeks and Romans did not even have a word. We are as completely cut off from the ancient outlook as if the Himalayas or the Alps stood between us. We can recover the ancient outlook only by study and effort. But since human nature does not change—or the gospel—it is worth the effort, and teachers, especially, must undertake it. All who are interested in the Bible, or concerned with the teaching of our religion, must place themselves at least in imagination in this ancient world from which the Bible comes. The background of the New Testament is far closer to its foreground than is often recognised; it is not like those distant landscapes seen through an open window or door in many a Renaissance portrait.

Hence we cannot claim that our subject is detached and abstract, without relation to present-day religious concerns, or even to theological interests. The idea of a "pure" history, written in a pure and timeless prose, accurate and scientific and unconcerned with the imagination of either writer or reader, and of a "pure" literary criticism, conducted in a vacuum of intellectual contemplation, seems to have gone by the board these days. What bearing have the data of first-century Christian history upon the life and faith of the Church today? The answer, even fifty years ago, would have been, "Much every way. Unless the Gospels can be accepted as literal and exact narratives of recent events in Palestine, we cannot view them otherwise than as forgeries or frauds, however pious." But we know a little more, today, about all ancient literature, including the religious writings, and we are now prepared to accept such a statement as the following, from a review of the volume of essays in honour of the late Professor T. W. Manson:

All the New Testament documents are the work of those who believed that Jesus of Nazareth had been crucified, had died, was risen from the dead, glorified, and had ascended to God. Such belief must have transformed whatever views they may earlier or might otherwise have formed of his earthly life, ministry and teaching, and no less the earlier meanings of such terms as they applied to him. As with "Messiah" and "*Logos*," when it is said of Jesus that he is Messiah or that "the *Logos* became flesh" in him, by and in those statements "Messiah" and "*Logos*" acquire a meaning which, in their totality, they had not before carried: their Christian context is more important for their meaning than their earlier history. Similarly, the New

Testament writers wrote for communities of their own day, and the reasonable assumption is that the meanings of the terms they use were intended to be those which their readers would assign to them: there is no reason to suppose that either writers or readers would have had in mind the varying meanings these terms had borne in their often long history.[7]

There was as little probability that the first readers of the New Testament would bear in mind the philological history of the terms it used as that they would foresee the later developments of Christian theology and attach the fully formulated orthodox definitions to them as they went along. It is a pity that some of these words were ever translated, for there are no equivalents in other languages, with identical colour, connotations, overtones. *Logos* should have been retained, for it means far more than "Word" (Goethe's correction, "In the beginning was the Deed" is wholly inadequate); and *Paraclete*, which the French retained, has at least five meanings which "Comforter," "Advocate," "Counsellor," "Helper," or "Guide" cannot possibly convey, even when all are taken together. Words like *Christ* and *Messiah*, which are transliterations, require explanation; and that is as it should be; people ought not to be led to think that some simple English equivalent is all that is needed, and that any casual reader can expound the theology of the New Testament at first glance.

We also recognise the crucial importance of the question raised in a recent number of *The Hibbert Journal* by Professor S. G. F. Brandon of Manchester:

Surely, if one is seeking to recommend Christianity as a faith of universal validity, the problem must be faced whether the post-70 A.D. synthesis achieved in the Synoptic Gospels truly represents the original form of the movement which stemmed from the life and teaching of Jesus of Nazareth.

The answer lies, as I shall try to demonstrate, in a further extension of the method, and application of the results, of the past hundred and fifty years of New Testament criticism, not by its abandonment. Restive souls would dismiss all "modern criticism" and begin *de novo*, taking the Gospels "just as they stand" and making of them whatever we can. Would anyone think of doing this in the classical field?—dismissing the researches of philologists, textual critics, archaeologists,

---

[7] *The Times Literary Supplement*, 25 Sept. 1959, p. 549.
[8] *The Hibbert Journal*, July 1959, pp. 404f.

editors and historians since the days of Bentley and Porson?
Hardly!

Take textual criticism: we have many times more resources,
in sheer number and amount, than our forefathers possessed,
even as recently as 1870, when work began on the English
Revised Version of the Bible. One may, of course, not be interested
in textual criticism, and may class it with crossword puzzles;
but that makes no difference. It is a discipline fundamental to
all study of the New Testament, to its translation, and to its
exegesis.

Take source criticism: there are still those who are un-
convinced by the evidence put forth to support the hypothesis
of two—or four, or more—sources or documents or collections
of tradition underlying the Synoptic Gospels (labelled Q, L,
M, etc.[9]); but the fact remains that the hypothesis (call it
nothing more) remains the simplest solution of the literary
problem involved in the relationship between the first three
Gospels. It meets the requirements of the canons of ancient
historiography, especially for literature in transition from tradition (what the Chadwicks of Cambridge called "oral" literature) to written books. It meets the conditions reflected in the
books themselves. It meets the requirements, as far as we understand them, of the on-going life of the early Church, chiefly (and
this is what really counts most) its liturgical life, i.e. the use of
the Gospels in public worship, along with, and supplementary
to, the Greek Old Testament.

Or take form criticism: there are some who view it as a
purely rationalistic attempt to "unstring the beads" in the
gospel narratives.[10] But this is surely a shallow judgment. Form
criticism has its limitations—very severe ones, since the period
is so far away, the finished Gospels so carefully written, and the
non-canonical traditions so late and unreliable. (What would
we not give for even a few of the writings of the "many" (Lk. 1.
1), who "took it in hand to draw up a narrative" of the events
in Jesus' life, his death and resurrection?) Nevertheless, as a

[9] For the significance of these algebraic symbols, see my book, *The Gospels,
Their Origin and Their Growth*, New York 1957, London 1959.
[10] See my *Form Criticism, A New Method of New Testament Research*, Chicago 1934,
or E. Basil Redlich, *Form Criticism, Its Value and Limitations*, London 1939. The
best introduction to form criticism, is still Martin Dibelius's *From Tradition to
Gospel*, London and New York 1935. This book certainly should be reprinted.

purely literary discipline which attempts to recover "the sources behind the sources," form criticism is not only inevitable but indispensable. It is as inevitable and indispensable in the study of the New Testament history as it is in that of the Old Testament, where the method originated. It may easily be exaggerated, pushed too far, and made to yield questionable "laws" governing oral tradition. But that is only because some modern scholars, trained in "scientific" method, have instinctively looked for laws and guiding principles and "social" constructions of myth, legend, and tradition. There is no substitute for common sense—which is really quite uncommon—in any branch of study; or for the keen, delicate "sound judgment" of a scholar who has spent a lifetime (more or less!) among his chosen documents, and knows them expertly, as a symphony conductor knows the music of the great masters and "reads" a composition and interprets it without looking at a note. I would rather know what John McNeill thinks about an idea one meets in a chapter of Calvin's *Institutes*, its antecedents, the books or schools or teachers who influenced Calvin, the way his mind took hold of the idea—perhaps traditional, perhaps ultimately Scholastic in origin—and worked upon it, producing eventually what we read in his final edition, than hear what a hundred tyros have to say after six weeks of diligent study. This is what form criticism requires: expert, unerring, almost preternatural skill in interpreting the antecedents and the course of development of the gospel pericopes. In brief, it requires literary insight and sensitiveness of an extraordinary calibre; pedestrian exposition will not do. Therefore literary criticism is both inevitable and indispensable, but it must be expert and understanding. It is like brain surgery, for which, Sir William Osler said, "a seaman's grip and a lacemaker's touch" are both required. Hence it is not only form criticism that needs to be criticised, but also form critics. We must realise, however, that rejection—or ridicule—is not criticism. And I believe that it is still very important to take into account both the old Jewish traditional literature, especially the Haggadic and Midrashic, the beginnings of which are clearly traceable in the Old Testament and the Apocrypha, and also the Hellenistic literary antecedents and milieux which the heralds of the gospel encountered as soon as they crossed the borders of

Palestine—and probably even earlier still, since Hellenism had also penetrated Palestine.

There is no getting away from this transitional character of the early New Testament period, not only down to A.D. 100 but even long afterwards, in certain areas.[11] Papias of Hierapolis, about the year 130, was still talking about the "living and abiding voice" of tradition, which he much preferred to written records. Ignatius of Antioch, on the contrary, about A.D. 110, preferred the written "archives"—though he was perhaps referring to the Old Testament, viewed as a collection of prophetic oracles. Irenaeus of Lyons, about 185, clearly recognised the oral foundation of the gospel narratives, and so did Eusebius of Caesarea, about 325, and so did everyone else in the ancient Church. It is only our modern world, with its unique development of literacy and of accurate recording, its exclusive reliance upon the printed word, and its consequent scepticism relative to "mere word of mouth" and "mere legend or tradition," that tends to view the Gospels as purely personal and private literary compositions, and their circulation in the Church as "publication." The whole ancient world, for almost the whole period of human history, relied upon the spoken word far more than we moderns are accustomed to do. For us, the maxim, *littera scripta manet*, is absolutely binding; but it was not always thus.

Far more of ancient history was traditional than most persons realise. Form criticism should really be called "tradition criticism" or "form history" (*Formgeschichte* was the original German word for it). And it is as applicable to Herodotus and Livy and other ancient historians as it is to the Gospels—to all but the pedestrian annalists and chroniclers, or to men like Polybius or Tacitus who used documents. Anyone who wrote history with imagination, with insight, with a flair for interpretation, with a sense of the deeper implications, especially social and religious, of events as they transpired, with a feeling for the profound past and the immense future of what was happening, still happening, and about to happen: in brief, anyone who wrote *Heilsgeschichte* or its equivalent, necessarily invites the study and analysis of his original sources, the oral sources

[11] This is one major thesis of my *Introduction to New Testament Thought*, New York 1950.

behind the written ones, and the whole development of his story or stories in the light of literary parallels wherever found. For the writers of the Gospels were not historians pure and simple (are there any such persons?) but evangelists; and their story was the story of the proclamation of redemption. Moreover, their sources, Jewish, Semitic, Palestinian for the most part, were now circulating in Greek, as the common treasure of the Gentile churches. The meaning of the very terms they used, especially the most important ones—such as Prophet, Messiah, *Logos*, Lord, Son of God—these were all understood and used in the sense and with the meaning given them in the Gentile churches. These meanings had a prehistory not only in Semitic thought and speech but in Hellenistic. Hence the Hellenistic antecedents and background are always fully as important, and sometimes even more important, than the original Semitic, Aramaic, Palestinian Jewish, or Jewish Christian—i.e. Christian Jewish—background. It is this background of circumambient Hellenism that we ought to examine.

The first question to consider in an historical approach to the New Testament is the nature of the New Testament writings and their relation to the Christian Church whose sacred books they have always been. Two generations ago, it was assumed that the New Testament collection contained a body of historical documents upon the basis of which the beginnings of Christianity could be reconstructed. But it is now perfectly clear that these are quite inadequate for any such purpose and use. They are too fragmentary in form and too few in number to provide the desired reconstruction. Conditions in the early Church or in the apostolic mission or in the life of Jesus are presupposed but not explained. For example, it was once believed that the origins of the Christian ministry could be traced from the "records" in the New Testament. But this is true only in broadest outline. Many questions remain which are simply unanswered, e.g. what was an apostle, or a deacon, or a presbyter, in the middle of the first century, say in the period of Paul's missionary activity?

The picture of the early Church which we can reconstruct from the New Testament is like a jig-saw puzzle from which half the pieces are missing. What was the ministry like in

Palestine in Paul's time? "Apostles and elders," as in Acts xv? "High priests and prophets," as in the Didache? "Elders and evangelists," as in Asia Minor in the middle chapters of Acts (e.g. xiv. 23)? Or "bishops and deacons," as at Philippi (see Phil. i. 1)? Or was it somewhat different in the Aegean area, under Paul's influence (this was the main scene of his missionary activity)? Or in Anatolia, after the apostle had moved on to the West? Or in Italy, before he arrived there? And what were the conditions in Egypt? Here we are utterly in the dark for the whole first century and more of the Church's earliest history. The late Canon B. H. Streeter and Professor Karl Holl agreed in recognising a variety of types in the apostolic age. Their view has been challenged but is still the most probable. These questions are baffling, frustrating, intriguing, for they simply cannot be answered. The problem is difficult enough when we get into the more fully documented late second century, or the third, or the fourth. But it is quite impossible of solution, with the data we now possess, for the first century. Hence the books on the origins of the ministry are largely concerned with hypotheses—that is to say, with guesses—and with inferences from later Christian conditions, or from Judaism, or even from Hellenistic-Roman cults. This is a very unsatisfactory situation, especially when the New Testament scholar is asked to contribute to the discussion of a proper ministry for the ecumenical Church of today and tomorrow.

We could spend a long time listing the inadequacies of our documents for purposes of historical reconstruction: the conflict in chronology between the Synoptics and John, between Acts and the letters of Paul; the manifold problems of the life of Jesus, his teaching, his own "self-consciousness" (as it is now called), his sense of mission (prophetic or messianic or both), the events and the forces which led to his death, and so on.

There is also the indubitable fact of partiality in the evidence. Only one side is heard from—the victors in the struggle for dominance. What were the views of the opposition, e.g. "those about James," the pillar apostle in Jerusalem, or Peter and those who shared his views and his scruples at Antioch? Much the same is true in Judaism: the Sadducean literature (if there was any) has completely disappeared: only the Pharisaic has survived. The same situation exists in many other areas of history:

for example the one-sided documentation in much of Roman history, where the records of the old patrician families were completely annihilated during the Civil Wars; where the reign of Tiberius is recorded chiefly by his enemies; where the "opposition under the Caesars" has to be reconstructed largely by inference. It is also true of far later periods, as Garrett Mattingly points out in *The Armada*,[12] where a great many of the data exist only in fragmentary form, and where for some important scenes and movements in that crucial struggle there are none at all. In the case of the New Testament, it is enough to say that the confident optimism of the two decades following 1890 is no longer shared by most biblical scholars. These twenty-seven writings are *not* primarily a collection of historical sources, cherished by the Church because they shed a full light upon the period of its origin.

Another mistaken assumption is that the New Testament contains the classic statement of Christian theology—a view not only as old as William Chillingworth and *The Bible Only the Religion of Protestants* (1637) but far older. In fact it was the major presupposition of both patristic and Scholastic theology, i.e. of dogmatic theology in its widest definition. Only, unlike some modern writers, the Church fathers and the Schoolmen, and likewise the old Protestant theologians, took the Bible in its wide sense as *Biblia sacra*, including Old Testament as well as New, and also the Apocrypha in some instances—at least parts of the Apocrypha.

But, once more, the modern view of the New Testament discounts or ignores this conception of the nature and purpose of the biblical writings. "Systematic" theology, which is our preferred term, is something far more than "dogmatic" theology, and certainly something very different from "biblical" theology. Time was when our fathers could assume that these three were one, at least one in the sense of fundamental agreement. And of course this is still basically true. The three are inseparable, like the roots of three trees growing in close contact with each other. But dogmatic theology goes beyond biblical theology—the whole presupposition of "dogma," i.e. of officially and authoritatively defined doctrine, involves a logical process and a strict definition of terms which are foreign

[12] Boston 1959; London 1960 as *The Defeat of the Spanish Armada*.

to both the Hebrew Old Testament and the Greek New Testament. And systematic theology goes beyond dogmatic not only in content but in method: it includes apologetics and philosophy of religion, it looks off across the surrounding fields of modern science, cosmology and astronomy, biology, anthropology, world history, psychology, even psychotherapy and psychoanalysis (as in Paul Tillich's system).

And why not? If we are to have a theology adequate for our times, as the Schoolmen, especially Anselm and Aquinas, provided one for their days, these things must be included. A mere restatement of the dogmas set forth by the early Councils, or of the major "religious ideas" found in the Bible, is not what we require and demand. A true systematic theology must stand on its own feet, deal adequately and fairly with the data of biblical revelation, ecclesiastical tradition, and Christian experience, and at the same time it must provide a central unity of interpretation which will deal adequately and fairly with all human knowledge, scientific and other. Such a "philosophical" theology is the great quest of our times in the religious realm. It is the goal of the long search of such religious and philosophical thinkers as William Temple and Paul Tillich: nothing less than a unified religious and theological world view. It would be, and is, a great mistake to pretend that this world view is to be found in the New Testament or in the Bible as a whole. (This is where Rudolf Bultmann's demand for "demythologisation" finds its justification.) True, some of the indispensable elements and presuppositions of such a view are to be found here; and from our standpoint it is clear that apart from the New Testament and its normative religious influence such a unitary view is completely impossible; but it is not *all* here, nor is it reasonable or just to force upon the New Testament the systematic theological views of today—or of the thirteenth century or the sixteenth. To interpret the New Testament in such a fashion is only to take the rabbit out of the hat after first inserting it, as Kant said of the theistic arguments. Such interpretation is circular in direction and simply does not reach the most essential and most precious treasure the New Testament possesses and enshrines for all time.

Nor is there any valid reason for demanding that every systematic theology must find its principles fully anticipated in

Scripture. To be vital, a religion must be a present possession—
"alive and on the march," as G. K. Chesterton described it.
So must a theology also be, if it is to be the theology, i.e. the
rational description and explanation of this vital religion and
its intellectual presuppositions. Not that systematic theology
and biblical theology are opposed, or even sharply divided;
only, they must not be identified, or one compelled to support
the other.

Furthermore, we are now more fully aware of the process by
which faith is formed—any faith—and by which theology in
turn undertakes to work out the presuppositions of religious
experience. William Golding's observation is often quoted; it is
profound and true: "What men believe is a function of what
they are; and what they are is in part what has happened to
them." This I take to be a succinct statement of what is often
called Existentialism (i.e. as far as it concerns religion). At least
it states what many of us, an increasing number, hold to be
true. We cannot accept anything which we do not recognise as
having meaning for our own life-situation, or the world in
which we live; and what we conceive or feel to be our own life-
situation is obviously the result of our own experience. Even to
take something "on faith," without demonstration of its truth
or probability, implies a recognition of its relevance or value,
and we must accept *someone's* authority for stating it. There is
no use in trying to escape this situation. Modern theology must
frankly accept the condition and work under it.

What then are the sacred scriptures of the New Testament,
and what is their purpose, if they are neither a collection of
historical records nor a quarry of hard granite for the erection of
a consistent and philosophical system of theology? The answer
must be found in the earliest use made of them, which was
obviously liturgical. Certainly this had been true of the Old
Testament, the books read aloud in the Jewish synagogue and
finally included in its "canon" about A.D. 100. The book of the
Law of the Lord which Ezra read to the assembled Jews in
Jerusalem, presumably in the year 397 B.C., was the Torah or
some large part of it.[13] To this were soon added the Former and

[13] See my book, *Translating the Bible*, Greenwich, Conn. and Edinburgh 1961,
pp. 7–11.

the Latter Prophets, and finally the Writings, as read (for the most part) in the synagogue lectionary, the last-named including the "Rolls" (*Megilloth*) which were read on festivals. Translated into Greek, with the addition of certain other books found only in that language (these were later called the "Apocrypha"), this collection of sacred scriptures of "the Old Covenant" (i.e. "the Old *Testament*") formed the Bible (τὰ βιβλία, "the books," II Tim. IV. 13) of the early Gentile Christian Church. To it were added certain Christian writings, the ten letters of Paul, the four Gospels, the epistle (or homily) addressed "To Hebrews," the seven so-called "Catholic" epistles, the Acts of the Apostles, the three Pastoral Epistles, and the book of Revelation, i.e. the Apocalypse of John. These were all Greek books, whatever their origin, or whatever the language of their underlying sources, and they were added to the Greek Bible by Greek-speaking Christians for reading publicly in the services of the Greek-speaking Gentile churches in the West. Eventually they came to be known as the *New* Testament in distinction from the older collection, which was based on the Septuagint.

The authority, the inspiration, the sacredness of all these books was fully recognised as the New Testament canon grew in clarity and certainty of definition. And it was *because* they were the sacred books read at public worship, along with the sacred books of the Old Covenant (whose authority, it appears, no early Christian ever questioned before the time of Marcion), that the New Testament books came to be viewed as reliable historical sources and as containing data for theological statements, especially in refuting "novelties" and perversions of Christian truth, e.g. Docetism and Gnosticism. (The theory that the New Testament Canon was the result of a hurried assemblage of authoritative documents to refute or outbid Marcion is a very partial and one-sided interpretation of the evidence.) That these books were not at first viewed as infallible historical documents is clear from Luke's reference to his predecessors (Lk. I. 1–4), and from the "corrections" in the gospels, Luke's and Matthew's corrections of Mark, and John's reinterpretation of the whole earlier evangelic tradition. (If one objects to the word "earlier," then let us say "non-Johannine.") The same is true of Luke's reinterpretation of Paul—supposing that he was acquainted with at least some of Paul's letters. Or take for example the reinterpretation or further unfolding of Christian doctrine in the Epistle to the Hebrews; or the one-sided apocalyptic emphasis found in the Book of Revelation; or the reinterpretation of Paul in the Pastoral Epistles. We need not go outside the New Testament itself to find this unity in diversity, this diversity in unity, this process of reinterpretation and re-emphasis—though it is very marked in the Apostolic Fathers and in the whole history (so far as it is recoverable) of second-century Christianity. Uniformity begins with Irenaeus, about A.D. 185, but the process had a long way to go before achieving anything like the fixed and immutable theology presupposed by the fifth- and sixth-century Fathers.

Stated briefly, then, the proper historical approach to the New Testament begins with the recognition that these books, together with the Greek Old Testament, formed the lectionary of the early Church. Our point of view accordingly is not, and never can be, that of the Day of Pentecost in the year 30 or thereabouts, but that of some decades later, say the turn of the century about A.D. 100. These were the books which the Church had produced, preserved, set apart as sacred and inspired, as "useful for edification," "profitable for teaching, for reproof, for correction, and for training in righteousness" (II Tim. III. 16), and therefore read publicly in the Church's services of worship along with the Septuagint. All this took place from a very early time—perhaps from the time the first copies were read in the Christian assemblies (see Col. IV. 16; Mk. XIII. 14). The historical value of these books was not questioned: they were assumed to be historically true and trustworthy records of the past; but their main significance was not as historical documents. Their theological importance was equally unquestioned, though in the first few decades of the Church's history the questions to be settled by appeal to the Scriptures were more often practical than theological—this was the period prior to the rise of Christian Gnosticism and Docetism. Thereafter the appeal to the Old Testament (on the doctrine of Creation and the nature of man, the inspiration of prophecy, and the authority of the Law) was matched by an appeal to the Christian books, especially to Paul and the Gospels (on the doctrine of the Incarnation, the reality of Christ's human nature, the Resurrection, the Parousia and the Final Judgment). But the New Testament collection was no more the result of a theological test than of an historical. These were the apostolic writings, written by apostles or at least by "apostolic men," as Eusebius called them,[14] at the behest of the apostles, and they enshrined the genuine, valid, unquestioned *apostolic tradition*.

When theological—or even historical—questions arose, as the result in part of divergent interpretations of the Old Testament, or of contact with current Hellenistic-Oriental speculation, it was the most natural thing in the world for the Church to appeal to its own sacred archives, the divinely inspired books which were read at public worship, viz. the Greek Old Testament now supplemented by the Greek Christian writings which were destined in time to be known as the New Testament. They were not compiled (perhaps by some committee, as the Muratorian Canon assumes) in order to provide the Church with proper lections—only anthologists do that sort of thing for religious sects, especially sects of the eclectic type. But they were the only available sacred books of *apostolic* origin, and so they were read, along with the Greek Old Testament. Their arrangement as lections took place very early, as Archbishop Philip Carrington has shown in the case of Mark,[15] and as Professor George Kilpatrick has hinted in the case of Matthew,[16] and as the late B. W. Bacon assumed for John.[17] The result, as seen from the historical viewpoint, is a very fragmentary collection of sources; and it might have been vastly more so if Acts or Luke-Acts had not survived. But, as we have already observed, we must recognise how fragmentary is all documentation of ancient history (and even of modern)—for example, English history from *c.* 400 to 597. The popular present-day impression that "source material" is unlimited for every period and area in the past, and needs only to be investigated, is completely wrong.

Finally, the Christian conception of the inspiration of the New Testament writings resulted not only from a transfer or extension of Jewish veneration for the Hebrew scriptures (and also for additional books belonging to various sects, e.g. those

[14] *Church History*, II. 17. 2.
[15] See his *Primitive Christian Calendar*, Cambridge 1952, and *According to Mark*, Cambridge 1960.
[16] *The Origins of the Gospel according to St Matthew*, Oxford 1946.
[17] *The Gospel of the Hellenists*, New York 1933.

of the group at Qumrân,[18] or the Essenes described by Josephus, or the Therapeutae described by Philo); but it also resulted in some measure from the influence of contemporary pagan veneration for canons (i.e. standard lists[19]) of religious or philosophical works, not to mention the more abstruse and esoteric books derived, at least ostensibly, from the Oriental religions. Such collections as the Golden Words of Pythagoras, the sayings attributed to Zoroaster, the Chaldean Oracles, the Hermetica, the Orphic Hymns—or the forerunners of these writings—were on a par, for many persons, with the almost sacred writings of Plato, Epicurus, and Zeno venerated by the philosophers. But none of these writings, so far as we know, was formed into a lectionary for public reading at services of worship:[20] this feature was peculiar to the Jewish synagogue and the Christian Church. Primarily and essentially, then, the Hebrew-Christian scriptures were the sacred writings of a religion, read in its liturgy; their historical or exegetical or theological use and authority were secondary to the liturgical. And it makes a very great difference in the interpretation of the New Testament whether or not this principle is recognised.

[18] See titles listed in the bibliography at end of this volume, V, §B.
[19] See my *Introduction to New Testament Thought*, pp. 78–81.
[20] See *Corpus Hermeticum*, ed. A. D. Nock and A. J. Festugière, vol. I, Paris 1945, Preface.

# Chapter VII

## Paul the Pharisee

The gift of accurate self-appraisal is rare in human history. Within our own lifetime we have seen the rise and fall of many who entirely mistook their own importance in the life of mankind, especially in its political organisation and direction. But it is also true that more modest men and women often do not realise the contribution they have made—or are making—to the whole world. John Wycliffe was such a person, the translator of the Bible into Middle English in the days of Chaucer, and the "morning star" of the Reformation. He could not understand why so much concern was felt about his movement and his teaching, and why "every sparrow twittereth thereof." To his mind, he was only an Oxford don trying to do something for the propagation of the Gospel and the dissemination of knowledge about the true Law of God set forth in Scripture. But what he really did was launch a tidal wave of reform which spread and increased as it rolled steadily onward. He could not possibly have foreseen the full and final consequences of his work. But on the other hand there are towering personalities who believe themselves to be commissioned by God for tremendous tasks, with consequences for time and eternity, men who stand on the threshold of new ages, or even, as they assume, at the beginning of the "last days" which lead to the end of the world.

One such man was Paul, perhaps the greatest example of this type of prophet, preacher, and missionary known to Christian history. He was not only a prophet and apostle, but a profound interpreter of the inner life. He laid the foundations of a reinterpretation of Christianity, which to this day has never worked out in detail the full implications of his principles—and he certainly never worked them out himself. In his own self-estimation he was an emissary of the Risen and Glorified Christ, the Heavenly Lord, sent on a flying journey throughout the Gentile world to call all men to prepare for the coming Judg-

ment. This transcendent "vision of the end," and of the part
God had called him to play in it, sustained him through all his
trials and tribulations, until his martyrdom in Rome at the end
of his course. On this hasty mission he tried to reach all men
and proclaim the gospel to them. Jerusalem, Damascus,
Tarsus, Antioch, Cyprus, Pamphylia, Galatia, Macedonia,
Achaia, the Province of Asia, finally Rome—the whole eastern
Mediterranean world was his mission field, and he even looked
forward to visiting Spain, if it was possible to get there. He was
in fact "the" apostle to the Gentiles, as he claimed, and it was
his conception of this responsibility that he must reach, directly
or indirectly, every human being outside the pale of Judaism.

All this he undertook to accomplish in the course of a dozen or
fifteen years! Other apostles were commissioned to present the
gospel to the Jews: his mission was to the Gentiles. It is no
wonder if he had little time to consider the possibility that the
world might *not* come to an end, that the present "age" might
last on indefinitely, and that the approaching Judgment
would take place after death and not in this present aeon. In
fact, he seems to have come to this conclusion before he died
(see Phil. 1. 23); but it was not the mainspring of his earlier
preaching, which was apocalyptic-eschatological, as we say,
i.e. oriented toward the coming transformation of all things.
Nor did he spend much time in introspection and self-analysis
(though he tended that way), and he left us no "spiritual
odyssey" of the kind modern romantics have produced. He
could scarcely be expected to appraise himself in the light of
later centuries, and he certainly did not try to write an autobiography—or what some German writers call a "psychography," a self-analysis of motives, qualifications, reactions to
experience, insights into reality, limitations due to ignorance.
We may be sure that he would have been surprised to be classed
with the "ecstatics" of later Hellenistic religion, who walked
with their heads in a cloud and scarcely touched the soil of
common earth with light ethereal tread. And I doubt if he
would have recognised himself the creator of "Paulinism," as
he was viewed three generations ago. This is not to say that he
was not the creator of Paulinism! But you cannot always get a
complete, not always an accurate answer from any man of
whom you inquire: Who art thou? Every one of us carries an

image of himself which is somewhat distorted. But so does everyone of everyone else. Only God knows us as we really are. But we can clear up the image somewhat by careful study, perhaps more successfully by study of the image of others than of ourselves. (There is a lesson in this. Our Lord said, "Judge not, that you be not judged." Half the schisms and dissensions in Christian history would have been impossible, I believe, if Christians had really tried to understand the mind and outlook of the opposition.) And so our approach to Paul may well begin with the question, How far was his own self-appraisal correct?

It is one of the paradoxes of the New Testament that the Apostle Paul, who probably did most to free Christianity from observance of the Jewish Law, insisted most vigorously upon his upbringing as a Pharisee. "If any other man thinks he has reason for confidence in the flesh, I have more: circumcised on the eighth day, of the people of Israel, of the tribe of Benjamin, a Hebrew born of Hebrews; *as to the Law a Pharisee*, as to zeal a persecutor of the church, as to righteousness under the Law blameless" (Phil. III. 4–6). The author of Luke-Acts goes farther and makes Paul insist that he is still a Pharisee, when on trial for his life before the Jewish Sanhedrin and before the Roman procurator and King Agrippa. "Brethren, *I am a Pharisee*, a son of Pharisees; with respect to the hope[1] and the resurrection of the dead I am on trial" (Acts XXIII. 6; cf. XXIV. 10–16, XXVI. 4–8, XXVIII. 20). The historical authenticity of this representation has been questioned, but its probability is strong. That surviving traces of Paul's own self-estimate should reach us via the Acts of the Apostles is not at all unlikely, and the question is involved in the authorship of that book. It is the Epistle to the Philippians that sets forth Paul's strong claim to Pharisaic antecedents and upbringing; and it is at Philippi that the "we-sections" begin (Acts XVI. 10–17, XX. 4–16, XXI. 1–17, XXVII. 1, XXVIII. 16; the passages in Acts where the author shifts from the third person singular and plural to the first person plural: "we" went instead of "he" or "they"). The mutual bearing of these two facts may have some importance in this

[1] "The Hope," i.e. the Messianic hope of Israel, not merely the hope of resurrection.

connexion, though precisely what this was is a matter of speculation. The language Paul uses in the rhetorical passage in Philippians (III. 4b–11), especially the phrase κατὰ νόμον, reflects
a favourable and highly appreciative attitude towards Pharisaism. In Pauline idiom, the κατά clearly implies "as far as
concerns" or (R.S.V.) "as to," i.e. a full rendering of the account or relation (cf. Rom. I. 3 f.); and this attitude is the one
also found in Rom. VII. 12, "So the Law is holy, and the com-
mandment is holy and just and good." Thus the paradox to
which we have referred goes back to Paul himself; he never
drew the final inference, the total rejection of the Mosaic Law.
How could he have drawn it? Was the Law not a divine revelation? Was its source not the wisdom and the saving purpose of
God? Had it not led men to Christ (cf. Gal. III. 19–IV. 7)? The
problem of its past and permanent value in the history of salvation is the central subject of the first half of Romans.

It was his attitude toward the Law, then, which characterised
the Pharisee, according to Paul, and distinguished him from all
other Jews. This also has ample support in ancient literature.
Following the re-establishment of the Jewish state after the
Exile, and especially after the long twenty-five-year Macca-
baean War of Independence in 168–143 B.C., the party of "the
pious," the Hasidim, redoubled their efforts to achieve a complete observance of the sacred Law, not only personally but on
the scale of the nation as a whole, viewed as the Covenant
People, who had been given "a Law whereby they should live
and not die" (cf. Lev. XVIII. 5). The Law was their guide, their
stay, their goal; yet it was more than a code of law; it was teaching, revelation, the Word of God. This is repeatedly affirmed,
for example in Psalm CXIX, the long acrostic poem on the divine
revelation, whose seeming simplicity, as Canon Liddon once
observed, overlies vast depths of spiritual insight and meaning:
"Thy Word is a lamp to my feet, and a light to my path" (vs.
105). It was the party of the Hasidim with their undying
devotion to the sacred Law, for which they were quite ready to
lay down their lives in the struggle with Antiochus, which
eventually produced, or became, the party of the Pharisees.

Pharisaism was a puritanical movement, separatist, completely devoted to the observance of the requirements set forth
in the Torah, and at the same time devout and earnest in culti-

vating the inner life of personal consecration and obedience to the will of God. In modern usage, alas, this central drive and emphasis in Pharisaism has been lost sight of. A popular dictionary defines "Pharisee" as a member of an ancient Jewish sect which "held to the letter rather than the spirit of Mosaic law and tradition." From this definition the *descensus facilis* leads swiftly to another: "One who is more observant of religious ritual than actively benevolent; a self-righteous person; a prig"; and Pharisaism is equated with "formalism, self-righteousness, hypocrisy." I am not criticising the excellent *Macmillan's Dictionary*; it is only too faithful in recording current English usage. But surely Paul did not claim to have been reared in this kind of religion—if it can be called religion. Whether or not he still claimed to be a Pharisee at the date reflected in Acts, clearly he viewed his religious upbringing in Pharisaism as an asset, a limited asset, but not a liability. Our modern Protestant theology must recover a fairer appraisal of the central aim and purpose of Pharisaism if it is to deal fairly, not only with Judaism, but also with the Apostle Paul. For Judaism was without doubt the noblest and purest monotheistic religion in the ancient world; and Pharisaism was its noblest, purest expression—not Sadduceeism, which was ultra-conservative and reactionary; nor Essenism, which was one-sided, pietistic, and semi-monastic; nor Zealotism, which was politically-minded and bent on revolution.

Not only in his attitude toward the Law, as the source and record of a divine revelation, but in his allegiance to the great religious affirmations of the early Pharisees (we cannot call them "doctrines," for there was no ecclesiastical authorisation of Jewish teaching), Paul remained a Pharisee to his dying day. The absolute oneness, uniqueness, and sovereignty of God; His creation of the world; His self-revelation, to Moses and the prophets, in Scripture, and in nature and in human history as well; the freedom of the human will, and the consequent possibility and the patent historical fact of human sin and disobedience; the frailty of human nature and the inevitability of death; the possibility, and the hope, of a resurrection from among the dead; the glorious future Reign of God, over a redeemed and transformed universe; the central characteristic of all God's dealings with mankind, His mercy and grace, triumphing over vindictive justice; the sending of a Redeemer, the Messiah, to act as God's Agent in the restoration of the divine rule upon earth (Paul the Christian, of course, recognised him in "the Man Christ Jesus" who had become the Risen and Glorified Lord, not only of the Church but of the whole created universe, as described in Phil. II. 5-11); the necessity of some rational ground in the divine purpose for even the most abhorrent and self-contradictory processes or events, such as the suffering and martyrdom of the righteous (for Paul, this meant above all the death of Christ on a cross); the possibility and the necessity of deeper and fuller applications of the principles set forth in revelation—as for example in the famous Pharisaic device known as the *prosbol*, to offset the consequences of a literal observance of the rule requiring cancellation of debts every seven years (for Paul, this was carried further into the principle of freedom whereby a fresh religious movement, guided by the Holy Spirit, could free itself from its own past heritage and revise its own standards rather than be smothered or strangled by them: a principle not often invoked in later Christian history, but clearly indispensable)—*all* these principles and beliefs are rooted in Pharisaism, and they help to account for the man Paul of Tarsus and his immense influence upon nascent Christianity.

It is true that some of these beliefs and views have parallels, either remote or close at hand, outside the Old Testament and Judaism, and hence beyond the range of Pharisaic interest or influence. Man's frailty and false hopes were recognised by Homer—see *Odyssey* XVIII. 130 ff.:

> Nothing feebler is nourished by earth than man,
> Of all that breathe and move about upon it.

Similarly, man's inward anxiety even in the midst of outward prosperity and apparent happiness (something Homer was not thinking about) was described by Lucretius (*De rerum natura*, VI. 9-42). It is also biblical:

> Man being in honour hath no understanding,
> But is compared unto the beasts that perish
>
> > (cf. Ps. XLIX. 12).

Moreover, Paul's list of virtues in Gal. v. 22f. reaches its climax in "self-control," which is thoroughly Greek; and it is followed by the typically Greek anticlimax of understatement, "Against *such* [surely] there is no law!" But these are the soft and more delicate virtues, of the kind found in Virgil and other non-Stoic, non-Cynic writers, and in the tracts and traditions of the Jewish teachers (e.g. The Testaments of the Twelve Patriarchs), an ethical teaching which grew in sheltered gardens, under the influence of religious ideas and of a more or less spiritual view of life. Paul's ethics, not merely his "theology," is also Pharisaic, religious, pietistic. It is by no means the revolutionary social or political ethics which denounced slavery and threatened tyrants and demanded world brotherhood at once.

Still another principle of Paul's religious outlook and teaching, one which he owed to his Jewish inheritance and specifically to Pharisaism, was the superiority of rational and volitional piety to emotional. The best example of this characteristic Pauline outlook is found in his manner of dealing with the outbreak of corybantic paganism in the church at Corinth (1 Cor. xii–xiv). The γλωσσολαλία or "speaking with tongues" was an ecstatic, irrational kind of utterance, which was supposed to be the language of angels or of spiritual devotion or of divine inspiration (a "spiritual gift"); but it meant nothing at all unless or until it was "explained" by someone specially skilled or in possession of the parallel "gift" of "interpretation" —the interpretation was no doubt likewise supposed to be inspired. Though Paul himself was able to "speak in tongues more than you all," "in church" he would rather speak five words with his mind, in order to instruct others, than ten thousand words in a "tongue" (ch. xiv. 18 f.). And the "fruit of the Spirit," i.e. the outward evidence of possession by the Holy Spirit, was not γλωσσολαλία, or even the working of miracles, but the ethical virtues (as above); "love, joy, peace, patience, kindness, goodness, faithfulness, gentleness, self-control." Anyone who fails to recognise in this passage the characteristic emphases of ancient Jewish ethics simply does not know ancient Judaism; anyone who fails to recognise in it the characteristic emphasis found in the teaching of Jesus simply does not know the Gospels.

Paul's freedom in carrying forward the development of Old Testament religious teaching, and also that of Jesus, is apparent on almost every page of his epistles. For example, slavery. In the Old Testament this was a recognised social institution, as it was elsewhere in ancient law, but it was modified by the requirement (not always observed) that Hebrew slaves must be set free. But Paul considers the Christian slave of a Christian master (i.e. owner), or even the Christian slave of a pagan master, better off as a slave than as a freedman, in view of the approaching end of the age (1 Cor. VII. 20–4; Philem. 16; Col. III. 22–IV. 1; Eph. VI. 5–9; 1 Tim. VI. 1–2). Or take the difference between Jew and Gentile, which in the Old Testament tended to break down (see Is. XIX. 23–5) but which for Paul no longer existed: "In Christ Jesus neither circumcision nor uncircumcision is of any avail, but faith working through love" (Gal. V. 6; cf. 1 Cor. VII. 19). It cannot be said that this, or anything like this, was the teaching of the Pharisees. Many of them would have been baffled, not to say horrified, by the distinction between circumcision and "keeping the commandments of God." Had not circumcision been specifically commanded by God, as the sign of membership in the divine Covenant (Gen. XVII. 9–14)? Nevertheless, many of them recognised that righteousness, wherever found, was precious in God's sight; and the principle of a spiritual interpretation which Paul stressed, even beyond the letter of the Law, was one toward which Pharisaism was already moving. For Paul, Christianity was the fulfilment not only of the Law and the Prophets but also of the teaching of those spiritual guides of ancient Judaism whose highest claim, like his own, was to be faithful interpreters of the oracles of God, the revealed will and purpose of the Father in heaven. The paths they followed were not closely parallel; indeed, they were widely divergent—note the difference between Paul's letters and any tractate of the Mishnah, the traditional exegesis of the Old Testament Law handed down in the schools by the Tannaim; yet they had a common origin and shared in varying degrees a common impetus, viz. the quest for a free and positive spiritual life under the guidance of both the written word and the loving Spirit of the Most High.

It is not necessary to maintain the strict historicity of the statement attributed to Paul in Acts XXII. 3, according to which he had been a pupil of Gamaliel I (cf. ch. V. 33–9). Perhaps the only exaggeration in the statement is the length of time assumed. Nor is it necessary to ignore the varieties of religious thought within Pharisaism, which was a religious, i.e. a pietistic, movement, not theological. Josephus claimed to be a Pharisee (see his *Vita*, appended to the *Antiquities* as BK. XXI); and there were others. Paul's Pharisaism was surely tinged by ideas common in the Graeco-Roman world surrounding the Western Diaspora. For him, for example, the words Sin, Death, Judgment, Wrath, Wisdom, Power were always written with capitals, we might say, as quasi-substantive entities in the spiritual world. But it is the over-arching and all-embracing fact of his fundamental Pharisaism, for all his repudiation of its details, which provides the key to Paul's complex, paradoxical, dynamic, creative religious genius.

But how are we to account for the harsh language he uses about the Law, about his own people the Jews, about the Pharisees? Jewish readers of Paul's letters are completely baffled by what they read there—Sholem Asch told me he had no difficulty with the Gospels, but when he came to Paul he was utterly incapable of understanding him. How can Paul take the attitude he does to his own people and their religion? Can he have been really a Jew and shared the Jewish way of life and faith? Was he ever a "good" Jew, observing the sabbaths and festivals of the Jewish year, the lections and prayers of the synagogue, the food regulations, the normal and wholesome requirements which the ancestral religion laid upon every member of the chosen people? I must say that I think Paul's anti-Judaism has been exaggerated. Take a concordance and look up the passages where he refers to Jews and the Law—he never mentioned Pharisees or Pharisaism, except in one passage (Phil. III. 5) where he mentions his upbringing (much as Josephus does). The passages where he criticises the Jews are usually offset by words of favour or generalisation—as in Rom. III. 1 ff., where he suddenly switches (in vs. 5) from "the Jews" to "us" and "our" wickedness. If one reads his words without prejudice, it will be clear that he never condemns except reluctantly, and then with a sudden realisation that "*all* have sinned," not just his own people.

His words about the Law are more serious, and here one must fall back upon the findings of religious psychology for a clue to Paul's conversion, its antecedents, its course, its results. Like all converts, he now "adored what once he had burned, and burned what once he had adored"—the same thing one finds in millions of cases of religious crisis and *volte face*. Not pagan idolaters only, but Catholics turned Protestant in the sixteenth century, Puritans and Independents in the seventeenth, not to mention the long wars of "religion" and the catastrophic divisions of Christendom over political or theological or even merely personal ecclesiastical disputes—were ever harsher words uttered than by nominal Christians against one another in such situations? Paul was a Semite: and Semites do not mince words in argument—see the Old Testament, for example, or the Koran: in the one the Canaanites, in the other idolaters are "for burning." See also the Gospels, where the tradition of Jesus' teaching, in its present form (e.g. the tirade against "scribes and Pharisees, hypocrites" in Mt. XXIII), is full of vituperation and invective: many scholars now think the chapter reflects the mood of the late first century, after the separation of the Church from the synagogue, rather than the mind of Jesus. But it is absurd to credit Semites with more than a fair share of the capacity for invective—look at the world around us today! Read any morning paper!

Furthermore, Paul was undoubtedly one of the "twice-born," who had once been a "sick soul" and never wholly overcame his handicap—God often uses such men more effectively than the "once-born," for they are usually able to see into human distress and anxiety far more deeply and understandingly than others. His eager, energetic, dynamic leadership led him into hasty decisions which surely he must later have regretted: for example, it was scarcely a preamble to canon law when Paul wrote to the wild Galatians (ch. v. 18), "If you are led by the Spirit you are not under the Law." Such a rule simply ignored the necessary course of education, discipline, nurture, edification and spiritual enlightenment which must precede such a launching into the deep as the direct guidance of the Holy Spirit. What could he possibly have replied to the Corinthians, if they had read this letter and had then reminded him, "Yes, that is precisely what we are doing here in Corinth—and oh, what a glorious time we are having!" One wishes Paul had written far more, including an autobiography, and that he had lived to be eighty, and had *then* told us what his final summing up came to. Plato lived to be eighty, and his final views are somewhat different from his earlier, as we may see by comparing the *Laws* with the *Republic*. But there are other contrasts: "the style is the man," and Plato's broad, rich harmonies are like deep-toned organ music, harmonies like Bach's or Mozart's; Paul's notes are single sharp trumpet blasts of startling shrillness which "stab men's spirits broad awake." "If the bugle gives an indistinct sound, who will get ready for battle?" (1 Cor. xiv. 8)—that is Paul's own figure, true to his whole mind and purpose, his missionary career, and his message. Once more, we are required to reconstruct the career and the mind of Paul with only half the necessary data. If we could but follow him through boyhood and youth, through his period of fanatical devotion to the anti-Christian (or anti-"Nazarene") party as a persecutor, and then through the mysterious crisis which changed his life and made him turn suddenly into a propagandist for the new faith—if we only possessed such data as these we should be able to draw a far more satisfactory picture of the "mind of Paul" and explain some of the baffling paradoxes he presents. What he says of the Law is often like the twitching of a very deep old wound.

There are several modern books on the theme of "Jesus the Jew," insisting, as against the "Aryan" nonsense of Houston Stewart Chamberlain and others, that Jesus was completely Jewish in ancestry, environment, background, characteristic ideas, standards, and aims. It is only against this Jewish background that the finest elements in his gospel, some of which distinguish it from the background by a strong contrast, begin to stand out. The same would be true of Paul, if only people studied him as an ancient Jew—the kind of man Adolf Deissmann described, a living man, a religious devotee and propagandist under the early Roman Empire: "Ein anatolischer und antiker Paulus, ein *homo novus* aus der Masse der Vielen und Kleinen herauswächst."[2] We have no quarrel with those who

---

[2] "An ancient Anatolian Paul, a *homo novus* who emerged from the mass of the many and the little." *Homo novus*, a "new man," was the term for *parvenus* who rose to position in the public life of Rome without family, funds, name, or other backing.

prefer to study Paul's theological significance, and who trace
the beginnings of ideas that grew later into mighty systems,
Augustine's, Luther's, Calvin's; but the way to begin is to study
him as a man, a religious man, a man whose life was centred in
obedience to the will of God and in the inner transformation
which his "new being" in Christ involved. We must study him
the way John Colet studied and expounded him in 1496,
when, fresh from his residence in Italy and his association with
Marsiglio Ficino and the humanists, he lectured at Oxford
on St Paul, and insisted that the epistles of the Apostle should
be treated as one would treat those of Cicero, and thus find
how they differed (p. 29). Or as the poet Coleridge read the Bible
—"like any other book," thus finding how it stood apart from all
others. For Paul himself, we might say at this point, holy
Scripture was something fresh and new and directly revealing,
though he had studied it all his life; for now at last he had
found the key and clue to it: it all led up to Christ, set the stage
for Christ, hinted and beckoned in his direction, packed away
deep mysteries of divine purpose in even the lowliest happenings
and their record, so that in the fullness of the time men would
not fail to recognise their deliverer, the Son of God who was
coming to save mankind. But the story was plainly told, the
word was near, and in men's hearts to conceive (Rom. x. 8).
That was the marvel of it: a simple story of a small people, in
whom all the earth should be blessed—or bless themselves, as
the R.S.V. now translates; but at the heart of the tale is a
glowing mystery of divine love and divine self-sacrifice, self-
humiliation, reaching its climax in the cross of Christ and his
glorification (Phil. II. 5–11). For Paul, the familiar Scriptures
took on a wholly new meaning. But it was the Jewish Bible,
which he had learned to read as a child, and it was still fundamentally Jewish in its meaning and implications: Judaism
fulfilled, universalised, catholicised. It was "Catholick Judaism," as certain old writers affirmed.

I have tried elsewhere to describe Paul as a figure in history,[3]
noting not only his use of the Bible, his loyalty to Judaism, his
independent attitude toward Greek philosophy, and various
other factors in his mind and personality. He was an implacable

[3] "The Historical Paul," in *Early Christian Origins: Studies in Honor of Harold R.
Willoughby*, ed. Allen Wikgren, Chicago 1961.

opponent of racialism, discrimination, intolerance, and of fanaticism of any kind. He was an absolutely fearless leader, willing to stake his life in a cause worthy of it. He had a profound respect for law and order, and he viewed the Roman Empire as God's creation, not the devil's—as the apocalyptists held. Like Jesus, he was anti-Zealot, and would have stood with King Agrippa II in his opposition to the Jewish War in 66. He was an intense and profound monotheist; not a theorist, not a philosopher, but a man who found the centre of his being in God. Important as was his Christology, it never obscured his awareness of God. Like all deeply Christian theists, for him belief in God, trust in God, obedience to God came first, and was the indispensable presupposition of his doctrine of Christ. The shallow modern cliché, "the Christlike God," would have sounded pagan, or blasphemous, or at the least darkly obscure to Paul, and so gravely in need of interpretation that it had better not be used. Nor was he in any danger of "trying to put the Bible in the place of God," a modern theological tendency against which Leonard Hodgson has warned us in his Page Lecture (1958). Paul's view of the Church as the true Israel, in direct continuity with the ancient people of God—this is another idea which cannot be derived anywhere but from the Old Testament and Judaism. The primacy of ethics in his religion, not as something separate, like the ethics of Aristotle or the Stoics, but integral and inseparable from the religious faith by which his ethics were inspired—this too was profoundly Jewish and Pharisaic.

All these and other characteristics are recognisably Paul's. Not that he is an easy person to describe or to make out: he is as complicated and involved as any other ancient Jew, as any other man of any age, ancient or modern. But how he managed to keep all these elements in equilibrium—not always a smooth and silent equilibrium, but like G. K. Chesterton's figure of the Catholic Church, "reeling but erect"; how he managed to live with himself, and not fly apart in all directions; how he overcame the immense tension within himself, bringing every thought and motive into obedience to Christ; how he could live with a faith too hot to pour into intellectual moulds, like bronze castings that burst the clay forms in many a Greek artist's studio (we have some of them); how he could live by that faith and yet despair of putting it in words, only hinting that the greatness of the idea was beyond description or utterance—all this leads us in one direction: *Paul was a mystic*. At the very heart of his religious life (which was his whole life) glowed a union with the divine person which transcended language and even thought. "Oh, the depth of the goodness and mercy of God!" "What eye has not seen nor ear heard, nor has it entered the heart [i.e. the mind] of man to conceive—such things God has prepared for those who love him!" (1 Cor. 11. 9; cf. Rom. XI. 33). This is not frothy emotionalism, but the topmost peak of the religious approach to God, where the next step is off into a realm beyond space and time and concrete thought, where only a projection of the idea can be attempted—"beyond the flaming ramparts of the world."

Mysticism, of which there was a fair amount in ancient Judaism, in spite of the caricatures of Judaism drawn by modern critics, is the attempt to put in words, or, failing words, somehow to convey an impression of the absolute Reality which cannot be described yet nevertheless can be experienced —as in Augustine's "moment of intelligence," or Boehme's *Aurora*, or Pascal's blazing "fire," or Paul's "heavenly vision" on the way to Damascus and the "great light" that accompanied it. He was a Pharisee who *might* have taken the road to legalism —and been in misery all his days: he did not take to the law, even the sacred Law, or the Torah, God's revelation, viewed as law. Instead, he took the other road, which also lay open to an ancient Pharisee, viz. the road to the heavenly city which led through dark valleys of renunciation, long hours of prayer, of "wrestling with God," of waiting to hear the divine voice, in a life of complete dedication to the divine will. The modern world does not know much about this kind of religion; perhaps modern Judaism knows it as little as modern Christianity does. But it has been found in many areas in the past, in Judaism, in Catholicism, in paganism, in Islam, and in other religions; and also in more modern and more recent times: e.g. among the Chassidim in Poland two centuries ago; at Little Gidding; at Gethsemani, Kentucky; in prison camps and at lonely outposts on the desert. For wherever God is, there you may find a mystic: and where is there any place where God is not? Wrapped in the peace that "passeth all understanding," Paul lived his

busy, hazardous, active, even tumultuous life as the servant of
Christ, a Pharisee to his dying day, a saintly Jew who found the
centre of his being "hid with Christ in God."

But he wrought more mightily than he knew. The world did
not come to an end in the first century, nor did the Roman
Empire; yet the stream of vital faith and experience opened up
by Christ, shared and interpreted by Paul, continued to flow
on and on and on and has never run dry. That too is mystical:
for the river of living water is a constant, unceasing, ever-
enriching experience of God in Christ. Alas, that men ever
thought they could collect it in buckets or barrels or cisterns, or
even in brackish reservoirs of rationalism! Or that it could be
converted into a rigid system of thought, along with the rest of
the world's systems, and supported by irrefutable logic, rather
than by faith and prayer and love and holy living!

Paul's self-appraisal was correct. He *was* a Pharisee, but a
Pharisee who had found Christ (or been found by him, Phil.
III. 9). This discovery had transformed his whole outlook on
life and religion, on God's self-revelation and God's purposes,
on the meaning of salvation and the hope of the life to come.
And yet, for all this transformation, he was still a Pharisee, and
remained one all his life. He was no Hindu or Stoic or Egyptian
or Roman or Greek; he was no philosopher or intellectual
theorist; he was not even a theologian, in the commonly
accepted sense, and he certainly was no medieval Schoolman.
Instead, he was a first-century Jew, reared in the religion of his
fathers and striving with all his soul for "the hope of Israel."
His Judaism was not the orthodox variety current in Palestine—
at least not the kind that became current before long, in the
period following the destruction of Jerusalem and the revival of
the Jewish schools. Instead it was the Judaism of the Western
Diaspora, already tinged with Hellenism through use of the
Greek language and the consequent adoption of certain Greek
modes of thought. But it was still Pharisaic Judaism, rooted in
the Law and the Prophets and culminating in the prospective
fulfilment of the ancient promises, which were now recognised
to have begun to take place in the life of Jesus, his death and
resurrection, and to be still in process of fulfilment in the swiftly
moving events which now flowed from his exaltation and glori-

fication. Paul was one "upon whom the end of the ages had come," and who could look forward, as he believed, to the immediate realisation of the New World, for its powers were even now active in and through Christ's "body," the Church (see Heb. VI. 5; Mk. XVI. 20, for this early Church outlook). And it was from this unique vantage-point that Paul looked back upon the ancient Law, and saw it in what other Pharisees had looked for, but in vain. To Paul the Pharisee, Christ was the "end" of the Law (Rom. X. 4), not merely its abrogation but its final goal and consummation, its τέλος in the total purposes of God.

# Chapter VIII

# The Emergence of Early Christian Doctrine

W e are now in a position to view the course of development of the early Christian religion, as a whole, against its wider background in Hellenism. We can begin to make out its successive stages, the first tentative efforts to formulate its teaching (*doctrina*) in technical terms, its steady accumulation of scripture resources, its adoption of methods of apologetics and even of forms of worship and the titles of its appointed leaders from the surrounding world of Judaism and Hellenism—especially Hellenistic Judaism. Thus it was gathering up the treasure of the past and reminting its gold into something fresh and new. We may summarise these stages as follows:

1. Christianity began as a messianic movement within first-century Judaism. As a rule, messianic movements arise in crises, which may be partly political, partly economic—though the deeper causes are usually economic. Prophetism, in the Old Testament, likewise arose in crises, and its whole history is set in the framework of crisis, from the Philistine threat to the Assyrian, the Babylonian, the Seleucid, and the Roman. With the Seleucid crisis prophecy began to be transformed into apocalyptic.[1] The crisis which formed the setting for John's prophecy and that of Jesus was the impending destruction of Jerusalem and the Jewish state by Rome. Jesus' ethics of non-resistance was the only sane and practical view to be taken, like the view of Jeremiah in a similar crisis at the end of the seventh century before Christ. It was not "world renunciation" that Jesus taught, but the only possible *modus vivendi* for the Jews under the overwhelming military power of Rome, with its irresistible army of occupation, its inescapable taxation, and the quisling priests and princes who endeavoured to cushion this burden of foreign rule and keep up an appearance of continuity with the past. These are factors of the greatest import-

[1] On the distinction between the two, see my *Ancient Judaism and the New Testament*, ch. vi.

ance for understanding Jesus' message and the course of his career—including his arrest, trial, and crucifixion.

2. But it was not long before Christianity had crossed the borders of Palestine and was spreading far and wide in the vast world of Graeco-Roman-Oriental Hellenism under the early Roman Empire. Here a totally different political-economic background was to be found from that in Galilee and Judea in the twenties and thirties of the first century, one which had immense and far-reaching consequences for the preaching of the gospel of the risen and glorified Messiah Jesus.

3. The young Christian Church, the fresh religious movement known at first as the Nazarenes, crossed the borders of strict Judaism and began preaching to Gentiles at a very early date—much earlier than is commonly supposed.[2] In its earliest historical stage, the Christian movement was fundamentally and unmistakably Jewish, even Pharisaic, and messianic. But almost from the first it embraced "Hellenists," i.e. Greek-speaking Jews from the Diaspora.[3] These Hellenist Jews had already made advances toward the Gentiles. They "compassed sea and land to make one proselyte" (Mt. XXIII. 15), and their success in both East and West was remarkable. The story of Queen Helena of Adiabene and her son Izates, told by Josephus,[4] is a capital illustration of this missionary activity. Adiabene lay east of the Tigris, in north-west Iran or "Assyria" as it was still called in the first and second centuries. Professor Paul Kahle believes the first Aramaic or Syriac translation of the Old Testament was made for these Jews in Adiabene.[5] The New Testament also provides examples of converts to Judaism, i.e. proselytes, some of whom later became Christians (see Acts VI. 5, XIII. 43).

4. More than this, the Jews of the Western Diaspora had produced, partly through their translation of the Old Testament into Greek, a religious vocabulary which became of the

[2] See Acts VIII. 4f., 14, 25, Samaria; VIII. 26–39, the Ethiopian; x, Cornelius; XI. 1, 18, Gentiles; XI. 20–6, Antioch; XIII. 1–3, the mission to Cyprus; XV. 6–11, Peter's reference to the "early days" when the preaching to Gentiles first began.

[3] See Acts II. 5–11, the Greek-speaking Jews in Jerusalem at Pentecost; VI. 1–6, the Hellenist widows; VI. 5–6, the Hellenist "deacons"; VI. 9, IX. 29b, the Hellenist synagogues.

[4] *Jewish War*, II. 19. 2; IV. 9.11; V. 2.2, 3.3, 4.2, 6.1; VI. 6.3, 4; *Antiquities*, xx. 2–4; see also Eusebius, *Church History*, II. 12. 1–3.

[5] See the new edition of his book, *The Cairo Geniza*, Oxford 1959, pp. 270 ff.

greatest value and utility to the early Christian writers.[6] Some of the most important words in the Christian religious vocabulary were taken directly from the Graeco-Jewish writings, chiefly from the Septuagint. It is for this reason that the study of the Septuagint is indispensable to the New Testament student. The Jewish writers in Alexandria also set forth noble ethical teaching in Greek terms; the process began with the translation of Sirach into Greek in 132 B.C. (if not earlier), and included such a remarkable poem as that of Pseudo-Phocylides.[7]

5. Thus the Jews also penetrated the world of Hellenistic religious thought and, both influencing it and being influenced by it, they contributed to a development of ideas which led away from traditional Judaism. It is not unlikely that peripheral Jewish groups, found here and there in the Mediterranean world, especially in Egypt, Syria, and north-west Anatolia, helped to prepare the way for what was later to be known as Gnosticism—a *mélange* of speculation and piety which Paul Wendland not inaptly called "the theology of syncretism."[8] The traditional view, set forth by the Church fathers, traced Gnosticism to Simon Magus; but it is not unlikely that disappointment and disillusionment following the two unsuccessful wars against Rome in 66–70 and 132–5 led many Jews to shift their hopes to a purely "spiritual," cosmic, supramundane level.

The Christian movement was thus by no means limited to Judaism, either in Palestine or in the Western Diaspora. The apostles, evangelists, and missionaries ("preachers of the word") were soon preaching directly to Gentiles, i.e. to that large group of them who already had some inkling of what the gospel was all about, having been influenced by Jewish propaganda, worship, and sacred scriptures. From this it was only a short step to approach those Gentiles who had not been influenced in any degree by Judaism. Here the presuppositions were quite different, and—as Johannes Weiss, Adolf Harnack,

[6] See C. H. Dodd, *The Bible and the Greeks*, Part I. See above, pp. 24, 72, 80, 119.

[7] A translation of *The Maxims of Phocylides*, made by Burton Scott Easton, was published in the *Anglican Theological Review*, XIV (1932), pp. 222–8.

[8] See R. M. Grant, *Gnosticism and Early Christianity*, New York and Oxford 1959. And see above, Ch. III, *ad fin.*

and many others have pointed out—a deeper foundation had to be laid: monotheism, the doctrine of creation, the eternity of the moral law, the resurrection and Last Judgment, the divine nature of Christ, the messianic community and its supernatural destiny.[9]

Naturally these concepts were understood and interpreted against a very different background and in terms with very different presuppositions from those which were to be found in Judaism, either in Palestine or in the Western Diaspora. The consequence was a theological transformation of primitive Christianity whose beginning can be traced in the New Testament and which continued for many generations—not only until Irenaeus (c. A.D. 185), or the Council of Nicaea (A.D. 325), but down into Byzantine times; to some extent it has continued ever since.[10]

For example, the Gentile world, speaking generally, was not content to view God as a person, the Father, whose Son was the Messiah; or as the One who "raised up" and "sent" the Prophet Jesus as his messenger, agent, and anointed Messiah; or whose divine Spirit was "poured out" on certain men, a "power" or "inspiration" which led to exalted utterance of an authoritative message or "word" from God to his people, and also to miraculous cures and exorcisms or other "mighty works" (i.e. works of God, done through or for men). It is true that these features were also found in Graeco-Roman cults; but in this case there was much more to tell. The Gentile world insisted upon viewing God as a metaphysical entity or principle, and his "Son" and "Spirit" as substantive entities, distinct from "the Father" yet ineffably united and indeed identified with him. Of course the presupposition was the utter, complete, essential *reality* of this spiritual nature, beyond both the merely physical or phenomenological level of existence and also the noumenal, viewed as subjective or a mere distinction in thought.

---

[9] See Adolf Harnack, *The Mission and Expansion of Christianity in the First Three Centuries*, trans. from the 2nd German edition by James Moffatt, New York 1908; Johannes Weiss, *Primitive Christianity*, trans. by Four Friends and ed. by F. C. Grant, New York 1937; repr. as *Earliest Christianity* in Harper's Torchbook Series, New York 1959. See also Ch. V, above.

[10] See Edwin Hatch, *The Influence of Greek Ideas and Usages upon the Christian Church*, 1890; repr. in Harper's Torchbook Series, New York 1957; see also my book, *An Introduction to New Testament Thought*, New York 1950.

For a time, in the middle of the second century, the idea of two divine Persons was current in certain Christian circles—Justin Martyr used the expression "the Second God," about A.D. 150 (see his *Apology*, LVI. 11). But the view was only a halting point on a longer journey. By A.D. 180 Theophilus of Antioch was using the term Τρίας.

The final result was the doctrine of the Trinity, or rather the *Tri-unity* of God, which in spite of all the pressures upon the Church exerted by various theological thinkers or groups was not so much a metaphysical theory as an attempt to describe the presuppositions of New Testament language and to set limits to its proper use and interpretation. In brief, it was an attempt to formulate *the proper Christian way of speaking about God*, his Son, and the blessed Spirit. The terms were simple, and held close to the traditional terminology: God is "Three Persons in One." The Father is God, the Son is God, the Spirit is God. Yet the Father is not the Son, nor the Son the Father; the Father is not the Spirit, nor the Spirit the Father; neither is the Son the Spirit, nor the Spirit the Son. It is an inconceivable "mystery," beyond our comprehension, yet a necessary hypothesis, not so much an inference as a presupposition of all Christian thought about God, in Gentile terms. But the contrast with the earliest stage of Christian thinking, as reflected in the oldest parts of the New Testament, is unmistakable and undeniable. There was a real development of thought, from the beginning, from the earliest days of the Gentile mission and the founding of the Gentile churches.[11]

The chief Trinitarian text in the New Testament is the baptismal formula in Mt. XXVIII. 19: "Go therefore and make disciples of all nations [i.e. *in* all nations], baptising them in the name of the Father and of the Son and of the Holy Spirit, teaching them to observe all that I have commanded you." There have been many modern objections to this formula. Eusebius of Caesarea evidently read the passage simply "make disciples of [*or* from] all nations *in my name*, teaching them to observe all that I have commanded you." But Eusebius stands alone, and it may be that he either quoted from memory,

---

[11] See the articles on the Trinity in the new editions of Hastings' one-volume *Dictionary of the Bible* and the *Encyclopedia Americana*, or my *Basic Christian Beliefs*, ch. II.

paraphrased, or wished not to get entangled in theological debate over the matter. Conceivably, his own text may have been altered in transmission. But none of the explanations really meet the case. Further, the meaning of the saying is obviously, "make disciples, and teach them"—the insertion of the command to baptise (in the participial form, as if they would be made disciples by baptism, which is not the view of the earliest Church, which required a certain amount of Christian practice before baptism was permitted—see Justin Martyr, in his *Apology*, 61, 65 and other evidence) is in form much like other glosses, either written or oral, found elsewhere in both the holy Scriptures and ancient literature in general. But if so, it must be very early—so early that Matthew himself may have added the words. Presumably the baptismal formula is as old as the Matthean form of the Lord's Prayer, which most scholars assume to be identical with the form used in the Church at his time, rather than the Lucan form, which looks edited. At any rate, the baptismal formula sums up the experience of early Christians, even Christian Jews, as George Foot Moore insisted.[12] The conception of God as "Father" was inherited as an essential part of the Jewish liturgy and the daily prayers; the term "Son" covered their new-found faith in the Risen Christ (it could be either "Son of Man" or "Son of God"—Mk. xiii. 32 has the same usage); the term "Holy Spirit" was common in the early Church, which was aware of the divine presence in their midst and viewed this presence as the earnest and guarantee of the coming of the miraculous New Age which was to follow Christ's Parousia and the Last Judgment. Like other items in the Gospel of Matthew, this also was derived from the faith, worship, and tradition of the early Syrian-Palestinian Church around the end of the first century. The similar formula in the Didache (vii. 1–4) points likewise to an early date and to current church usage. If one thing is certain, the formula is not the invention of one man who mischievously "interpolated" the Gospel, as some people used to think. The fact that the formula is introduced among the post-resurrection sayings of Jesus would indicate that it did not belong among the old traditional "words of Jesus" handed down in the basic gospel sources. It is one of the briefest summaries of early Christian

[12] G. F. Moore, *Judaism*, VOL. I, p. 188.

belief about God, who is the Father; Christ, who is God's Son; the Holy Spirit, who is one with the Father and the Son, who "comes" upon the Church or upon individuals, and who not only guides into "all truth" (as in Jn. xvi. 13) but is the source of new moral and spiritual life for the Christian (Gal. v. 16–26). The line leading on from this brief summary to the fuller creeds of the second, third, fourth, and fifth centuries is clear; only the details are complicated and require careful study.

But the line leads backwards as well, even if not all the way to the explicit teaching of Jesus, e.g. in the Sermon on the Mount or elsewhere. The liturgical "grace" found at the end of ii Cor. xiii. 14) is probably apostolic and characteristically Pauline. The stage of Christian doctrine reached in Paul's time already assumed the pre-existence of the Son and his subordination to the Father (i Cor. viii. 6, xi. 3) not only prior to the Incarnation (Phil. ii. 5–11) but also at the final Consummation and for ever after (i Cor. xv. 24–8), though the precise relations between the divine Persons are never worked out by the Apostle. The same is true of the author of John and the Johannine Epistles, though the perfect unity of the Father and the Son is stressed over and again (e.g. Jn. x. 30). In the Epistle to Hebrews the Son is pre-existent (i. 1–4), but again no effort is made to define the precise relations between the divine Persons. It may be pointed out that the New Testament theology is neither "binitarian" (two persons only) nor "adoptionist" (Christ a man adopted by God and deified at the Resurrection); these were later views, and were pronounced heretical in the second century. In the development of this doctrine as in that of others the Church manifested a practical rather than a speculative interest, and the formulae used belong to the daily routine of worship, practice, and instruction in the Church— the instruction of converts, their baptism and pastoral supervision, the interpretation of the Old Testament, the life of Christian piety among the converted Gentiles, the "God-fearers" who had now become attached to the new faith. Once more, it is the right way of speaking about God, the proper way to use Christian language, that is far more important than any possible metaphysical implications—all these came later, and led to the Christological controversies of the third and following centuries. What we see in the New Testament is the language of direct, immediate religious experience, the experience of divine revelation and redemption, and the on-going experience of "salvation" (something far more than momentary rescue, it is a whole state of σωτηρία, safety, welfare, peace, security, the "glory of going on and not to fail"). And this led, before long, to a still fuller expression of the new life in Christ, in this spring-time of the Spirit which characterised the early decades of Church history.

Another "mystery" was the nature and mode of the Incarna-tion. The appearance of a prophet, even "the true Prophet" as the Clementines call him, was not enough. If he was now exalted to heaven, he must have come originally from heaven. If he is the eternal Son of God, he must have pre-existed as Son of God. The mode of his birth must have been appropriate to his pre-existence and incarnation: the Virgin Birth was the most probable and the most "congruous" assumption possible, based as it was on the Greek Bible (not the Hebrew), in the oracle promising a divine "sign" (in Is. VII. 14).

What is commonly described as the "divinity" of Christ has been a doctrine, i.e. a teaching, of the Christian Church from the beginning. It is true that the title "Lord" could be used in a very human sense—as in England today; but the researches of the past two generations into the language of the Hellenistic age, especially the vast work of Count W. W. von Baudissin,[13] has established the fundamentally religious or sacral signifi-cance of the title in the period we are considering. Even before the Church became mainly Greek, while it was still in the midst of the Palestinian Aramaic-speaking milieu, the use of *Mar*, *Mari*, *Maran*, *Marana* was clearly liturgical. It survives in the oldest liturgical "tag" in the New Testament, "Our Lord, come!" (I Cor. XVI. 22). And obviously it opened the way to a Christological interpretation of certain Old Testament pas-sages, for example Psalm CX: "The Lord says to my Lord" (*Mara . . . Mari* in the Syriac version to this day). How early the identification, and the problem, arose is clear from Mk. XII. 35-7. "David himself calls him Lord; so how is he his son?" According to von Baudissin, and the view is supported by a

[13] *Kyrios als Gottesname im Judentum und seine Stelle in der Religionsgeschichte*, 4 vols., Giessen 1926 ff. (ed. Otto Eissfeldt).

wide range of Hellenistic literature, inscriptions, and papyri, the term *Kyrios* (Lord) had come to mean *the invisible divine head of a cult*; and this is precisely what we find in the New Testament. It is not the sad recollection of a departed teacher and friend, not the glowing admiration for an heroic martyr, not the dutiful offices of a group of disciples in memory of a revered teacher, now departed—these purely modern theories will not hold good in the first century. What we see is the emergence of a cult, devoted to a present *Kyrios*, not a departed one; a divine or quasi-divine person, not a human teacher; a victorious Lord, risen from among the dead and about to come in glory to hold the Last Judgment: Christianity began with Christ's *Resurrection*, not his death, and not the Sermon on the Mount. It is the Risen and Glorified Lord of the Christian cult who is described as "Lord."

But the working-out of the implications of the term, especially with the Greek Old Testament open before them, led the early Christian leaders, teachers, and apostles to take new steps in interpretation. One of the most important Christological passages in the New Testament is Paul's description of Christ in Phil. II. 5–11. The doctrinal statement comes in almost incidentally: "Have this mind among yourselves, which you have in Christ Jesus"—that is, follow your great exemplar, who though "in the form of God," living a divine existence, a heavenly being, refused to share in the Titanic revolt of Satan, who undertook to seize the throne of God: for he did not think "equality with God" something to be seized (a ἁρπαγμόν, which does not mean something cherished, grasped, or clutched, but grabbed—the famous old Kenotic theory was wrong).[14] Instead, he utterly denied and abased himself, stripping off all his divine prerogatives, and even "took the form of a slave," born "in the likeness of men . . . in human form." And so he eventually became "obedient to death," i.e. to the extent of dying, even—unthinkable for a divine being!—death on a cross, the most shameful, the most painful, the most unbearable kind of death. But because of this total renunciation God has "highly

---

[14] See the article, "The Christmas Message," in *Anglican Theological Review*, xxx (1948), pp. 227–30; also ch. v, "Preaching in Holy Week" in the volume, *Preaching the Christian Year*, ed. Howard A. Johnson, New York 1957. In both articles the view stated above is expounded and defended.

exalted him," and given him "the name that is above every name," i.e. the title *Lord*, at the mention of which every knee must bow, "in heaven and earth and under the earth"—in Hellenistic thought this clearly means angels, daemons, men, and spirits of the dead—all must worship him.

This is the pattern of thought which underlies all of St Paul's Christology, and much of the rest of the New Testament. The Apostle did not live in the fourth century, and although it may be argued that had he lived then his theology would have been Nicene and orthodox, we must recognise that behind Nicaea lies a long course of doctrinal development, and that St Paul belongs to one of the earliest stages, great as was his contribution toward further development. In 1 Cor. xv. 23–8 he describes the process of further advance in the re-establishment of God's Kingdom (his sovereignty or reign) over this part of the universe, which has revolted and needs to be forcibly reunited to the eternal reign of God in the heavens (described in Psalm cxlv and assumed in the Old Testament). The reconquest is headed by the King's Son, now the Risen Christ. His rising from the dead (sometimes he is "raised from the dead" by God, sometimes he "rises") means the beginning of the conquest, for it is Christ's victory over Death. Stage after stage in the campaign leads to further conquests; every "rule, authority, and power" opposed to God (i.e. the revolting forces of evil) must be put down and annihilated, and Christ must continue to reign until he has "put all enemies under his feet"; the last enemy to be destroyed will be Death, already overcome and in flight—for Death is the power which chiefly opposes God, and its strength is sin which leads to actual death of those who yield to it. At last Christ will return victoriously from the war; he will gather his followers about him (vs. 23) and then hand over the reconquered, unified, and restored divine Kingdom to God the Father (vs. 24). This dramatic tale of Christ's victory and kingship and submission to the Father is also the pattern assumed in the Apocalypse of John, though there it is even more military and political and far less metaphysical in its implications. Evidently it was the pattern known to most early Christians, for whom the Christian calling meant enlistment in a "warfare from which there is no discharge." John Bunyan understood this tale perfectly and wrote it out in vivid detail in his *Holy War* (1682). It is too militant for modern taste; but in the martyr Church of the first three centuries it meant something. That the idea may go back to Jesus himself is clear from his own view of his ministry as set forth in Mk. III. 22–7; Mt. XII. 28; Lk. XI. 20. Christ's conquest of the daemonic world is the beginning of the End; whether or not there will be an earthly Armageddon with all the terror and tumult of battle is not said (except in the Apocalypse), but the result, the final conquest of evil, is already in process, and Christ is Victor and King even now, the Son of God who is steadily bringing all things to bow and obey their Creator.

The early Church made no attempt to explain the process or rationale of the doctrine of the Atonement.[15] Enough that it proclaimed the fact: as Paul wrote to the Christians in Rome, six or seven years before his martyrdom there, "Since we are justified by faith, we have peace with God through our Lord Jesus Christ" (Rom. V. 1). This was not the consequence of some legal process in the heavenly court, or in the mind of God: it was the overwhelming fact of current Christian experience; and it was no achievement of human effort but the gracious act of God. Whether or not the legal process of "justification" could be explained—men now being treated by God as if they were righteous when patently they were not, except by intention and fresh resolution—it was really only a metaphor, one of several which, as we have seen, Paul chose for the purpose of conveying the meaning of the profound, transforming experience of "newness of life" in Christ Jesus (Rom. VI. 4). These metaphors used by Paul were not meant to be taken serially, or simultaneously, nor co-ordinately, but alternatively, each one an effort to outdo the others in making precise and vivid the implications and the consequences of the transforming experience. New Testament theology is not, and was never designed to be, a "systematic" theology. It is purely the theology of the heart, the experiencing subject, the "man in Christ" (II Cor. XII. 2) who has been brought over from the kingdom of darkness into the kingdom of light (Col. I. 13—this was one of

---

[15] See article "Atonement" in the new edition of *Encyclopedia Americana*; also Hastings Rashdall, *The Idea of Atonement in Christian Theology* (Bampton Lectures for 1915), an older work which still repays careful study.

Paul's metaphors), has now been "reconciled to God" (or "with God"; II Cor. v. 18, 20), released from slavery (Gal. v. 1), bought or redeemed and set free (Col. 1. 14), adopted (Gal. IV. 5), cleansed from the pollution of sin (1 Cor. v. 7), acquitted at the bar of divine justice (Rom. VIII. 1), released from bondage, the slavery to the dark astral powers who rule this present world (Gal. IV. 3–5), given a new citizenship in heaven or the world to come (Phil. III. 20), reborn (Gal. IV. 28—possibly a term borrowed from the pagan mysteries; but where did the mysteries get it?), made a "new creature" or a "new creation" (II Cor. v. 17), made a partaker of the sacrifice of the death of Christ (Rom. VI. 3), a sharer in his sufferings, his death, his resurrection and glorification (Rom. VI. 5).

The "mystery" at the heart of this great experience was the "atonement" with God through Christ (the original form of this English word was the phrase, "at onement"). It was no "propitiation" of an angry God, for the whole action sprang from the divine initiative; nor was it even an "expiation," in the pagan sense, i.e. something required by the experts who could read signs and omens and find the way to restore normal relations with the invisible world or set men "right with God" once more. It was, in fact, not a concept but an inner realisation of what had already transpired, and it was closely bound up with the death of Christ. Most naturally, it was interpreted and stated in the language of sacrifice, the age-old Semitic and Mediterranean device for establishing right relations with God or the gods. But it was still far removed from the medieval Scholastic or Reformation or Post-Reformation theology which probed the "deep things of God" and came up with various mechanical or legal explanations—which as a rule did no credit to God or the New Testament revelation upon which they were presumably based.

It is sometimes a matter for surprise to readers of the New Testament to discover how very simple the primitive Christian doctrines were. We modern Christians are used to vast and complicated theological systems which attempt to combine and correlate all the data of the Bible and assign adequate reasons for every combination. The same kind of ingenuity was applied to the Old Testament by the rabbis, though their interests were practical, not metaphysical or dogmatic, and to the Koran by Islamic theologians, who were more theoretical. A good example of the New Testament outlook is the great ascription at the end of Romans (xvi. 25–7; some manuscripts locate it earlier), which may have been a later addition to the Pauline epistles, a kind of tailpiece such as the old artists added to Oriental books:

Now to him who is able to strengthen you according to my gospel and the preaching of Jesus Christ, according to the revelation of the mystery which was kept secret for long ages but is now disclosed and through the prophetic writings is made known to all nations, according to the command of the eternal God, to bring about obedience to the faith—to the only wise God be glory for evermore through Jesus Christ. Amen.

This ascription is representative of the whole of New Testament theology, which is basically biblical, not rational or philosophical, not systematic or even dogmatic, and certainly not Scholastic. The primitive Christian theology was originally and essentially a key to the prophecies of the Old Testament scriptures and to the Old Testament as a whole, viewed as a book of mystery and revelation; the clue to its real meaning was found in the experience of men who had been brought face to face with Christ, and discovered in him the meaning of life.

The other fundamental doctrines were likewise formulated in language and in concepts familiar to the Greek-speaking world of the eastern Mediterranean, rather than the Jewish or Semitic or even the Syrian and Iranian world. The first fifty years were probably the most crucial. Indeed, within less than twenty-five years the title "Christ" had become a proper name, no longer a mere translation of "the Anointed" or "the Messiah." In its place the new title of Jesus was the out and out divine one, Κύριος, "Lord."

But, as we have now seen, the earliest stages in this transformation were not marked by theological speculation; instead, the source closest at hand for every formulation of religious ideas or definition of theological terms, even the simplest, was the Old Testament, specifically the *Greek* Old Testament, the Bible of the early Church.

The early Church did not set out to be a school of theology. Instead, its primary aim was to interpret its ideas, its teaching, its beliefs in language which pagans could grasp and understand. The earliest Church had no acquaintance with Greek philosophy or its technical terminology; the only Greek literature the Church knew at first was the Greek Bible. The effort to find and employ proper technical terms for theological concepts, and to achieve consistency in doing so, came considerably later, beginning with the Gnostics and the apologists of the second century.

This earliest step toward explanation of the Christian faith in a new language was one of far-reaching importance—like a child's first efforts to walk or speak. Looking backward it appears to have been easy, like looking down a mountain-side after the peak has been won; looking down, the ledges melt into one another; in reality, every upward gain has been a dangerous and demanding one, achieved only by daring and persistence. In the development of early Christian doctrine this daring and persistence belonged to St Paul and men of his calibre and determination.

Thus from its first beginnings Christian theology was *biblical theology*. The Church's philosophical, metaphysical, systematic theology, like its dogmatic theology, came later— much later than the New Testament period, though its earliest efforts can be traced in the New Testament. Later theologians sometimes tended to forget the purpose of these earliest dogmatic definitions, which was to preserve and safeguard the biblical language enshrined in the liturgy, in Christian devotion, preaching, and teaching. As a consequence of this oversight, further definitions and explanations were proposed, chiefly of a theoretical nature; these definitions presupposed that Christian theology was in fact a consistent philosophical system, indeed an inspired one, and that logical inferences could safely be spun from single words or phrases, without regard to the "wholeness" or totality of the Christian faith: such words as "likeness," in Paul's phrase, "the likeness of sinful flesh" (Rom. VIII. 3); or "emptied himself," in the famous "kenotic" passage (Phil. II. 7); or "neither the Son" (in Mk. XIII. 32); or "no one knows the Son"—or "the Father" (in Mt. XI. 27). The old Gnostics were not the only ones who spun whole systems out of single phrases, or drew precarious further inferences from what were at first only private theories or inferences drawn from language only partly understood.[16]

This is the principle upon which we must insist if we are to understand and interpret correctly the religious literature of early Christianity. It was the literature of a Jewish messianic movement which became in time—in a very short time—a church, the "growing" Catholic Church of the first and second centuries. The Church's faith, worship, practice, rites, organisation, ministry, sacred books, methods of interpretation—all these were Jewish; but they were all in process of modification, adaptation, enlargement, re-emphasis from the day the earliest evangelists ceased speaking "to Jews only" and addressed themselves to "the Gentiles." The story of this transformation is the fascinating tale of the development of early Christian doctrine. It is sometimes told as if theology operated in a vacuum, and theologians spoke only to one another, and some of them (like a famous family in a famous rhyme) "spoke only to God." But the story is incomprehensible apart from Church history as a whole—the factors that were really determinative in this development were factors which involved and affected the Church as a whole. The ethos, the *Zeitgeist* of the whole eastern Mediterranean world, from Italy to Syria inclusive, and from Pontus and Macedonia to Egypt and Ethiopia, was one which profoundly affected every activity, every development, every effort and aspiration of the nascent and steadily growing Christian Church—its "theology" and its biblical interpretation as much as its prayers, its moral teaching, its missionary preaching and its martyrdoms. It was the world, and the age, of later Hellenism, the Hellenistic culture of the Near East under the early Roman Empire.

The beginning of this Hellenisation of the gospel can be traced in the New Testament. Such classic terms and phrases as "the only wise God" (Rom. xvi. 27), "who alone has immortality" (I Tim. vi. 16), "when the goodness [χρηστότης] and loving kindness [φιλανθρωπία] of God our Saviour appeared" (Tit. iii. 4; literally "our Saviour God"), "the appearing

---

[16] On the purpose of creeds I may refer to my *Basic Christian Beliefs*, New York and Edinburgh 1961, pp. 101 f., where the view stated above is more fully elaborated.

[epiphany] of the glory of our great God and Saviour Jesus Christ" (Tit. II. 13), or "the washing of regeneration" (Tit. III. 5), are all Hellenistic in tone and implication. So are the majestic conceptions of "the *Logos*," "the Son of God," "the Mediator," "the Saviour" whose "Body" is "the Church." But, more than all this, the whole movement of thought and use of language is in the direction of institutional religion, organisation, Canon Law, a fixed liturgy, officially defined doctrines (i.e. dogmas), and an equally specific ritual set forth by superior authority—all this natural, inevitable, historical process, beginning in the New Testament period, continued without ceasing for the next four hundred years, indeed for the next fifteen hundred. Some writers have viewed this "institutionalising" of Christianity as the "second Fall." But how Christianity was to have survived and be propagated otherwise than through an institution, a ministry, an organised religious life and activity, they do not say. And since the society in which the Church found itself (save for the fringe groups in the Middle East) was dominated by Rome, both in the West and the East (Byzantium was always "New Rome"), it was inevitable, and in the providence of God most fortunate, that the social and religious patterns to which Christianity adapted itself were Roman, i.e. Graeco-Roman, Roman under the influence of Greek ideas and intellectual standards. The whole historical development of Christianity is therefore inexplicable apart from the background and the antecedents provided in Roman Hellenism. If the Church in barbarian days demanded chiefly loyalty and obedience, it was in the interest of self-preservation and the maintenance of civilised society—though the demand outlived the need. If the Church undertook to define its doctrines by imperial authority, it was to prevent the splitting up of the Christian society into two, five, or a dozen warring sects—though the scope of these definitions was as a rule far less extensive than many modern writers have assumed. If the Church required explicit observance of prescribed ritual, a feature in Roman religion as old as its earliest beginnings and surviving in the Gubbio tablets, the festival of the Terminalia, the rustic sacrifices of Cato, and even in the saecular observance by Augustus, it was because the average person could not be trusted to get anywhere with an *ad lib*. or *ad hoc* performance of the sacred rites. If the chief stress in the interpretation and formulation of the gospel during the few generations between the earliest apostles and the councils of Nicaea, Constantinople, Ephesus, and Chalcedon lay in the area of Christology, it was because Christology was the main differential between Christianity and Judaism on the one hand and Christianity and paganism on the other. It followed the immense shift in Graeco-Roman religion from public cultus to personal religion, with its deep private convictions, prayer and devotion, and above all trust in a divine person—all of which was part of the "preparation for the gospel" made in the Hellenistic world. But the tendency could be carried too far, and Gibbon's famous gibe, the sundering of Christendom over a diphthong, still remains unanswered, and unanswerable. Men argued then—and still continue to argue—over the "person" of Christ, and the relations between his two "natures," the divine and the human, as if we could know everything about Christ but very little about God, whom he was sent to reveal in a life of perfect obedience and in words which were light and life. We can understand how, and more or less why, the development of early Christian doctrine took the course it did; but we can scarcely help regretting that the Church's interests and energies were channelled off in the direction of fruitless controversy and sectarianism. As a consequence of this Hellenistic-Roman influence, much of the vast potency of the gospel became neutralised, insulated, and has never been set free to this day. When, under the influence of the surrounding decline in scholarship and philosophy, and the substitution of rhetoric for clear and careful thinking, the Church let itself be satisfied with an ethic falling far short of the one set forth in the Gospels, and with a view of the world that merely took over and sanctioned or even consecrated the fading scientific outlook of the second and third centuries; when the Church adopted the world-renouncing ἄσκησις of dying paganism in lieu of its own transforming, life-giving inspiration; when it lowered the Christian conception of marriage to match more nearly the best that paganism could offer; when, in the midst of the terror and chaos of the barbarian invasions, the Church's prayers came to be mainly cries for help, for relief, for release from sin (which all agreed, pagan and Christian alike, had brought on the terrible conditions), for translation to another world—all this is understandable enough, but it has fettered and hamstrung the Christian religion for fifteen centuries, and leaves us in a situation where Christianity does not begin to meet the threatening challenge of our own dangerous present, from which there is no escape save by the solution of our problems, not their abandonment.

Thus the Church's Hellenistic-Roman heritage has been both a blessing and a bane; indispensable, in keeping Christianity alive through dark centuries when all human civilisation and culture, in the West, all religion and honour, all thought and learning seemed in process of extinction; a vast burden and liability when, after the rise of the new states and the emerging world culture of recent times, a religion which had transformed itself into systems of theology and codes of law now lacked the freedom and suppleness required to meet new issues and solve new problems. Our Reformation—and our Counter-Reformation—are only half begun.

The lengths to which purely dogmatic or speculative theology may be carried, without the slightest connexion with the New Testament, can be seen in the new dogmas of the Immaculate Conception and the Bodily Assumption of the Blessed Virgin and the more recent speculations regarding the mode of Christ's birth. It is now maintained by some writers that not only before but also during and after the birth of Jesus his Mother remained *virgo intacta*, without lesion or rupture of hymen.[17] Just as the Risen Christ was able to enter a room without passing through the door (Jn. xx. 19), so the Christ Child could enter this world without opening the womb of his Mother. Obviously, the former case is almost Docetic, Christ being a phantom who came and went (cf. Lk. xxiv. 31, 36), and the next step was to carry back this conception into his earthly life, before the Resurrection. (This *was* Docetism.) Obviously, in the case of his birth, the new conception is equally Docetic. Whatever the devout motive behind this speculation, it does no reverence to Christ or his Blessed Mother to make them both unreal and inhuman; instead, it

[17] See *The Mother of the Redeemer*, ed. Kevin McNamara, New York 1960. See also the *Living Church* (Milwaukee, Wisconsin,) 3 July 1960, pp. 10 ff., summarising a questionnaire sent to 500 clergymen of the Episcopal Church, and the editorial on p. 14.

robs the Incarnation of its meaning, if Christ was not born "as man." This theory is mythological, Gnostic, fundamentally unhistorical; and it really undermines the whole position which the early Church with its Apostolic writings, the New Testament, its Apostolic succession of authoritative teachers, its Apostolic creed repudiating the false doctrines of Gnosis, maintained heroically and successfully through the long centuries during which the theology of pagan syncretism continued to threaten its existence.

Too often, the early Church has been held responsible for the decline of interest in philosophy and science; but this was a characteristic of the "religious culture in decline," as T. S. Eliot describes it,[18] by which the Church was surrounded. Paul's view of the natural creation as "subjected to futility" and "in bondage to decay," "groaning in travail together until now" (Rom. viii. 20 f.), was hardly likely to encourage any scientific interest on the part of his readers, and it is a far cry from the "system of animate nature" described by modern biologists. It is closer to Tennyson's "Nature, red in tooth and claw," and both are somewhat Gnostic and reflect the antipathy of those to whom the details of biological research are repulsive. But it is the world-view of the first and second century, from which Gnosticism was an easy inference: either the powers of darkness had invaded and upset the harmonious cosmos of the good Creator, or the Creator himself was a lesser deity who bungled the job and let evil in—

As if some lesser god had made the world,
But had not force to shape it as he would.[19]

To this view Paul added his eschatological conviction that evil was temporary, and the "groaning" of all creation was the beginning of a "travail" of birth which would end when "the sons of God" were "revealed" (or manifested). The beginning of God's "new" creation was already visible to those who had eyes to see—it was as certain for Paul as it had been for Jesus—

[18] See his *Notes Towards the Definition of Culture*, New York 1948, p. 28. Cf. Nilsson, *Geschichte*, vol. ii, p. 682.
[19] Tennyson, *The Passing of Arthur, ad init.*

and the "subjection" of nature was the background of a divinely inspired "hope" (see the whole passage, Rom. VIII).

But in any case it is hardly fair to accuse the early Church of not fostering scientific studies—Christianity was not a civilisation but a religion. And the whole ethos of the times was becoming more and more averse to scientific research. Men preferred to argue *a priori* from the principles of reason that the earth was round—or flat—and that tides flowed up the beaches beyond the pillars of Hercules, and thus save the bother of investigation. Only Posidonius went all the way to Gibraltar to find out. As for experimental science there was almost none. If observational science was limited chiefly to astronomy; and if astronomy was the leading science; and if astronomy was limited to observation, without experiment, then it is no wonder that men generally lost interest in science, and that the Ptolemaic system became entrenched for thirteen centuries, from Claudius Ptolemaeus of Alexandria to Nicolaus Copernicus of Cracow.

Another charge against primitive Christianity is its failure to distinguish between theological terms and the living realities of religion. But, again, this was an inescapable characteristic of the times. The medieval struggle between Nominalism and Realism was already being prepared in the late classical period, and the wordy subtleties of theologians were the natural and inevitable product of the intellectual activities of the third to fifth centuries, and later.

But it was not only in the area of formulated doctrine and theology that the influence of Roman Hellenism was apparent and decisive: it was also dominant in ethics. Why did the Church do nothing about slavery? Or the emancipation of women? Again St Paul's advice to slaves, widows, the unmarried, and the unhappily married was all in one key: the time is short; "the form of this world is passing away," and "I want you to be free from anxieties." The end of the age is so near at hand that it is not worth the effort to change one's status. (See I Cor. VII, and note the eschatological *motif*.) The time came, under Constantine and his successors, when the Church might well have done more than it did to change social conditions; but, alas, the barbarian invasions were already wrecking Mediterranean society, and about all that could be done by intelligent, devout, earnest men and women was take refuge, for the duration, in whatever safe shelters they could find. Many found none, and perished.

In a totalitarian society, under the weakening military monarchy of Rome, whose first requirement was loyalty and obedience—and taxes—it was not strange that the Church, with its pronounced eschatological outlook, responded with an ethic of patience and humility. No one dreamed of an ethic of responsible citizenship, concerned not only with obedience to existing law but with the framing of just and humane laws— no one, that is, except the emperor and his advisers, and the students and teachers of law, who were hampered by the burden of accumulated edicts and traditions of interpretation. The average man felt no responsibility for the laws under which he lived, and the whole concept of the "consent of the governed" lay hundreds of years in the future.

It is this transitional character of the early Church, and of Roman Hellenism itself, which not only influenced the formulation of the gospel in the New Testament; it also influenced the interpretation and application of Christian teaching, both doctrinal and ethical, as it was handed down in the Graeco-Roman world of the first to fifth centuries. The pity is that the Church still adheres to its ethics as thus modified and centred in patience and humility, stressing these as if they were the cardinal virtues, instead of setting forth an ethic of responsibility, which is demanded by the age now upon us. Modern science, especially in the fields of psychology and psychiatry, has uncovered far more important and decisive aspects of human nature than the ancient world with its widespread demonology and its ideas of inherited pollution or guilt ever dreamed of. Nevertheless, underneath these ancient conceptions lay levels of human experience which we too, in turn, are required to understand and interpret and do something about, especially with the new tools of research, interpretation, and therapy now in our hands.

The traditional attitudes are still with us; they appear to be rooted in the New Testament and in the Church's earliest teaching; but they are found there only because they were the common assumptions of the first and second centuries, and are not of the essence of the gospel—which contains new and revolutionary principles for dealing with human problems, never envisaged in paganism. Take sex and marriage, for example, or race relations, or the phenomenon of religious antagonism. The Church did not create "anti-semitism," but it tolerated it, encouraged it, inflamed it from time to time, instead of stamping it out in the second century. But this is asking too much: the Jews were hated by Gentiles long before Christianity came on the scene, for the Jews refused to be absorbed into the pagan *mélange* of syncretism with its "many 'gods' and many 'lords'" (1 Cor. viii. 5), and to give up its unique institutions and its inspired Scriptures. After the two revolts of A.D. 66 and 132 in Palestine and the intervening eastern Mediterranean revolt of 117, the antipathy only increased among both Christian and non-Christian Gentiles; and although the Church claimed descent from Abraham (see Gal. iii. 29), it was only a metaphor, and actual Jews and Judaism were despised as "rejected by God" and therefore properly scorned by men. So began a tragedy which has run its gruesome course through the long centuries since. The climax under Hitler was the consequence of a dominant Church refusing to measure up to its responsibility. The roots of medieval and modern anti-semitism are no longer those of the first century but are theological, the consequence of dogmatic presuppositions (e.g. God's "rejection" of the Jews) which have never been thought through, or brought to the test of the spirit of Christ which is the essence of the gospel.

It is no use telling the oppressed, the disfranchised, the hungry, the persecuted, to be patient and humble. Worse than that, it is immoral and inhuman to do so. And it is without excuse, exegetically; for it is an attempt to universalise what was in origin only the soundest, sanest course open to a people who could not possibly better their state by appeal to the sword, and would only inevitably worsen it by revolution; and who, more than all that, expected—at least multitudes of them expected—the end of the present world any day.

Even the ancient Jewish ethics was an ethics of submission, acceptance, even submission to the "evil power" which ruled the contemporary world. Men were to have nothing—or as little as possible (see *Pirqe Aboth* 1. 10)—to do with rulers; for those who had tried it had either turned into collaborationists, apostates, and betrayers of their brethren or had been destroyed by the power they served. The hated tax-collectors of the New Testament period were hated because they collected tribute to be paid to Rome, whose occupying armies defiled the holy land with their idolatries. If patience and humility are writ large over the New Testament ethics, they are also characteristic of the ethics of the Pharisees. Both ethics were formulated in a totalitarian age, when no other ethics was practicable. An ethics based upon freedom and responsibility would have led directly to revolution—and extinction.

Thus, as Francis Burkitt of Cambridge said long ago, "The gospel ethics need criticism far more than the gospel miracles." The miracles fit hand in glove the religious outlook of the contemporary ancient world, both Jewish and pagan; the ethics are different, and for a specific reason. And there can be little doubt that the failure of religion to curb the militarism, greed, racial malice and political animosity of mankind during the past twenty-five centuries is owing chiefly to its adaptation to the world in which it lived: Caesarism, totalitarianism, the identification of the Byzantine and Catholic Churches with the state in East and West, the Protestant attempt to direct or control the state without identifying church and state, but giving the state a free hand in its supposedly separate sphere of action (conceived as independent of moral supervision), the sectarian principle of independence which only weakened or disintegrated the religious forces politically, the purely individualistic and nonsocial emphasis in much of the modern interpretation of the gospel (especially since the dismissal in disgrace of the "social gospellers")—all these help to account for the Church's failure, past and present. But the beginnings of these efforts go back to the New Testament period, when the religious ethics of Jesus,[20] at least as it was handed down in early Christian tradition, began to be warped into conformity with the demands of a worldwide, totalitarian, militaristic, thoroughly materialistic society. There lay the "fall"—not in the natural and normal growth of an institution or even the creation of dogmas, but in the accommodation of the ethics of the gospel to the standards of the heathen world. And from this corruption the Church has never wholly recovered. But nothing is more drastically needed today than

[20] Once more, not an ethical system but an ethic based wholly on religion.

its recovery, and the proclamation of an ethic based frankly on the Christian revelation of the final Reality, the whole truth about God and man.

It is sometimes said that the Church failed to establish peace with justice in the ancient world; but this is not only asking too much of a submerged sect, slowly gaining influence and position in a hostile environment, and coming to power only after it was too late to do much with a decadent society surrounded by greedy barbarians; it cannot be described as a failure because it was not even attempted. As G. K. Chesterton said, "Christianity has not failed—it has never been tried." And this is the tragedy, that a gospel meant for the healing of the nations accepted a lesser role and became only one more of "the world's great religions," leaving Hatred, War, Greed, Hunger, and Misery still the permanent rulers of mankind; and instead of one united body of believers it became a fissiparous crowd of competing sects, which preferred to do nothing rather than co-operate for the good of the human race or even for their own advantage. That is the tragedy, over which God himself must weep. "He came unto his own, and his own received him not." He came not only to the Jews, but to the whole human race, which was his creation. And his own refused to listen.

# Appendix

# A Note on *Religio Licita*

The question arises repeatedly, in almost every study of early Christianity, Why were the Christians persecuted? Another, closely related, question is this: Why did the earliest Christians claim to be Jews?—i.e. why did they insist that the Church was a "sect" or "way" within Judaism? Of course the very first Christians (or "Nazarenes") *were* Jews; but it was not long before born Gentiles were claiming descent from Abraham. In fact, Paul insisted that descent from Abraham was shared by those who were "in Christ" and "lived by faith," regardless of physical descent (Rom. IV. 11 f.; Gal. III. 7). And why was this tie broken and repudiated, first by Jews and then by Christians? And why did the Roman authorities at first accept the plea and later reject it? On what other grounds could the Church have claimed toleration in the first century? Or was there no other possible basis of recognition than identification with the mother-religion of Judaism? And was the claim made in the language of Roman law, viz. the right to recognition and toleration as a *religio licita*? Was this term used in the first century? Did it apply to Judaism? And was it the purpose of the author of Luke-Acts to show that Christians also were entitled to plead the privilege?

For fifty years and more, since the time of Theodor Mommsen, there has been a repeatedly adjourned debate over the question whether or not it was possible, under the early Roman Empire, to plead that Christianity was a *religio licita*, like Judaism. Writers on the Acts of the Apostles have been concerned with this question, as it is often claimed that the purpose of the author of Acts was to show that Christianity deserved to be viewed as such a religion. It is the modest purpose of this brief appendix to add a footnote to the discussion, from the point of view of the history of Roman religion, and to argue that the term was not used, and very likely could not have been used, before *c.* A.D. 250, or at least some time in the early third century.[1] In order to understand the situation we must consider the essential nature of Roman religion and its relation to the state.

As expounded by modern experts, the earliest stages of Roman religion assumed that the Roman lived "in the midst of a population of spiritual beings (*numina*) whose attitude toward him was a doubtful one, . . . continually influenced by what he did or said."[2] Consequently the Roman did everything in his power to live on good terms with them: the prescribed methods of maintaining the *pax deorum* were known to and were administered by the authorities of the state, "who by experience and tradition had learned how to deal with them." The religious function was therefore not only one of the functions of the state, but the most essential of all its functions, and, as in the Old Testament and in other early codes, there was no distinction

[1] For works prior to 1939 see *Cambridge Ancient History*, VOL. XII, p. 775 (h). For works published since then, see A. N. Sherwin-White, "The early persecutions and Roman Law again," in *Journal of Theol. Studies*, III (1952), pp. 199–213 (and see titles in footnotes). Sherwin-White surveys the course of the debate and favours the theory of Mommsen, viz. the *coercitio*, i.e. police action, rather than the "general law" assumption of many other writers, especially before Mommsen. See also Hans Lietzmann, *The Founding of the Church Universal* (=VOL. II of his *History of the Early Church*), English translation 1950, p. 155; Henri Leclercq, "Droit persécuteur," in *Dictionnaire d'archéologie chrétienne et de liturgie*, ed. H. Leclercq and H. Marrou, VOL. IV, PART II, cols. 1565–1648; Hugh Last, "The study of the persecutions," in *Journal of Roman Studies*, XXVII (1937), pp. 80 ff. The charge in Acts XVI. 21, "They advocate customs which it is not lawful for us Romans to accept or practice," is echoed by Tertullian, *Apology*, §§ 24, 27: *crimen laesae . . . romanae religionis*.

On the view that the Book of Acts as a whole is an apology for the new Christian religion, see *The Beginnings of Christianity*, edd. K. Lake and F. J. Foakes Jackson, VOL. II (1922), p. 179: Theophilus was "not a catechumen, thirsting for religious instruction, but . . . a Roman official concerned with the public safety and legal procedure. He had heard stories damaging to Christians, perhaps especially to Pauline Christians, and the purpose of the writer was to disabuse him of these slanders by putting before him the exact facts." The questions which would first occur to him would be two: "Were the Christians practising a lawful religion? Were they doing anything by word or deed which called for administrative action?" The only way the former question could be considered was by showing that Christianity was "lawful," i.e. the cultus of a recognised "race"; no new religion could be licensed—since the Empire, unlike some modern states (e.g. Israel) had no "Ministry of Cultus" which could deal with various "religions." Hence the apologists argued either (*a*) that Christianity was the true religion of Israel (a view shared by Luke, as is evident from both the Gospel and Acts), or (*b*) that the Christians were a *new* "race" or *natio* and were therefore entitled to practise and profess their own religion, new as it was to the various peoples within the Empire (*op. cit.*, p. 180).

[2] W. W. Fowler, in Hastings, *Encyclopaedia of Religion and Ethics*, VOL. X, p. 829.

between sacred and civil law: the *jus sacrum* belonged to the *jus civile*, as it still did in Cicero's *De legibus* (BKS. II–III). Hence the omnicompetence of the state left no room for the development of religion as a separate or separable institution. The modern conception of the "separation of church and state" would have seemed absurd to an early Roman, had it been conceivable. The element of fear and of concern for security against enemies, human and superhuman, immensely reinforced the control which the state exercised over both the religious and the civil affairs of its citizens. The social factor was also present: for the custodians of Roman tradition, in both its political and its religious aspects, were traditionally members of the nobility, i.e. they were patricians. The consequent conservatism of Roman religion was something which belonged to its very essence, irrevocable, irreformable—the most formidable political and religious system in the ancient world. By the beginning of the Republic, no plebeian or foreigner could have any part or share in the Roman cultus, either as priest or worshipper. The later admission of plebeians and the introduction of new deities and rites only modified this state-bound system, and by no means introduced a new religious attitude or marked any tendency toward the separation of "church and state," not even to the extent of suggesting the view that Roman religion was one among many possible religions, the one chosen and preferred by Rome above all others—as the Hebrews had chosen Yahweh, or rather had been chosen by him. For the Roman, the very existence of the state was bound up in its relations with the gods. Suppress the official, recognised, indispensable cultus, and the state would cease to exist.[3]

Such changes as were made in the cultus were achieved without any modification of the underlying principle. Foreign gods

---

[3] See Jean Bayet, *Histoire politique et psychologique de la religion romaine*, Paris 1957, pp. 59f. The word *religio* "condensed the necessities of the situation." It represented, to the ancients, the totality of the recognised obligations which bound men to the gods. From this arose the notion of reciprocal legal obligations (*fides*), exactness of rite to be paid the gods, vows, etc. Therefore what was *religiosus* was untouchable. Basically, Roman religion was a sense of inquietude (i.e. anxiety, *Angst*; Professor Bayet is writing of the psychology of Roman religion) *vis à vis* the gods—something which prepared for the great revolution in the first century, the vindication of the individual conscience versus the organisation of the state. Compare W. W. Fowler, *Religious Experience of the Roman People*, London 1911, esp. chs. I and XI.

were absorbed, as a rule, by identification with old Roman deities. Rome grew and expanded; but one could affirm that Rome *had never changed*, or had "changed only to remain the same" (as some modern apologists have affirmed of the Christian Church). The chief developments of Roman religion were in the direction of the complete regimentation of the Roman citizen, in thought, word, and deed. The devastating effects of the influence of Greek religious and philosophical thought, followed by the invasion of the lower levels of society by various Oriental cults, did little to weaken the attachment of the tradition-loving Roman to the state cultus: the Augustan "restoration" of the old religion swept in like a spring tide, once it got under way. "A revival of religious *life* it certainly was not, for what we understand by that term had never existed at Rome."[4] Instead, it was the restoration of the antique, traditional cultus upon which the continuance, or rather the very existence, of the state depended. The reaction of the newly established empire against the anarchy and excess of the last period of the Republic goes far to explain the intransigence of the Romans in dealing with the new Christian religion, which seemed not only to be "a setter-forth of strange gods" but the proponent of an inconceivable theory, viz. that Rome might exist with another cultus than that which (in theory) had existed from the beginning of the city. The view seemed as preposterous as the threat of the apocalyptists that *Roma aeterna* would soon come to an end. The very terms in which the proposal might have been discussed were lacking. *Religio* was not "a religion," but *religiousness*, devotion, zeal, scrupulousness, fidelity, piety, the exact observance of the explicit requirements of the state *vis à vis* the gods.[5] One might not really believe in *religio*, and might

---

[4] W. W. Fowler, in Hastings, *Encyclopaedia of Religion and Ethics*, VOL. X, p. 840.

[5] As Walter Otto said, in his essay on "*Religio* und *Superstitio*," in *Archiv für Religionswissenschaft*, XII (1909), pp. 533–54, "Neither in its origin nor its later history was *religio* limited to the sphere of what we call religion." "*Religio* was no matter of feeling, or of knowledge, or of faith.—Die *religio* ist, wie gesagt, kein Gefühl; weder dies, noch ein Wissen, ein Glaube." By contrast, Georg Wissowa's definition was too narrow, too modern, too evangelical and Schleiermacherian: "Grundlage und Voraussetzung [ist] . . . ein Gefühl der Abhängigkeit von den göttlichen Macht und Fürsorge (*religio*)." See his *Religion und Kultus der Römer*, 2nd edn. Munich 1912, p. 380.

In his new *Römische Religionsgeschichte*, Munich 1960, p. 39, Professor Kurt Latte sets forth a strictly historical definition of *religio*. "Religiosität bedeutet eben für

even view it as blind and foolish superstition; but this was no excuse for the failure to share in the public cultus—Varro's whole sceptical explanation of *religio* presupposes this. And what Lucretius condemned was not "religion" but fanaticism: *tantum religio* [i.e. religious zeal] *potuit suadere malorum*. It was religious*ness* that spelled the trouble: *Aber*glaube, "too much believing." The notion of a possible variety of "religions" simply did not dawn on people prior to, let us say, the middle of the third century. Partly the idea was the creation of Christian writers, especially the apologists; partly it was the result of the "conflict of religions" which resulted from the invasion of the West by the mystery cults.[6]

It is often assumed, in modern works on early Christianity and on the contemporary pagan world, that the old state cultus had fallen into abeyance and neglect, and that the new mystery religions had taken its place. But neither the surviving literary records nor archaeology support this view. Domitian's devotion to Jupiter is well known. Antoninus Pius's care for public worship was one of the notable features of his reign, and so was that of Marcus Aurelius, in spite of his personal devotion to philosophy. The inscriptions tell the tale. The overwhelming majority of dedications were made to the great gods of the

den Römer nicht eine Gesinnung, die die ganze Persönlichkeit prägt, sondern die ständige Bereitschaft, auf jedes Anzeichen einer Störung des gewohnten Verhält-nisses zu den Göttern mit einer begütigenden Handlung zu antworten und einmal übernommenen Verpflichtungen nachzukommen." Latte's whole book is strictly based upon the surviving data for ancient Roman religion; he is even more sceptical than Wissowa (in the good sense of historical *skepsis*) and does not piece out the evidence with probabilities in areas where our information is scanty. For this reason his work marks a new stage in modern research and promises to open a quite new approach to the subject—much as we still owe to his pre-decessors.

[6] One of the most important surveys of the history of the term is Warde Fowler's paper, "The Latin history of the word *religio*," in *Transactions* of the Congress for the History of Religions, 1908, reprinted in his *Roman Essays and Interpretations*, Oxford 1920, pp. 7–15. After noting the wide diversity in usage during the pre-Christian centuries, he advanced the view that Cicero gave the word a new turn: *religio* was specifically the *cultus deorum* and all that concerned it (see *De inventione*, II. 161, and *De legibus*, x. 25). The final change came, Fowler believed, in the second century, as a result of the rivalry of the various cults. The term now meant, on the whole and as a rule, not religion in general, nor the state cultus exclusively, but the cults of the separate religious movements, each of which was a *religio*. Thus Apuleius, *Metamorphoses*, XI. 14, speaking of Isis: *tunc e cohorte religionis unus*. This was only a step from the Octavius of Minucius Felix, or the apologies of Lactantius, Arnobius, and Tertullian: *nostra religio, vera religio*, and so on.

Roman state.[7] The Christian apologists' main attack was centred upon the traditional Roman cultus, not the new mystery rites; and the same was true of Augustine's heavy bombardment in his *City of God*. But it is doubtful if even the apologists would have been very much interested in the status of a tolerated cult, had such a conception existed before the third century.[8] What they were looking for, and arguing for, was a total substitution of Christian truth and the Christian way of life for the debased and outworn primitive rites and superstitions of the pagan world. As Origen stated it, at the close of his *Contra Celsum*, "If . . . everyone were to do the same as I, obviously the barbarians would also be converted to the word of God and would be most law-abiding and mild. And all other worship would be done away and only that of the Christians would prevail. One day it will be the only one to prevail, since the word is continually gaining possession of more souls."[9]

It is not difficult to imagine the view pagans would take of this announcement. It was their flat assertion of *No compromise* which made it clear to the Graeco-Roman world that the Christians were neither a sect nor a *natio*, but a new *religio*.[10]

[7] See those given in *Corpus inscriptionum latinarum*, ed. T. Mommsen, VOL. VI, Berlin 1876, and the examples in H. Dessau, *Inscriptiones latinae selectae*, Berlin 1892–1916, Chs. 11, 17, and Index.

[8] When Tertullian refers to *religio licita* he means Judaism, which is *certe licita*, and compared with which Christianity is a school or sect (not even a *collegium*). Thus *Apol.* 21.1: "It was under cover of the appeal to this ancient religion that the Christians hoped—according to the pagans—for recognition and toleration— *sub umbraculo insignissimae religionis, certe licitae*." But even this means only "lawful," or "tolerated," not authorised or recognised or licensed, as if the Roman government operated a licensing bureau for religious organisations! In legal terminology, up to this time at least, there appears to have been a recognised usage of *collegia licita*, but not *religio licita*, which, as I am arguing, was, from the Roman point of view, an impossible idea. Minucius Felix has the term *illicita* (*Oct.* 8.3), and also *inreligiosa* (8.1). What the Christians were charged with or suspected of doing was attempting to undermine religion, not *a* religion, not the Roman religion as one among many, but religion in general and in its totality, with which the Roman religion was identified, since it included the worship of *all* the gods (as he says in 6.1).

[9] *Contra Celsum*, VIII. 68, *ad fin.*; trans. H. Chadwick, Cambridge 1953, p. 505.

[10] The *Digest* refers to Judaism as a "*religio*" (e.g. XLVIII. 8. 11); but it is clearly the cultus of a distinct and recognised *natio*; it had only one temple, and that one far in the East, and long since destroyed; the synagogues were not temples or even shrines, but "houses of study" like the meeting-places of the philosophical schools. Therefore, traditionally, and despite the peculiarities of Jewish custom, Judaism did not look like a rival cult to that of the Roman state. Romans would have scoffed at the idea that the Empire might be converted to Judaism. Not so the threat of Christianity.

(continued on p. 178)

There can be little doubt of the apologetic aim of Luke-Acts. It is openly avowed in Lk. I. 1–4, and the contents of the two books bear it out. But the Lucan thesis is that Christianity is the New or the True Israel, and therefore entitled to share in the public toleration of Judaism,[11] rather than that it is an independent *religio licita*, which in the first century would have been an impossible anachronism.

The grounds upon which Jews had been granted their special privileges have often been described, e.g. by Emil Schürer in his *Geschichte des jüdischen Volkes*, esp. in VOL. III, §31 (4th edn. 1909), and by Jean Juster in *Les Juifs dans l'empire romain*, Paris 1914. One of the main sources is still Josephus, *Antiquities*, BK. XIV, with its wealth of inscriptions. These privileges dated from before the first century A.D., viz. from the time of Hyrcanus II, Antipater, and Herod.

The view of Maurice Goguel (see his *Naissance du Christianisme*, 1946, PT. V, esp. pp. 545 ff.), viz. that the persecution under Nero made it clear that Christians were *not* Jews and were therefore not entitled to appeal to membership in the Jewish *natio* as a ground for claiming liberty of worship, helps to explain the use of the term "for the name" or "in the name" in the early Gospel of Mark (e.g. IX. 41); but it does not help us when we come to Rev. III. 9, "the synagogue of Satan, who say that they are Jews and are not," or when we come to the apologists (e.g. Tertullian, *Apol.* §8, cited above). Perhaps the unmasking of the pretenders (as pagans would call it) or the separation of the Church from the synagogue (as Christians would view it) did not take place simultaneously in all parts of the Empire; nor did the gradual process (for it was surely that) take place at a uniform rate in all localities.

[11] This was the view of the late Burton Scott Easton, set forth in his lectures at the Virginia Theological Seminary on *The Purpose of Acts* (London 1936), reprinted in the volume of his collected papers entitled *Early Christianity* (Greenwich, Conn., and London 1955).

# CHRONOLOGY

| B.C. | |
|---|---|
| 347 | Death of Plato |
| 339 | Xenocrates heads the Academy |
| 335 | Aristotle settles in Athens |
| 323 | Death of Alexander the Great |
| 322 ff. | Eudemus of Rhodes and Theophrastus of Eresus |
| 322 | Death of Aristotle |
| 321 | First production of Menander |
| 316–307 | Demetrius of Phalerum in Athens. His legislation, incl. condemnation of funeral extravagance |
| 314 | Freedom of Greek cities proclaimed by Antigonus<br>Polemo becomes head of the Academy |
| 312 ff. | Seleucus restores the Didymeion |
| 312 | Official cult of Hercules in Rome. Birth of Theocritus |
| 310 | Zeno of Kitium founds the Stoa at Athens |
| 308 | Brilliant observance of the Dionysia at Athens by Demetrius of Phalerum |
| 307 | Proposal of Sophocles son of Amphicleides that philosophical schools be abolished in Athens<br>Exile of Theophrastus; recalled in 306<br>Antigonus and his son Demetrius Poliorcetes receive cultic honours in Athens |
| before 306 | Introduction of the cult of Sarapis as imperial cultus by Ptolemy I Soter in Alexandria |
| 306 | Epicurus founds his school at Athens |
| 304 | Cult of King Ptolemy I in Rhodes<br>Demetrius Poliorcetes honoured as σύνναος of Athena in Athens |
| 302 | Initiation of Demetrius Poliorcetes in the Eleusinian mysteries.<br>Cultic honours for Demetrius and his father Antigonus |
| 301 | Battle of Ipsus; death of Antigonus |
| c. 300 | Euhemerus of Messene, friend of Cassander. His "Sacred Book" promulgating "Euhemerism"<br>Euclid of Alexandria: *Elements* [of Geometry] |
| 294 | Demetrius Poliorcetes takes Athens and becomes King of Macedonia |

B.C. 293   Removal of the cult of Asclepius from Epidaurus to the
           island in the Tiber

292        Completion of the Helios Colossus at Rhodes

291        Hymn of Hermocles to Demetrius Poliorcetes

288        Dedicated gifts of Seleucus and Antiochus sent to Didyma

288–1      Lysimachus supports the cultus at Samothrace

287–212    Archimedes

286        Removal of the cult-image of Bryaxis (Sarapis) from
           Sinope to Alexandria

283        Death of Demetrius; his son Antigonus Gonatas takes his title

283–246    Ptolemy II, King of Egypt, patron of letters

280        Dedicated gift of Pyrrhus of Epirus at Dodona.
           Aristarchus of Samos: heliocentric astronomy

279        Procession (πομπή) of Ptolemy Philadelphus at
           Alexandria. Inauguration of the Ptolemaia

278–7      The Gauls threaten Delphi. Founding of the Soteria, at
           first annual, later quadrennial and made panhellenic

277–6      Plundering of the Didymeion by the Gauls

276–5      Aratus of Soli at court of Antigonus Gonatas

275        Pyrrhus returns from Italy

270        Death of Epicurus

           Cult of Arsinoe Philadelphus. Theocritus: *Adoniazusae*

262        Death of Zeno

262–232    Cleanthes head of the Stoic school: his *Hymn to Zeus*

262–190    Apollonius of Perga: *Conics*

c. 250     Cult of the Muses in Thespiae. Arcesilas head of the New
           Academy. Beginning of the Greek translation of the Old
           Testament (the Septuagint)

246        Eratosthenes head of Alexandrian Library

238        Egyptian astronomers invent leap year

232–206    Chrysippus head of the Stoic school

228–7      Destruction of the Colossus of Rhodes by an earthquake;
           large collections for its restoration

227        Divine honours for Ptolemy III Euergetes in Athens; the
           Phyle Ptolemais
           Decline of Egyptian naval power under Ptolemy
           Philopator, who claimed descent from Dionysus

225        Eratosthenes measures the circumference of the earth

221        Delian dedicatory gift of Antigonus Doson after the battle
           of Sellasia

after 220  Artemidorus of Perga recognised in Thera as a god, by
           the Pythia

B.C. after 220   Epiphany of Artemis Leucophryene in Magnesia on the Maeander

216   Carthaginian victory at Cannae

215   Venus Erycina and Mens honoured with a temple on the Capitol at Rome

214   Birth of Carneades

213   Colossus of the hero Aratus at Epidaurus, as son of Asclepius

207   *Hymn to Juno* of Livius Andronicus

206   θεωροί sent from Magnesia on the Meander
Founding of the Leucophryena. Similar festivals established in Teos, Didyma, and elsewhere

204   Death of Chrysippus
Cultus of Magna Mater (Cybele) of Pessinus brought to Rome
Ennius brought to Rome by Cato; Latin translation of Euhemerus

c. 200   Divine honours for Attalus I of Pergamum at Athens; the Phyle Attalis.
Aretalogy of Sarapis on Delos

after 200   Hero-cult in the testament of Epicteta of Thera

198   Beginning of Seleucid domination in Palestine

196   Freedom of the Greek tribes proclaimed by Flamininus at the Isthmia
Temple of Zeus Sosipolis on the Maeander founded by the Magnesians after a successful war with Miletus

195   First temple of the goddess Roma erected at Smyrna

189   Battle of Magnesia; Antiochus III defeated by the Romans

187   Antiochus III of Syria smitten while plundering the temple of Baal in Elymais

186   *Senatus consultum* on the Bacchanalia in Italy

185   Ben Sirach (Ecclesiasticus) in Hebrew; translated into Greek 132 B.C.

184   Great victory of Eumenes II of Pergamum over the Gauls—probably the occasion for erection of the great altar in 180
Birth of Panaetius

183   Heroic honours given to Philpoemen by the Achaeans

174 ff.   Antiochus IV Epiphanes undertakes vast temple constructions in Hellas e.g. the Olympieion at Athens, but leaves much unfinished

173   Two Epicurean philosophers expelled from Rome

B.C. 168     Battle of Pydna, and end of the Macedonian Empire
             Desecration of the Temple in Jerusalem; Maccabaean
                 Revolt

    165      Rededication of the Temple in Jerusalem
    161      Expulsion of Greek philosophers and teachers from Rome
    155      Carneades, Critolaus, and Diogenes arrive in Rome as
                 envoys
    147      Temples of Juppiter Stator and Juno Regina
    146      Destruction of Corinth and of Carthage by the Romans
 c. 140      Apollodorus of Athens (author of *Concerning the Gods*)
                 in Pergamum
    140      Hipparchus of Nicaea discovers trigonometry and the
                 precession of the equinoxes
  138-7      First Pythais of the Athenians sent to Delphi
    135      Panaetius teaches in Rome
    133      Attalus III bequeathes the Kingdom of Pergamum to the
                 Romans
 129 ff.     Restoration of the temple of Artemis Leucophryene in
                 Magnesia
    129      Death of Carneades
 c. 129-110  Panaetius of Rhodes head of the Stoa in Athens
 c. 117      Amphictyonic decree regarding the territory of Delphi
             Hero-cult of Polybius in the cities of Achaia
    106      Birth of Cicero
     99      The so-called Temple Chronicle of Lindos
     92      Regulation of the mysteries at Andania
             Latin rhetores suppressed by the censors
  90-51      Posidonius of Apamea teaches in Rhodes
     88      Siege of Rhodes by Mithridates. Epiphany of flame-
                 spewing Isis
     86      Sulla devastates Athens and surrounding territory
     83      Sulla brings the text of Aristotle's works to Rome
     81      *Senatus consultum* on the Asylia of Lagina
  74-73      Dedication of a statue of Aion at Eleusis by Q.
                 Pompeius and his two brothers
     73      *Senatus consultum* on Amphiaraos of Oropus
     72      Antiochus IV of Commagene deposed
before 67    The pirate scourge; Greek temples plundered
     64      Pompey in Syria; end of Seleucid monarchy
     63      Pompey captures Jerusalem
  c. 63      Cult of Pompey in Mytilene
     55      T. Lucretius Carus: *De rerum natura*

B.C. 50–10   The Wisdom of Solomon (written in Alexandria?)

48   Assassination of Pompey

45   The Julian calendar inaugurated

45–44   Cicero: *De natura deorum, De officiis,* and *Tusculans*

44   Julius Caesar assassinated 15 March

43   Cicero murdered, 7 December

40   Virgil: Fourth Eclogue

35   Theophanes of Mytilene honoured after his death as Zeus Eleutherios

31   Battle of Actium

31 ff.   After the battle of Actium, temples were erected to Roma and Augustus
Cult of Livia and Julia as Hestia on the Athenian acropolis

29   Dedication of a temple to Divus Julius in the Forum

27   Beginning of emperor-worship. "Augustus" assumed as a title. Inauguration of the Caesareia. Death of Varro
Agrippa builds the first Pantheon

19   Death of Virgil; publication of the *Aeneid*

17   Saecular celebration of Augustus; Horace: *Carmen saeculare*

9   Dedication of the Ara Pacis Augustae in the Campus Martius

1   Restoration of the sacred books and the Asylia of Nysa on the Maeander. Chaldeans, Egyptians, Jews and others expelled from Rome

A.D. 14   Death of Augustus. Cult of the Divine Augustus. Coronation of Tiberius. "Epiphany of Great Pan"

21   Lists of the priests of Apollo at Halisarna on Cos

29 or 30   Death of Jesus

37 (?)   Conversion of Paul
Temple of Divus Augustus on the Palatine consecrated

41   The affair of Caligula's statue in Jerusalem
Philo of Alexandria (30 B.C.–A.D. 45) heads legation to the Emperor

42   Decree of the Arcadian Lycosurians regarding the cult of Despoina

c. 45   Paul and Barnabas at Lystra

c. 50–61   Paul's epistles

52   Epistle of Claudius to the Delphians

55   Seneca: *De Clementia*

A.D. 64       Persecution of the Christians at Rome under Nero.
              Deaths of Peter and Paul (62, 64?)

67            Nero in Greece
              Banishment of L. Annaeus Cornutus

68            Gospel of Mark (Luke, c. 90; Acts c. 95; Matthew,
                 c. 110; John, c. 125)

60–140        Epictetus. Apollonius of Tyana

70            Capture of Jerusalem by Titus

c. 45–125     Plutarch of Chaeronea, priest at Delphi

75–79         Josephus: *Jewish War*

80            Opening of the Colosseum at Rome
              Destruction of the Capitoline temple by fire; restored
                 and rededicated in 82

90            Council of Jewish rabbis at Jamnia

93            Philosophers expelled from Rome; Epictetus goes to
                 Nicopolis

94            Josephus: *Antiquities*

c. 95         The Apocalypse of John

c. 100 (or
  c. 135)     The Didache

100           Claudius Ptolemaeus: *System of Astronomy* (the *Almagest*);
                 catalogue of stars

104–171       Alexander of Abonuteichos. Lucian of Samosata

105           Dion of Prusa: *Discourse at Olympia*

111           Pliny the Younger sent to govern Bithynia

115–17        Jewish revolt in N. Africa and Cyprus. Destruction of
                 Greek temples in Cyrene

116           Decree of Avidius Nigrinus concerning the sacred
                 territory of Delphi

124           Hadrian arrives in Athens and visits Eleusis.
              Human sacrifice forbidden by Hadrian

125           Hadrian initiated as a μύστης at Eleusis
              Death of Plutarch

129           Hadrian initiated as an ἐπόπτης at Eleusis

130           Completion of the Olympieion at Athens.
              The Pan-Hellenic League and its Festival.
              Death and deification of Antinous

125–177       Restoration of many ruined temples in Greece by
                 Herodes Atticus

132–5         Second Revolt of the Jews in Palestine. Martyrdom of
                 Rabbi Akiba

A.D. 149–50    T. Flavius Cleitosthenes restores ruined temples and
                civic buildings at Thera

  c. 150       II Peter (latest book in the New Testament)
                Apuleius of Madaura: *Metamorphoses*

  155          Justin Martyr: *First Apology*

  155 ff.      Aelius Aristides, the rhetor, a zealous devotee of
                Asclepius: *Sacred Discourses*

  c. 160       Edict of C. Popillius Carus Pedo concerning the Artemis
                of Ephesus

  161–180      Marcus Aurelius, the Stoic emperor; Galen court physician
                Iobaccheia at Athens

  c. 163       S. Julius Antoninus, senator, from Nysa on the Maeander,
                a benefactor of the sanctuary at Epidaurus.

  170–80       Dionysus-mystae at Tusculum; the great Bacchic
                inscription

  174          Marcus Aurelius begins his *Meditations*

  174 ff.      Pausanias: *Description of Greece*

  177          Martyrdom of Christians at Lyons and Vienne

  182          Burning of the Telesterion at Eleusis

  c. 186       Irenaeus: *Adversus haereses*

  188 ff.      Epistle of the Emperor Commodus to the Eumolpids
                at Eleusis

  190–203      Clement head of the Catechetical School in Alexandria

  193–211      Lucius Septimius Severus emperor

  197          Tertullian: *Apologeticus*

  203          Passion of S. Perpetua

  204          Saecular festival of Septimius Severus

  210          Completion of the compilation of the Mishnah by Rabbi
                Judah

  211–17       Caracalla emperor

  211          All free men in the Empire made citizens of Rome by
                Caracalla

  218–22       Elagabalus emperor. Cultus of the Syrian Gods of
                Emesa taken to Rome.
                Philostratus: *In Praise of Apollonius of Tyana*

  221          Appearance of a "New Alexander" in Moesia and Thrace

  222–35       Alexander Severus emperor. His mother Julia Mammaea
                friendly to Christians

  185–254      Origen of Alexandria

  232          Origen removes to Caesarea

  242          Mani begins preaching his new religion in Persia,
                20 Mar.

A.D. 244 Plotinus at Rome

248 Origen: *Contra Celsum*

250–1 Persecution of Christians by Decius

Public dole on Syrus with offerings to Hestia

251 Cyprian: *On the Lapsed, On the Unity of the Catholic Church*; he was martyred in 251

262 The historian Herennius Dexippus is ἀγωνοθέτης at the Great Panathenaia

The Neoplatonist Porphyry at Rome

263–4 Destruction of the Artemision at Ephesus by the Goths. The temple at Didyma preserved from the Goths

267 ff. Severe devastation of Athens by the Herulians: defence by Dexippus

270 Death of Plotinus

270–5 Aurelian emperor. Cult of the Sun: temple of Sol Invictus dedicated in Rome

303 Persecution of Christians by Diocletian

305–13 Cultus in the sanctuary of Zeus Panamaros in Caria

312 Constantine conquers Maxentius at the Mulvian Bridge ("In this sign conquer")

313 Christianity tolerated in the Roman Empire

c. 312–15 Delphic decree with the ancient cult formulae

313 First edition of Eusebius's *Church History*

314 Council of bishops at Arles

315 Arch of Constantine erected in Rome

325 First ecumenical Christian Council at Nicaea, under Constantine. Athanasius vs. Arius

337 Baptism of Constantine on his death-bed by Eusebius of Nicomedia

341 Constantius prohibits the offering of pagan sacrifices

348–410 Prudentius the Christian poet

354 Decree by Constantius closing all pagan temples and prohibiting all sacrifices

361 Baptism and death of Constantius

361–3 Julian emperor. Attempted restoration of the old Greek religion; the Helios cult. The Neoplatonist Sallustius

375 The Hero Achilles warns Attica of an earthquake

379–95 Reign of Theodosius I

381 Council of Constantinople

382 Removal of the altar of Victory in the Senate House

387 Baptism of Augustine (*d.* 430). Taurobolium at Athens

390 Destruction of the Serapeum

A.D. 392     Theodosius I prohibits all pagan cults

393     Last observance of the Olympieia in the Altis at Athens

395     Barbarity of the Goths in Athens. The acropolis saved
by the epiphany of the Hero Achilles

396–430     Augustine Bishop of Hippo in North Africa

407     Withdrawal of the legions from Britain

410     Sack of Rome by Alaric

429     The Vandals in Africa

431     Council of Ephesus

before 450     Destruction of the Athenian Asclepieium under
Theodosius II

432–61     St Patrick in Ireland

440–61     Pope Leo I: his *Tome* sent to the Council of Chalcedon

450–85     The Neoplatonist Proclus in Athens

451     Council of Chalcedon

455     Sack of Rome by the Vandals

485     Marinus, the disciple of Proclus, returns to Epidaurus

524     Execution of Boethius at Athens

527–65     Reign of Justinian I

529     Closing of the philosophical schools in Athens

530–4     Codification of Roman law by Tribonian: *Digesta*,
*Institutiones, Novellae*

532     Building of Hagia Sophia begun at Constantinople

# FOR FURTHER READING

The subject of this book is so vast that any bibliography looks too long. It is not supposed that every student will read all the titles named. Some will be available in one library, others elsewhere, and only a few great collections will include all. But the books here named are all valuable, and each of them will lead the reader on to further researches. Many include their authors' own bibliographies. I have listed enough titles to enable the student to start where he likes. There is good reading "all along the line."

Fuller lists will be found in *A Bibliography of Bible Study for Theological Students*, Princeton Theological Seminary Library, 1948, and in Ch. XI of my book, *How to Read the Bible*, New York 1956; Edinburgh 1959. See also the bibliography in the Torchbook edition of Edwin Hatch, *The Influence of Greek Ideas on Christianity*, New York 1957, pp. xix–xxxv, and the one in the Torchbook edition of Johannes Weiss, *Earliest Christianity*, New York 1959, VOL. I, pp. xiii–xxii. For the Gospels and Acts, see the bibliography in my book, *The Gospels, Their Origin and Their Growth*, New York 1957; London 1959, pp. 203–7. For the Graeco-Roman world, there are ample lists in J. A. Nairne's *Classical Hand-List*, 3d edn. revised and enlarged by B. H. Blackwell, Oxford 1953. Books currently in print can be located in *Books in Print*, or *The Cumulative Book Index*. The new series of volumes in the Library of Congress Catalogue names the chief centres in the United States where each of the rarer books may be found.

## I. HISTORY

### A. General

BENGTSON, HERMANN. *Einführung in die alte Geschichte*. Munich 1949; 3rd edn. 1959. The best handbook introductory to the study of ancient history.

BREASTED, J. H. *Ancient Times*. 2nd edn. New York 1935.

*Cambridge Ancient History*. 12 vols. with 5 vols. of plates. Cambridge 1923–39. Excellent bibliographies in each volume.

ROBINSON, C. A. *Ancient History. From Prehistoric Times to the Death of Justinian*. New York 1951.

ROSTOVTZEFF, M. I. *A History of the Ancient World*. 2 vols. Oxford 1926–7; 2nd edn. 1930.

### B. Greek History

BENGTSON, HERMANN. *Griechische Geschichte von den Anfängen bis in die römische Kaiserzeit*. Munich 1950; 3rd edn. 1960.

BOTSFORD, G. W. *Hellenic History*, revised by C. A. Robinson. 2nd edn. New York 1939; 4th edn. 1956.

FERGUSON, W. S. *Greek Imperialism*. London and Boston 1913.

—— *Hellenistic Athens*. London 1911.

## C. Roman History

BOAK, A. E. R. *History of Rome to A.D. 565.* 3rd edn. New York 1943; 4th edn. 1955.

―――― "The First Century," in *Encyclopedia Americana*, VOL. XI, pp. 258-62.

CHARLESWORTH, M. P. *The Roman Empire.* London 1951.

FRANK, TENNEY. *Roman Imperialism.* New York 1914.

GIBBON, EDWARD. *The Decline and Fall of the Roman Empire.* VOL. I, London 1776; many later editions.

GRANT, F. C. "The Second Century," in *Encyclopedia Americana*, VOL. XXIV, pp. 511–14.

JONES, H. S. *Companion to Roman History.* Oxford 1912.

## D. The Provinces

BOUCHIER, E. S. *Syria as a Roman Province.* Oxford 1916.

DOWNEY, GLANVILLE. *A History of Antioch in Syria.* Princeton 1961.

DUCKWORTH, H. T. F. "The Roman provincial system," in *The Beginnings of Christianity*, edd. F. J. Foakes Jackson and Kirsopp Lake, VOL. II, London 1922.

MAGIE, DAVID. *Roman Rule in Asia Minor.* 2 vols. Princeton 1950.

MOMMSEN, THEODOR. *The Provinces of the Roman Empire*, trans. W. P. Dickson. 2 vols. New edn. London 1909.

STEVENSON, G. H. *Roman Provincial Administration.* Oxford and New York 1939.

## E. Roman Government and Law

BERGER, ADOLF. *Encyclopedic Dictionary of Roman Law.* Philadelphia 1953.

BUCKLAND, W. W. *A Manual of Roman Private Law.* 2nd edn. Cambridge 1939.

―――― *Textbook of Roman Law from Augustus to Justinian.* 2nd edn. Cambridge 1932.

KASER, MAX. *Das römische Privatrecht.* 2 vols. Munich 1955–9.

ROBY, H. J. *Roman Private Law in the Times of Cicero and the Antonines.* 2 vols. Cambridge 1902.

SHERWIN-WHITE, A. N. *The Roman Citizenship.* Oxford 1939.

### Texts

The Corpus of Roman Law. VOL. I, *The Theodosian Code*, trans. Clyde Pharr. Princeton 1952.

*Fontes iuris romani antejustiniani*, edd. S. Riccobono, F. Baviera, and C. Ferrini. 3 vols. Florence 1940–3.

GAIUS. *The Institutes of Gaius*, trans. F. de Zulueta. 2 vols. Oxford 1946–53.

JUSTINIAN. *The Digest of Justinian*, trans. C. H. Monro. 2 vols. Cambridge 1904–9.

―――― *The Institutes of Justinian*, trans. J. B. Moyle. Oxford 1883.

## F. Economic Conditions

BARROW, R. H. *Slavery in the Roman Empire.* London 1928.

BELOCH, K. J. *Die Bevölkerung der griechisch-römischen Welt.* Leipzig 1886.

CAVAIGNAC, E. *Population et capital dans le monde méditerranéen antique*. Strasbourg 1923.

*An Economic Survey of Ancient Rome*, ed. Tenney Frank. 5 vols. Baltimore 1933–40.

FRANK, TENNEY. *An Economic History of Rome*. 2nd edn. London and New York 1927.

GLOTZ, GUSTAVE, *Ancient Greece at Work*. London and New York 1926.

GRANT, F. C. *The Economic Background of the Gospels*. Oxford 1926.

———— "The economic background of the New Testament," in *The Background of the New Testament and its Eschatology*, edd. W. D. Davies and D. Daube, Cambridge 1956, pp. 96–114.

HEITLAND, W. E. *Agricola: A Study of Agriculture and Rustic Life in the Graeco-Roman World from the Point of View of Labour*. Cambridge 1921.

———— *The Roman Fate*. Cambridge 1922.

———— *Iterum*. Cambridge 1925.

OERTEL, F. "The economic unification of the Mediterranean region: industry, trade, and commerce," in *Cambridge Ancient History*, VOL. X, ch. xiii.

———— "The economic life of the Empire," in *Cambridge Ancient History*, VOL. XII, ch. vii.

PAUL, LOUIS. *Ancient Rome at Work*. London and New York 1927.

ROSTOVTZEFF, M. I. *The Social and Economic History of the Hellenistic World*, 3 vols. Oxford 1941.

———— *The Social and Economic History of the Roman Empire*. Oxford 1926; new edn., 2 vols., 1957.

*Studies in Roman Economic and Social History*, ed. P. R. Coleman-Norton. Princeton 1951.

TOUTAIN, JULES. *Economic Life of the Ancient World*. London and New York 1930.

WESTERMAN, W. L. *The Slave Systems of Greek and Roman Antiquity*. Philadelphia 1955.

### G. Geography

BUNBURY, E. H. *History of Ancient Geography among the Greeks and Romans*. 2 vols. London 1879; repr. 1960.

CARY, M. *The Geographic Background of Greek and Roman History*. Oxford 1949.

GROLLENBERG, L. *Atlas of the Bible*. Edinburgh and New York 1956.

RAMSAY, WILLIAM. *The Historical Geography of Asia Minor*. New York 1890.

———— "Roads and travel" (in the New Testament), in Hastings' *Dictionary of the Bible*, VOL. V, Edinburgh and New York 1904, pp. 375–402.

TOZER, H. F. *A History of Ancient Geography*. Cambridge 1897; 2nd edn., ed. M. Cary, 1935.

WEISS, J. "Kleinasien in der apostolischer Zeit," in *Realencyklopädie für protestantische Theologie und Kirche*, 3rd edn., VOL. X, Leipzig 1901, pp. 535–63.

WRIGHT, G. E., and F. V. FILSON, *Historical Atlas to the Bible*. New edn. Philadelphia 1956.

## II. HELLENISTIC CIVILISATION

### A. General

BAUMGARTEN, F., F. POLAND, and R. WAGNER. *Die hellenische Kultur.* 3rd edn. Leipzig and Berlin 1913.

—— *Die hellenistische-römische Kultur.* Leipzig and Berlin 1913.

—— *The Culture of Ancient Greece and Rome* (abbreviated trans.). Boston 1926.

BIEBER, MARGARETE. *Hellenistic Sculpture.* New ed., New York 1961.

BOTSFORD, G. W., and E. G. SIHLER. *Hellenic Civilization.* New York 1915.

BURCKHARDT, J. *Griechische Kulturgeschichte,* ed. Jakob Oeri. 4 vols. Berlin 1898–1902; abbreviated edn., 1 vol., Berlin 1934.

BURY, J. B., E. A. BARBER, EDWYN BEVAN, and W. W. TARN. *The Hellenistic Age.* Cambridge 1923.

CARCOPINO, JÉROME. *Daily Life in Ancient Rome.* New Haven 1940.

DILL, SAMUEL. *Roman Society from Nero to Marcus Aurelius.* London 1904; New York 1956.

—— *Roman Society in the Last Century of the Western Empire.* New York 1899; 2nd edn. 1910.

DROYSEN, J. G. *Geschichte des Hellenismus.* 2 vols. Hamburg 1833–43; new edn., 6 vols. in 3, Gotha 1877–8; revised edn. 1952–3.

FESTUGIÈRE, A. J., and P. FABRE. *Le Monde gréco-romain au temps de Notre-Seigneur.* 2 vols. Paris 1935.

FOWLER, W. W. *Social Life at Rome in the Age of Cicero.* London 1908.

FRIEDLÄNDER, LUDWIG. *Roman Life and Manners under the Early Empire,* trans. J. H. Freese and L. A. Magnus. 4 vols. London 1910–13.

FYFE, THEODORE. *Hellenistic Architecture.* Cambridge 1936.

GLOTZ, GUSTAVE, *The Greek City and its Institutions.* London 1929.

GRANT, F. C. "Hellenismus," in *Die Religion in Geschichte und Gegenwart,* VOL. III, 3rd edn. Tübingen 1959, cols. 209–12.

—— "The world into which Christianity came," in *The Bible Companion,* ed. William Neil. London and New York 1960, pp. 73–94.

GRANT, MICHAEL, *The World of Rome.* London 1960.

GRUPP, G. *Kulturgeschichte der römischen Kaiserzeit.* 2 vols. Munich 1903–4.

HALLIDAY, W. R. *The Pagan Background of Early Christianity.* Liverpool 1926.

JONES, A. H. M. *The Cities of the Eastern Roman Provinces.* Oxford 1937.

—— *The Greek City from Alexander to Justinian.* Oxford 1940.

KAERST, J. *Geschichte der hellenistischen Zeitalter.* 2 vols. Berlin 1901–9; new edn., under title *Geschichte des Hellenismus,* 1926–7.

KAHRSTEDT, ULRICH. *Kulturgeschichte der römischen Kaiserzeit.* 2nd edn. Bern 1958.

LEWIS, N., and M. REINHOLD. *Roman Civilization.* 2 vols. New York 1951–5.

LICHT, HANS. *Sittengeschichte Griechenlands.* 2 vols. and supplement, Stuttgart 1925–8; new edn., 1 vol. 1960.

OLIVER, J. H. "Hellenism," in *Encyclopedia Americana,* VOL. XIV, pp. 84, 84 a-f.

OTTO, W. *Kulturgeschichte des Altertums.* Munich 1925.

TARN, W. W. *Hellenistic Civilisation.* 3rd edn., revised by G. T. Griffith, London 1952.

TOYNBEE, A. J. *Hellenism: The History of a Civilisation.* London 1959.

WENDLAND, PAUL. *Die hellenistisch-römische Kultur in ihren Beziehungen zu Judentum und Christentum.* Tübingen 1907; revised edn. 1912.

The survey chapters in the *Cambridge Ancient History*, dealing with art, literature, religion, law, economics, and other aspects of civilisation, are immensely valuable, as are the bibliographies and chronological tables at the end of each volume.

### B. Education

BOUSSET, WILHELM. *Jüdisch-christlicher Schulbetrieb in Alexandria und Rom.* Göttingen 1915.

FREEMAN, K. J. *Schools of Hellas.* London 1907; 3rd edn., ed. M. J. Rendall, 1922.

*From Alexander to Constantine*, ed. and trans. Sir Ernest Barker. Oxford 1956. Passages and documents illustrating the history of social and political ideas.

GWYNN, A. *Roman Education from Cicero to Quintilian.* Oxford 1926.

JAEGER, WERNER. *Paideia: The Ideals of Greek Culture*, trans. Gilbert Highet. 3 vols. Oxford 1943–5.

MARROU, H. I. *A History of Education in Antiquity*, trans. G. Lamb. London and New York 1956.

NILSSON, MARTIN P. *Die hellenistische Schule.* Munich 1955.

SANDYS, J. E. *A History of Classical Scholarship*, VOL. I. Cambridge 1903; reprinted 1960; abbreviated edn. 1915.

### C. Science

FARRINGTON, BENJAMIN. *Science and Politics in the Ancient World.* London 1939.
——— *Science in Antiquity.* London 1936.

HEATH, T. L. *Aristarchus of Samos.* Oxford 1913; reprinted 1960.
——— *History of Greek Mathematics.* 2 vols, Oxford 1921.

SARTON, GEORGE. *A History of Science.* 2 vols. to date. Cambridge, Mass. 1952–9. VOL. II is entitled *Hellenistic Science and Culture in the Last Three Centuries B.C.*

### D. Literature

There are many good histories of Greek and Latin literature. Good ones to begin with are Gilbert Murray, *History of Ancient Greek Literature* (1897, repr. 1927) and J. W. Mackail, *Latin Literature* (1895). The present-day student has the great advantage of access to the Loeb Classical Library; begun in 1912, it now numbers over 400 vols. Each volume contains a critical text faced by a good English translation. All of the important classical authors are included. It is published by Heinemann in London and Harvard University Press in the U.S.A. Other good editions with French translations are to be found in the Budé series (Paris), the Librairie Garnier, and the Didot series (with Latin translations of Greek works). The famous Teubner texts, published in Leipzig, have text only, without translation; so also have the Oxford Classical Texts. Bohn's Classical Library and the Oxford Library of Translations have translations only, without the original texts.

## III. GRAECO-ROMAN RELIGION

### A. Greek Religion, General

ADAM, JAMES, *Religious Teachers of Greece*. 2nd edn. Edinburgh 1909.

BEVAN, EDWYN R. *Later Greek Religion*. London 1927.

BIDEZ, JOSEPH, and FRANZ CUMONT. *Les Mages hellenisés*. 2 vols. Paris 1938.

BOER, WILLEM DEN. *De Godsdienst van den Grieken*. Leiden 1948.

BOUCHÉ LECLERCQ, A. *Histoire de la divination dans l'antiquité*. 4 vols. Paris 1879–82.

CAMPBELL, LEWIS. *Religion in Greek Literature*. London 1898.

DEUBNER, L. *Attische Feste*. 1932; new edn. Berlin 1956.

DIETERICH, ALBRECHT. *Nekyia*. 1893; 2nd edn. Leipzig 1913.

DÖLGER, FRANZ JOSEPH. *Sol Salutis*. Münster (Westf.) 1920.

EDELSTEIN, EMMA J. and LUDWIG. *Asclepius*. 2 vols. Baltimore 1945.

FARNELL, LEWIS RICHARD. *Cults of the Greek States*. 5 vols. Oxford 1896–1909.

——— *Greece and Babylon*. Edinburgh 1911.

——— *Greek Hero Cults and Ideas of Immortality*. Oxford 1921.

——— *Outline History of Greek Religion*. London 1920.

FASCHER, ERICH. *Prophētēs*. Giessen 1927.

FESTUGIÈRE, A. J. *L'Idéal religieuse des Grecs et l'évangile*. Paris 1932.

——— *Personal Religion among the Greeks*. Berkeley 1954.

*Die Fragmente der griechischen Kultschriftsteller*, ed. A. Tresp. Giessen 1914.

GERNET, LOUIS, and ANDRÉ BOULANGER. *Le Génie grec dans la religion*. Paris 1932.

GRANT, F. C. *Hellenistic Religions: The Age of Syncretism*. New York 1953. Sources.

GREEN, WILLIAM CHASE. *Moira: Fate, Good and Evil in Greek Thought*. Cambridge, Mass., 1944.

GUTHRIE, W. K. C. *The Greeks and their Gods*. London and Boston 1950.

——— *Orpheus and Greek Religion*. London 1935; 2nd edn. 1952.

HALLIDAY, W. R. *Greek Divination*. London 1913.

KERÉNYI, C. *The Gods of the Greeks*. London and New York 1951.

KERN, OTTO. *Die Religion der Griechen*. 3 vols. Berlin 1926–38.

*The Legacy of Greece*, ed. R. W. Livingstone. Oxford 1921.

LIVINGSTONE, R. W. *The Greek Genius and its Meaning to Us*. 2nd edn. Oxford 1915.

——— *Greek Ideals and Modern Life*. Oxford 1935.

——— *The Mission of Greece*. Oxford 1928.

——— *The Pageant of Greece*. Oxford 1923.

MOORE, C. H. *The Religious Thought of the Greeks*. Cambridge, Mass., 1925.

MURRAY, GILBERT. *Five Stages of Greek Religion*. Oxford 1925; paperback edn. New York 1955.

NESTLE, WILHELM. *Griechische Religiosität*, 3 vols. Berlin 1930–3.

NILSSON, MARTIN P. *Geschichte der griechischen Religion.* VOL. I. Munich 1940; 2nd edn. 1955; VOL. II. Munich 1950.
—— *Greek Piety.* Oxford 1948.
—— *Greek Popular Religion.* New York 1940; 2nd edn. 1947.
—— *History of Greek Religion.* Oxford 1925; revised edn. 1949.
—— *Opuscula Selecta.* 3 vols. Lund 1951 ff.
—— *Die Religion in den griechischen Zauberpapyri.* Lund 1948.
NOCK, A. D. *Conversion. The Old and the New in Religion from Alexander the Great to Augustine of Hippo.* Oxford 1933.
—— "The development of paganism in the Roman Empire," in *Cambridge Ancient History,* VOL. XII, 1939, ch. xii.
—— "Religious attitudes of the ancient Greeks," in *Proc. Amer. Philosophical Society,* LXXXV (1942).
OLIVER, JAMES H. *The Athenian Expounders of Sacred and Ancestral Law.* Baltimore 1950.
OTTO, W. F. *Die Götter Griechenlands,* 2nd edn. Frankfurt am Main 1950. Eng. trans. *The Homeric Gods,* trans. M. Hadas. New York 1955.
—— *Priester und Tempel in hellenistischen Aegypten.* 2 vols. Leipzig 1905–8.
PARKE, H. W. *A History of the Delphic Oracle.* Oxford 1939; 2nd edn., 2 vols., 1956.
QUANDT, W. *Orphei hymni.* Berlin 1951.
RAMSAY, WILLIAM M. "Religion of Greece and Asia Minor," in Hastings' *Dictionary of the Bible,* VOL. V, Edinburgh and New York 1904, pp. 109–56.
*Religionsgeschichtliche Versuche und Vorarbeiten,* edd. R. Wunsch and A. Dieterich. Giessen 1903 ff.
ROHDE, ERWIN. *Psyche: Seelencult und Unsterblichkeitsglaube der Griechen.* 8th edn. Tübingen 1925. Eng. trans. *Psyche: The Cult of Souls and Belief in Immortality among the Greeks.* London and New York 1925.
ROSE, H. J. *Ancient Greek Religion.* London 1946.
STENGEL, PAUL. *Die griechischen Kultusaltertümer.* 3rd edn. Munich 1920.
—— *Opferbräuche der Griechen.* Leipzig 1910.
THOMSON, J. A. K. *The Greek Tradition.* 2nd edn. New York 1927.
TURCHI, NICOLA. *La Religioni di Grecia e di Roma.* Milan 1950.
WEINREICH, OTTO. *Antike Heilungswunder. Untersuchungen zum Wunderglauben der Griechen und Römer.* Giessen 1909.
—— *Gebet und Wunder.* Stuttgart 1929.
WIDE, SAM, and MARTIN P. NILSSON. *Griechische und römische Religion.* 4th edn. Leipzig 1931.
WILAMOWITZ-MOELLENDORFF, ULRICH VON. *Der Glaube der Hellenen.* 2 vols. Berlin 1931–2.
ZIELINSKI, THADDEUS. *The Religion of Ancient Greece,* trans. from Polish by G. R. Noyes. London 1926.

## B. The Mysteries

ANGUS, SAMUEL. *The Mystery Religions and Christianity.* New York 1925.
—— *The Religious Quests of the Graeco-Roman World.* New York 1929.

ANRICH, GUSTAV. *Das antike Mysterienwesen in seinem Einfluss auf das Christentum.* Göttingen 1894.

CARCOPINO, JÉROME. *Aspects mystique de la Rome païenne.* Paris 1942.

*Corpus inscriptionum et monumentorum religionis mithraicae,* ed. M. J. Vermaseren. 2 vols. The Hague 1956–60. Sources.

CUMONT, FRANZ. *Les Mystères de Mithra.* 3rd edn. Brussels 1913. Eng. trans. of 2nd edn. *The Mysteries of Mithra,* trans. T. J. McCormack. London and Chicago 1903.

———— *Les Religions orientales dans le paganisme romain.* Paris 1906; 4th edn. 1929. Eng. trans. of 2nd edn. *Oriental Religions in Roman Paganism.* Chicago 1911.

———— *Textes et monuments figurés relatifs aux mystères de Mithra.* 2 vols. Brussels 1895–9.

EITREM, SAMSON. *Orakel und Mysterien am Ausgang der Antike.* Zürich 1947.

*Fontes historiae mysteriorum aevi hellenistici,* ed. N. Turchi. 1923. Sources.

GEDEN, A. S. *Select Passages illustrating Mithraism.* New York 1925. Sources.

GRESSMANN, HUGO. *Die orientalischen Religionen im hellenistisch-römischen Zeitalter.* Berlin 1930.

GUTHRIE, W. K. C. *Orpheus and Greek Religion.* London 1935; 2nd edn. 1952.

JACOBY, ADOLF. *Die antiken Mysterienreligionen und das Christentum.* Tübingen 1910.

JEANMAIRE, HENRI. *Dionysos.* Paris 1951.

KERN, OTTO. *Die griechischen Mysterien der klassischen Zeit.* Berlin 1927.

———— *Orpheus: Eine religionsgeschichtliche Untersuchung.* Berlin 1920.

———— *Orphicorum fragmenta.* Berlin 1922. Sources.

LAGRANGE, M. J. *Les Mystères: l'Orphisme.* Paris 1937.

LINFORTH, IVAN M. *The Arts of Orpheus.* Berkeley 1941.

LOBECK, C. A. *Aglaophamus: sive, De theologiae mysticae graecorum causis libri tres.* 2 vols. Königsberg 1829.

LOISY, ALFRED. *Les Mystères païens et le mystère chrétien.* Paris 1913: 2nd edn. 1930.

MACCHIORO, VITTORIO. *Zagreus.* Florence. 1920.

MAGNIEN, V. *Les Mystères d'Eleusis.* Paris 1950.

MYLONAS, G. E. *Eleusis and the Eleusinian Mysteries.* Princeton 1961.

OTTO, W. F. *Dionysos: Mythos und Kultus.* 2nd edn. Frankfurt am Main 1942.

PETTAZZONI, RAFFAELE. *I Misteri.* Bologna 1923.

REITZENSTEIN, RICHARD. *Die hellenistischen Mysterienreligionen.* 3rd edn. Leipzig 1927.

———— *Hellenistische Wundererzählungen.* Leipzig 1906.

TURCHI, NICOLA. *Le Religioni misteriche del mondo antico.* Milan 1948.

WILLOUGHBY, HAROLD R. *Pagan Regeneration.* Chicago 1929.

## C. Gnosticism

BOUSSET, WILHELM. *Hauptprobleme der Gnosis.* Göttingen 1907.

BURKITT, F. C. *The Church and Gnosis.* Cambridge 1932.

CROSS, F. L. *The Jung Codex.* New York 1955. On the Coptic Gnostic library discovered at Nag Hammadi in 1945; see also articles in *Vigiliae Christianae* 1947 ff.

DORESSE, JEAN. *Les livres secrèts des Gnostiques d'Egypte.* Paris 1958.
———— *L'Evangile selon Thomas, ou les paroles secrètes de Jesus.* Paris 1959.
FAYE, EUGÈNE DE. *Gnostiques et gnosticisme.* Paris 1913. Eng. trans. 1960.
GRANT, ROBERT M. *Gnosticism: A Sourcebook of Heretical Writings from the Early Christian Period.* New York and London 1961.
———— *Gnosticism and Early Christianity.* New York and London 1959.
———— and D. N. FREEDMAN. *The Secret Sayings of Jesus according to the Gospel of Thomas.* New York and London 1960.
GUILLAUMONT, A., *et al. The Gospel according to Thomas.* Leiden and New York 1959.
JONAS, HANS. *The Gnostic Religion.* Boston 1958. Has a very full bibliography.
LEISEGANG, HANS. *Die Gnosis.* Leipzig 1924; 4th edn. 1955; French trans. of 3rd edn. 1951.
PÉTREMENT, SIMONE. *Le Dualisme chez Platon, les Gnostiques, et les Manichéens.* Paris 1947.
QUISPEL, GILLES. *Gnosis als Weltreligion.* Zürich 1951.
SCHOEPS, H. J. *Urgemeinde, Judenchristentum, Gnosis.* Tübingen 1956.
VOLKER, WALTHER. *Quellen zur Geschichte der christlichen Gnosis.* Tübingen 1932.

## D. Hermetism

*Corpus hermeticum,* edd. A. D. Nock and A. J. Festugière. 4 vols. Paris 1945–54.
DODD, C. H. *The Bible and the Greeks.* PT. II. London 1935.
FESTUGIÈRE, A. J. *L'Hermétisme.* Lund 1948.
———— *La Révélation d'Hermes Trismégiste.* 4 vols. Paris 1944–54.
REITZENSTEIN, RICHARD. *Poimandres.* Leipzig 1904.
SCOTT, WALTER. *Hermetica.* 4 vols. Oxford 1924–36.

## E. Roman Religion

*The Acts of the Pagan Martyrs,* ed. H. A. Musurillo. Oxford 1954.
ALTHEIM, FRANZ. *A History of Roman Religion,* trans. H. Mattingly. London 1938.
BAILEY, CYRIL. *Phases in the Religious Life of Ancient Rome.* Berkeley 1932.
———— *Religion in Virgil.* Oxford 1935.
CARCOPINO, JÉROME. *La Basilique pythagoricienne de la Porte Majeure.* Paris 1944.
———— *Virgile et le mystère de la IVe eglogue.* Paris 1943.
CARTER, JESSE BENEDICT. *The Religion of Numa.* New York 1906.
———— *The Religious Life of Ancient Rome.* Boston 1911.
CICERO, MARCUS TULLIUS. *De divinatione,* ed. A. S. Pease. 2 vols. Urbana, Ill., 1920–3.
———— *De natura deorum,* ed. J. B. Mayor. 3 vols. Cambridge 1880–5.
———— *De natura deorum,* ed. A. S. Pease. 2 vols. Cambridge, Mass., 1955–8.
CUMONT, FRANZ. *After Life in Roman Paganism.* New Haven 1922.
———— *Lux Perpetua.* Paris 1949.
FARQUHARSON, A. S. L. *Marcus Aurelius, His Life and His World,* ed. D. A. Rees, Oxford 1951.

FOWLER, W. W. *The Religious Experience of the Roman People.* London 1911.
—— *Roman Essays and Interpretations.* Oxford 1920.
—— *The Roman Festivals of the Period of the Republic.* London 1899.
—— *Roman Ideas of Deity.* London 1914.
FRIEDLÄNDER, LUDWIG. *Sittengeschichte Roms.* 10th edn. 1921–3. Eng. trans. of 2nd edn. *Roman Life and Manners under the Early Empire,* trans. L. A. Magnus. 4 vols. London and New York 1909–13.
GEFFCKEN, JOHANNES. *Der Ausgang des griechisch-römischen Heidentums.* Heidelberg 1920; repr. with supplement 1929.
GLOVER, T. R. *The Conflict of Religions in the Early Roman Empire.* 11th edn. London 1927.
GRANT, F. C. *Ancient Roman Religion.* New York 1957. Sources.
GRÉNIER, ALBERT. *The Roman Spirit in Religion, Thought, and Art,* trans. from French. New York 1926.
GUTERMAN, SIMEON LEONARD. *Religious Toleration and Persecution in Ancient Rome.* London 1951.
HALLIDAY, W. R. *History of Roman Religion.* Liverpool 1922.
LABRIOLLE, P. DE. *La Réaction païenne. Étude sur la polémique antichrétienne du 1er au 6e siècles.* Paris 1934.
LATTE, KURT. *Römische Religionsgeschichte.* Munich 1960.
*The Legacy of Rome,* ed. Cyril Bailey. Oxford 1923.
MARCUS AURELIUS. *The Meditations of Marcus Aurelius,* ed. A. S. L. Farquharson. 2 vols. Oxford 1944.
NOCK, A. D. "Religious developments from the close of the Republic to the death of Nero," in *Cambridge Ancient History,* VOL. X, 1934, ch. xv.
—— "The development of paganism in the Roman Empire," in *Cambridge Ancient History,* VOL. XII, 1939, ch. xii.
*La Regalità Sacra: The Sacral Kingship. Contributions to the Central Theme of the VIIIth International Congress for the History of Religions* (Rome, April 1955), ed. R. Pettazzoni. Leiden 1959.
ROSE, H. J. *Ancient Roman Religion.* London 1948.
ROSTOVTZEFF, M. I. *Mystic Italy.* New York 1927.
TAYLOR, L. R. *The Divinity of the Roman Emperor.* Middletown, Conn., 1931.
TURCHI, NICOLA. *La Religione di Roma antica.* Bologna 1939.
WISSOWA, GEORG. *Gesammelte Abhandlungen zur römischen Religions- und Stadtgeschichte.* Munich 1904.
—— *Religion und Kultus der Römer.* Munich 1902; 2nd edn. 1912.

## F. Astrology

BOLL, F., and C. BEZOLD. *Sternglaube und Sterndeutung: Geschichte und Wesen der Astrologie.* 4th edn. Berlin 1931.
CUMONT, FRANZ. *Astrology and Religion among the Greeks and Romans.* New York 1912.
—— *L'Egypte des astrologues.* Brussels 1937.
GRESSMAN, HUGO. *Die hellenistische Gestirnreligion.* Leipzig 1925.

See also the bibliography at the end of the article μάγος, in W. F. Arndt and F. W. Gingrich, *Lexicon to the Greek New Testament.* Cambridge and Chicago 1957.

### G. Demonology

EITREM, S. *Some Notes on Demonology in the New Testament.* Oslo 1950.
TAMBORNINO, J. *De antiquorum daemonismo.* Giessen 1909.
WEINEL, H. *Die Wirkungen des Geistes und der Geister im nachapostolischen Zeitalter.* Tübingen 1898.
WÜNSCH, R. *Geisterbannung im Altertum.* Breslau University Festschrift, 1911.

See also the bibliography at the end of the article δαιμόνιον, in W. F. Arndt and F. W. Gingrich, *Lexicon to the Greek New Testament*, Cambridge and Chicago 1957.

## IV. PHILOSOPHY

### A. General

CAIRD, EDWARD. *The Evolution of Theology in the Greek Philosophers.* 2 vols. Glasgow 1904.
DECHARME, PAUL. *La Critique des traditions religieuses chez les Grecs.* Paris 1904.
DIELS, HERMANN, and WALTHER KRANZ. *Die Fragmente der Vorsokratiker.* 6th edn., 3 vols. Berlin 1951–2. Sources.
*Doxographi graeci*, ed. Hermann Diels. 1879; repr. Berlin 1929. Sources.
*Fragmenta philosophorum graecorum*, ed. F. W. A. Mullach. 3 vols. Paris 1860–81. Sources.
FREEMAN, KATHLEEN. *Ancilla to the Pre-Socratic Philosophers.* Oxford 1948.
—— *The Pre-Socratic Philosophers; A Companion to Diels.* Oxford 1946.
JAEGER, WERNER. *The Theology of the Early Greek Philosophers*, trans. E. S. Robinson. Oxford 1947.
KIRK, G. S., and RAVEN, J. E. *The Presocratic Philosophers.* Cambridge 1957.
MORE, PAUL ELMER. *Hellenistic Philosophies.* Princeton 1923.
RITTER, HEINRICH, and L. VON PRELLER. *Historia philosophiae graecae.* 9th edn., ed. E. Wellmann. Gotha 1913. Sources.
UEBERWEG, FRIEDRICH, and KARL PRAECHTER. *Grundriss der Geschichte der Philosophie.* VOL. I, *Das Altertum.* 12th edn. Berlin 1926.
WINDELBAND, WILHELM. *Geschichte der abendländischen Philosophie im Altertum.* Munich 1923.
—— *Lehrbuch der Geschichte der Philosophie.* 1891; 11th edn. revised by E. Rothacker, Tübingen 1924.
WUNDT, M. *Geschichte der griechischen Ethik.* 2 vols. Leipzig 1908–11.
ZELLER, EDUARD. *Grundriss der Geschichte der griechischen Philosophie.* 13th edn. Leipzig 1928. Eng. trans. *Outlines of the History of Greek Philosophy*, trans. L. R. Palmer. New York 1931.
—— *Die Philosophie der Griechen.* 3 vols. in 6. Latest edns. Leipzig 1920–3. Eng. trans. of individual volumes London 1876–97.

### B. Stoics

ARNOLD, EDWARD VERNON, *Roman Stoicism.* Cambridge 1911.
BEVAN, EDWYN R. *Stoics and Sceptics.* Oxford 1913.

BONHÖFFER, ADOLF F. *Epiktet und das Neue Testament.* Giessen 1911.
*Frammenti degli Stoici antichi*, ed. N. Festa. 2 vols. Bari 1932–5.
HICKS, R. D. *Stoic and Epicurean.* New York 1910.
MARTHA, CONSTANT. *Les Moralistes sous l'empire romain.* Paris 1865.
POHLENZ, MAX. *Die Stoa.* 2 vols. Göttingen 1948–55; new edn. 1959.
SHARP, DOUGLAS S. *Epictetus and the New Testament.* London 1914.
*Stoicorum veterum fragmenta*, ed. Hans von Arnim. 4 vols. Leipzig 1903–24.
Sources.

### C. Epicureans

BAILEY, CYRIL. *The Greek Atomists and Epicurus.* Oxford 1928.
*Epicurea*, ed. Hermann Usener. Leipzig 1887. Sources.
*Epicurus*, ed. and trans. Cyril Bailey. Oxford 1926. Includes sources.
FESTUGIÈRE, A. J. *Epicurus and his Gods*, trans. C. W. Chilton. Oxford 1955.

### D. Middle Platonists, Eclectics

ADAM, JAMES. *The Vitality of Platonism.* Cambridge 1911.
ALMQUIST, HELGE. *Plutarch und das Neue Testament.* Uppsala 1946.
FESTUGIÈRE, A. J. *Contemplation et la vie contemplative selon Platon.* 2nd edn.
   Paris 1950.
OAKESMITH, JOHN. *The Religion of Plutarch.* London 1902.
REINHARDT, KARL. *Kosmos und Sympathie.* Munich 1926.
——— *Poseidonius.* Munich 1921.
WITT, R. E. *Albinus and the History of Middle Platonism.* Cambridge 1937.

### E. Neoplatonists

ARNOU, R. *Le Désir de Dieu dans la philosophie de Platon.* Paris 1921.
BREHIER, EMILE. *La Philosophie de Plotin.* Paris 1928.
FULLER, B. A. G. *The Problem of Evil in Plotinus.* Cambridge 1912.
GLOVER, T. R. *Life and Letters in the Fourth Century.* Cambridge 1901; new
   edn. New York 1924.
INGE, W. R. *The Philosophy of Plotinus.* 2 vols. 3rd edn. London 1929.
KRISTELLER, PAUL OSKAR. *Der Begriff der Seele in der Ethik des Plotin.* Tübingen
   1929.
PLOTINUS. *Ennéades*, ed. and trans. Emile Bréhier. 8 vols. Paris 1924–38.
——— *The Enneads*, trans. Stephen Mackenna. 5 vols. London 1917–30;
   revised edn. 2 vols., London 1956; 1 vol. 1959.
PROCLUS. *Elements of Theology*, ed. and trans. E. R. Dodds. Oxford 1933.
SALLUSTIUS. *Concerning the Gods and the Universe*, ed. and trans. A. D. Nock.
   Cambridge 1926.
SYNESIUS. *Letters of Synesius of Cyrene*, ed. and trans. Augustine Fitzgerald.
   Oxford and London 1930.
———*The Essays and Hymns of Synesius of Cyrene*, ed. and trans. Augustine
   Fitzgerald. London 1926.
WHITTAKER, THOMAS. *The Neoplatonists.* 2nd edn. Cambridge 1918.

## V. JUDAISM

### A. General

ABRAHAMS, ISRAEL. *Studies in Pharisaism and the Gospels.* 2 vols. Cambridge 1917–24. *Companion to the Daily Prayer Book.* London 1914; new ed. 1922.

BACHER, WILHELM. *Die Agada der Tannaiten.* 2 vols. Strassburg 1884–90.

BEVAN, EDWYN. *Jerusalem under the High Priests.* London 1904.

BONSIRVEN, JOSEPH. *Le Judaïsme palestinien au temps de Jésus-Christ.* 2 vols. Paris 1934–5; abr. edn. 1950.

BOUSSET, WILHELM, and HUGO GRESSMANN. *Die Religion des Judentums.* 3rd edn. Tübingen 1926.

BRÉHIER, EMILE. *Les Idées philosophiques et religieuses de Philon d'Alexandrie.* 2nd edn. Paris 1925.

COHON, S. S. "Pharisees", in Hastings' one vol. *Dictionary of the Bible,* new ed. by H. H. Rowley and F. C. Grant. Edinburgh and New York 1962.

DAUBE, DAVID. *The New Testament and Rabbinic Judaism.* London 1956.

DAVIES, W. D. *Paul and Rabbinic Judaism.* London 1948.

ELBOGEN, ISMAR. *Der jüdische Gottesdienst.* Leipzig 1913; 2nd edn. Frankfurt am Main 1924.

EPSTEIN, ISIDORE. *Judaism: A Historical Presentation.* London 1959.

FARMER, W. R. *Maccabees, Zealots, and Josephus.* New York 1956.

FINKELSTEIN, LOUIS. *The Pharisees.* 2 vols. Philadelphia 1938.

FOERSTER, WERNER. *Neutestamentliche Zeitgeschichte.* VOL. I, *Das Judentum Palästinas zur Zeit Jesu und der Apostel.* Hamburg 1940; 2nd edn. 1955.

FRIEDLÄNDER, M. *Textbook of the Jewish Religion.* London 1907.

GAVIN, FRANK S. B. *The Jewish Antecedents of the Christian Sacraments.* New York 1928.

GOODENOUGH, ERWIN R. *An Introduction to Philo Judaeus.* New Haven 1940.

GRANT, F. C. *Ancient Judaism and the New Testament.* New York 1959; 2nd edn. Edinburgh 1960.

LIEBERMANN, SAUL. *Greek in Jewish Palestine.* New York 1942.

——— *Hellenism in Jewish Palestine.* New York 1950.

MARMORSTEIN, ARTHUR. *The Old Rabbinic Doctrine of God.* 2 vols. London 1927–37.

METZGER, BRUCE. *Introduction to the Apocrypha.* London and New York 1957.

MOORE, GEORGE F. *Judaism in the First Centuries of the Christian Era. The Age of Tannaim.* 3 vols. Cambridge, Mass., 1927–30.

OESTERLEY, W. O. E. *History of Israel.* VOL. II. Oxford 1932.

——— *The Jewish Background of the Christian Liturgy.* Oxford 1925.

———, H. LOEWE, and E. J. ROSENTHAL. *Judaism and Christianity.* 3 vols. New York 1937–8.

PFEIFFER, R. H. *History of New Testament Times, with an Introduction to the Apocrypha.* New York 1949.

PREISKER, HERBERT. *Neutestamentliche Zeitgeschitchte.* Berlin 1937.

*A Rabbinic Anthology,* edd. C. G. Montefiore and H. Loewe. London 1938.

SCHECHTER, SOLOMON. *Some Aspects of Rabbinic Theology.* London 1909.

SCHÜRER, EMIL. *Geschichte des jüdischen Volkes im Zeitalter Jesu Christi*. 3 vols. 4th edn. Leipzig 1901–9. Eng. trans. of 2nd edn. *A History of the Jewish People*, Edinburgh and New York 1892.

STEWART, ROY A. *Rabbinic Theology: An Introductory Study*. Edinburgh 1961.

VOLZ, PAUL. *Die Eschatologie der jüdischen Gemeinde im neutestamentlichen Zeitalter*. Tübingen 1934.

WOLFSON, Harry A. *Philo*. 2 vols. Cambridge, Mass., 1947

## B. The Dead Sea Scrolls

BURROWS, MILLAR. *The Dead Sea Scrolls*. New York and London 1956.

———— *More Light on the Dead Sea Scrolls*. New York and London 1958.

GASTER, THEODOR. *The Dead Sea Scriptures in English Translation*. New York 1956, London 1957; revised edn. New York 1960.

SCHUBERT, KURT. *The Dead Sea Community*. New York 1959.

*The Scrolls and the New Testament*, ed. Krister Stendahl. New York 1957.

VERMÈS, GÉZA. *Discovery in the Judean Desert*. New York 1956.

## C. The Diaspora

BELL H. I. *Jews and Christians in Egypt*. London 1924.

DODD, C. H. *The Bible and the Greeks*, PT. I. London 1935.

JUSTER, JEAN. *Les Juifs dans l'empire romain*. 2 vols. Paris 1914.

REINACH, THEODORE. "Diaspora," in *The Jewish Encyclopedia*, VOL. IV, New York 1904, pp. 559–74.

SCHÜRER, EMIL. "Diaspora," in Hastings' *Dictionary of the Bible*, VOL. V, Edinburgh and New York 1904.

## D. Texts

*The Apocrypha* in Revised Standard Version of the Bible. New York 1957.

*The Apocrypha and Pseudepigrapha of the Old Testament*, ed. R. H. Charles. 2 vols. Oxford 1914.

ISHMAEL, RABBI. *The Mekilta of Rabbi Ishmael*, ed. J. K. Lauterbach. 3 vols. Philadelphia 1933–5.

JOSEPHUS. *Works*, ed. H. S. Thackeray. 9 vols. Loeb Classical Library. London and Cambridge, Mass. 1926 ff.

*The Mishnah*, trans. H. Danby, Oxford 1933.

PHILO JUDAEUS. *Works*, edd. F. H. Colson and G. H. Whitaker. 10 vols. and supplement, 2 vols. Loeb Classical Library, London and Cambridge, Mass. 1929 ff.

STRACK, H. L. *Introduction to the Talmud and Midrash*. Philadelphia 1931.

# VI. THE EARLY CHURCH

## A. History

BARDY, S. *The Church at the End of the First Century*. London 1938.

BIGG, CHARLES. *The Church's Task under the Roman Empire*. Oxford 1905.

———— *Origins of Christianity*. Oxford 1909.

BURKITT, F. C. "The Christian Church in the East," in *Cambridge Ancient History*, VOL. XII, 1939, ch. xiv.

CAIRD, G. B. *The Apostolic Age.* London 1955.

CARRINGTON, PHILIP. *The Early Christian Church.* 2 vols. Cambridge 1957.

CASE, SHIRLEY JACKSON. *The Evolution of Early Christianity.* Chicago 1914.

——— *The Social Triumph of the Early Church.* Chicago 1933.

*Christianity in the Light of Modern Knowledge* (a collective work). London 1929.

CRAIG, C. T. *The Beginning of Christianity.* New York 1943.

CULLMANN, OSCAR. *The Early Church.* Philadelphia 1956.

——— *Peter: Disciple, Apostle, Martyr.* Philadelphia 1953.

——— *The State in the New Testament.* New York 1956.

DAUBE, D., and DAVIES, W. D. See under V.A.

DIX, DOM GREGORY. *Jew and Greek.* London and New York 1953.

DUCHESNE, LOUIS. *Early History of the Christian Church.* 3 vols. London and New York 1909–24.

EASTON, BURTON SCOTT. *Early Christianity.* Greenwich, Conn., 1954.

——— *The Pastoral Epistles.* New York 1947. (Especially the word studies, pp. 171 ff.)

ENSLIN, MORTON SCOTT. *Christian Beginnings.* New York 1938; paperback edn. 1956.

GOGUEL, M. *Jésus et les origines du Christianisme.* VOL. I, *La Vie de Jésus*, Paris 1932; Eng. trans. *The Life of Jesus*, trans. Olive Wyon, London and New York 1933. VOL. II, *La Naissance du Christianisme*, Paris 1946; Eng. trans. *The Birth of Christianity*, trans. H. C. Snape, London 1953; VOL. III, *L'Église primitive*, Paris 1948.

GRANT, F. C. "Organization of the Early Church," in *Twentieth-Century Encyclopedia of Religious Knowledge.* Grand Rapids 1955, VOL. II, pp. 823–5.

GRANT, ROBERT M. *The Sword and the Cross.* New York 1955.

HARNACK, ADOLF. *The Mission and Expansion of Christianity in the First Three Centuries*, trans. from 2nd German edn. by James Moffatt. New York 1908. 4th German edn., 2 vols., Leipzig 1923.

——— *Bible Reading in the Early Church.* London 1912.

HOMO, LÉON. *De la Rome païenne à la Rome chrétienne.* Paris 1950.

JAEGER, WERNER. *Early Christianity and Greek Paideia.* Cambridge, Mass. 1961.

KNOPF, RUDOLF. *Das nachapostolische Zeitalter.* Tübingen 1905.

LEBRETON, JULES and J. ZEILLER. *The History of the Primitive Church.* VOL. I, *The Church in the New Testament.* New York 1949.

LIETZMANN, HANS. *Geschichte der alten Kirche.* 4 vols. Berlin 1932 ff. Eng. trans. *History of the Early Church*, trans. Bertram Lee Woolf. London 1937 ff.; New York 1938 ff.

——— "The Christian Church in the West," in *Cambridge Ancient History*, VOL. XII, 1939, ch. xv.

——— *Messe und Herrenmahl.* Bonn 1926. Eng. trans. *Mass and Lord's Supper*, trans. Dorothea H. G. Reeve. Leiden 1953.

MEYER, EDUARD. *Ursprung und Anfänge des Christentums.* 3 vols. Stuttgart

PFLEIDERER, OTTO. *Primitive Christianity*, trans. W. Montgomery. 4 vols. New York 1906–11.

RAMSAY, WILLIAM M. *The Church in the Roman Empire before A.D. 170.* 10th edn. New York 1913.

SCOTT, ERNEST F. *The Beginnings of the Church.* New York 1914.

——— *The Varieties of New Testament Religion.* New York 1947.

SRAWLEY, J. H. *The Early History of the Liturgy.* 2nd edn. Cambridge 1949.

STREETER, B. H. *The Primitive Church.* New York 1930.

——— "The rise of Christianity," in *Cambridge Ancient History*, VOL. XI, 1936, ch. vii.

VAN DER MEER, F., and C. MOHRMAN. *Atlas of the Early Christian World.* Edinburgh and New York 1958.

WEISS, JOHANNES. *History of Primitive Christianity.* Eng. trans. ed. F. C. Grant. 2 vols. New York 1937. Reprinted as *Earliest Christianity*, 2 vols., New York 1959.

WERNLE, PAUL. *The Beginnings of Christianity*, trans. G. A. Beinemann. 2 vols. New York 1903–4.

### B. The Background of Early Christianity

ANGUS, SAMUEL. *The Environment of Early Christianity.* London 1914.

BARRETT, C. K. *The New Testament Background.* London 1957. Sources.

BELL, H. I. *Cults and Creeds in Graeco-Roman Egypt.* Liverpool 1957.

BEVAN, EDWYN R. *Hellenism and Christianity.* London 1921.

——— *Sibyls and Seers.* Cambridge, Mass., 1929.

BULTMANN, RUDOLF. *Primitive Christianity in its Contemporary Setting.* New York 1956.

——— *Der Stil der paulinischen Predigt und die kynisch-stoische Diatribe.* Göttingen 1910.

BURKITT, F. C. "Pagan philosophy and the Christian Church," in *Cambridge Ancient History*, VOL. XII, 1939, ch. xiii.

CASE, SHIRLEY JACKSON. *The Origins of Christian Supernaturalism.* Chicago 1946.

CLEMEN, CARL. *Primitive Christianity and its Non-Jewish Sources*, trans. Robert G. Nisbet. Edinburgh 1912.

COCHRANE, CHARLES NORRIS. *Christianity and Classical Culture.* Oxford 1940.

DIBELIUS, MARTIN. *Botschaft und Geschichte: Gesammelte Aufsätze.* 2 vols. Tübingen 1953–6.

FAIRWEATHER, WILLIAM. *Jesus and the Greeks.* Edinburgh 1924.

FIEBIG, PAUL. *Die Umwelt des Neuen Testaments.* Göttingen 1926.

HALLIDAY, W. R. *The Pagan Background of Early Christianity.* Liverpool 1926.

*Het oudste Christendom en die antieke Cultuur*, edd. J. H. Waszink, W. C. van Unnik, and Ch. de Beus. 2 vols. Haarlem 1951.

KITTEL, GERHARD. *Die Religionsgeschichte und das Urchristentum.* Gütersloh 1931.

KNOX, WILFRED L. *Some Hellenistic Elements in Primitive Christianity.* London 1944.

KRAFT, H. "Antike und Christentum," in *Religion in Geschichte und Gegenwart*, 3rd edn., Tübingen 1957, VOL. I, cols. 436–49.

LIETZMANN, HANS. *Kleine Schriften.* VOL. I, *Studien zur spätantiken Religions-geschichte.* Berlin 1958.

MACGREGOR, G. H. C., and A. C. PURDY. *Jew and Greek, Tutors unto Christ.* New York 1936.

NOCK, A. D. "Early Gentile Christianity and its Hellenistic background," in *Essays on the Trinity and the Incarnation,* ed. A. E. J. Rawlinson, London 1928.

WENDLAND, PAUL. *Die hellenistisch-römische Kultur.* Tübingen 1907; 2nd edn. 1912.

## C. The New Testament

BAUER, WALTER. *A Greek-English Lexicon of the New Testament and Other Early Christian Literature,* trans. and edd. W. F. Arndt and F. W. Gingrich. Cambridge and Chicago 1957.

*The Beginnings of Christianity,* edd. F. J. Foakes Jackson and Kirsopp Lake. 5 vols. London 1920–33.

BORNKAMM, GÜNTHER. *Jesus of Nazareth,* trans. J. and F. McLusky and J. M. Robertson. London and New York 1960.

CARRINGTON, PHILIP. *According to Mark.* Cambridge 1960.

―――― *The Primitive Christian Catechism.* Cambridge 1940.

――――*The Primitive Christian Calendar.* Cambridge 1952.

DEISSMANN, ADOLF. *Paul.* 2nd edn. London 1926; repr. New York 1957.

DIBELIUS, MARTIN. *A Fresh Approach to the New Testament and Early Christian Literature.* New York 1936.

―――― *From Tradition to Gospel.* New York 1935.

―――― *Jesus,* trans. C. B. Hedrick and F. C. Grant. Philadelphia 1949.

―――― *Paul,* ed. W. G. Kümmel, trans. F. Clarke. New York 1953.

―――― *Studies in the Acts of the Apostles.* New York and London 1956.

DODD, C. H. *The Apostolic Preaching and its Developments.* New York 1950.

―――― *The Interpretation of the Fourth Gospel.* Cambridge 1953.

EASTON, B. S. *Early Christianity: The Purpose of Acts, and other Papers,* ed. F. C. Grant. Greenwich, Conn., and London 1955.

GOODSPEED, E. J. *An Introduction to the New Testament.* Chicago 1937.

GRANT, F. C. *The Gospels, their Origin and their Growth.* New York 1957; London 1959.

―――― *How to Read the Bible.* New York 1956; Edinburgh 1959.

――――*Translating the Bible.* Greenwich, Conn., and Edinburgh 1961.

GRANT, R. M. *The Earliest Lives of Jesus.* London 1961.

HAENCHEN, ERNST. Commentary on Acts in *Meyer-Kommentar.* Göttingen 1956; new edn. 1959.

HEARD, RICHARD G. *An Introduction to the New Testament.* New York 1950.

HOSKYNS, EDWYN C., and F. N. DAVEY. *The Fourth Gospel.* London 1928; 2nd edn. 1938.

―――― *The Riddle of the New Testament.* New York 1931.

*The Interpreter's Bible,* VOLS. VII–XII. New York and Edinburgh 1951 ff.

JOHNSON, S. E. *Jesus in His Homeland.* New York 1957; London 1958.

JÜLICHER, ADOLF, and ERICH FASCHER. *Einleitung in das Neue Testament.*

7th edn. Leipzig 1931. Eng. trans. of 1st edn., *Introduction to the New Testament*, trans. Janet Penrose Ward, London 1904.

KENYON, FREDERIC. *Our Bible and the Ancient Manuscripts*, new edn. ed. A. W. Adams. London 1958.

KITTEL, GERHARD. *Theologisches Wörterbuch zum Neuen Testament.* Stuttgart 1933 ff.

McNEILE, ALAN HUGH. *An Introduction to the Study of the New Testament*, Oxford 1927; 2nd edn., ed. C. S. C. Williams, 1953.

MOFFATT, JAMES. *Introduction to the Literature of the New Testament.* New edn. Edinburgh 1918.

NOCK, A. D. *St Paul.* London 1938.

SCOTT, ERNEST F. *The Literature of the New Testament.* New York 1932.

*The Study of the Bible Today and Tomorrow*, ed. Harold R. Willoughby. Chicago 1947.

## D. New Testament Teaching

BONSIRVEN, J. *Exégèse rabbinique et exégèse paulinienne.* Paris 1938.

BULTMANN, RUDOLF. *Theology of the New Testament.* 2 vols. New York 1951–5.

BURROWS, MILLAR. *An Outline of Biblical Theology.* Philadelphia 1946.

CARRÉ, HENRY BEACH. *Paul's Doctrine of Redemption.* New York 1914.

DAVIES, W. D. *Paul and Rabbinic Judaism.* London 1948.

DIBELIUS, MARTIN. *Gospel Criticism and Christology.* London 1935.

*Environmental Factors in Christian History*, edd. John T. McNeill, Matthew Spinka, and Harold R. Willoughby. Chicago 1939.

FOSDICK, HARRY EMERSON. *A Guide to Understanding the Bible.* New York 1938.

GRANT, F. C. *The Gospel of the Kingdom.* New York 1940.

—— *An Introduction to New Testament Thought.* New York and Nashville 1950.

JOHANSSON, NILS. *Parakletoi.* Lund 1940.

KNOX, JOHN. *Criticism and Faith.* New York and Nashville 1952.

——*Jesus, Lord and Christ.* New York 1958.

KNOX, WILFRED L. *St Paul and the Church of the Gentiles.* Cambridge 1939.

—— *St Paul and the Church of Jerusalem.* Cambridge 1925.

PARSONS, ERNEST WILLIAM. *The Religion of the New Testament.* New York 1939.

PERCY, ERNST. *Untersuchungen über den Ursprung der johanneischen Theologie.* Lund 1939.

PRAT, FERDINAND. *The Theology of St Paul*, trans. John L. Stoddard. 2 vols. London 1945.

RICHARDSON, ALAN. *A Theological Word Book of the Bible.* New York 1951.

SCHOEPS, HANS JOACHIM. *Theologie und Geschichte des Juden-Christentums.* Tübingen 1949.

—— *Urgemeinde, Judenchristentum, Gnosis.* Tübingen 1955.

——*Paul: The Theology of the Apostle in the Light of Jewish Religious History.* London and Philadelphia 1961.

Seitz, O. J. F. *One Body and One Spirit. A Study of the Church in the New Testament.* Greenwich, Conn., 1960.
Stauffer, Ethelbert. *New Testament Theology.* New York 1955.

### E. Early Christian Literature

Altaner, Berthold. *Patrologie: Leben, Schriften, und Lehre der Kirchenväter.* 2nd edn. Freiburg 1951.
Cayré, Fulbert. *Manual of Patrology and History of Theology,* trans. H. Howitt. 2 vols. Paris 1936–40.
Cross, F. L. *The Early Christian Fathers.* London 1960.
Deissmann, Adolf. *Light from the Ancient East.* London 1908; rev. edn. 1922.
Goodspeed, Edgar J. *A History of Early Christian Literature.* Chicago 1942.
Norden, Eduard. *Agnostos Theos.* Leipzig 1913.
—— *Die antike Kunstprosa.* 2 vols. Leipzig 1898; repr. with supplement 1909.
Quasten, Johannes. *Patrology.* 4 vols. Utrecht 1950 ff.
Stählin, Otto. "Die altchristliche griechische Literatur" in *Geschichte der griechischen Literatur,* ed. W. von Christ, vol. ii, Pt. 2. 6th edn. Munich 1924.

### Texts

#### (i) Series

Ancient Christian Writers: The Works of the Fathers in Translation, edd. J. Quasten, J. C. Plumpe, and W. J. Burghardt. Westminster, Md., and London 1946.
Ante-Nicene Christian Library, edd. A. Roberts and J. Donaldson. Edinburgh 1867–97, Buffalo 1885–96; reprinted Grand Rapids, Mich., 1956.
Fathers of the Church, edd. R. J. Deferrari *et. al.* New York 1947 ff.
Library of Christian Classics, edd. John Baillie, John T. McNeill, and Henry P. van Dusen. Philadelphia and London 1953 ff.
Nicene and Post-Nicene Fathers, edd. P. Schaff and H. Wace. 2 series. New York and Oxford 1886–1900; reprinted Grand Rapids, Mich., 1956.
Sources chrétiennes, edd. H. de Lubac, J. Daniélou, and A. Mondésert. Paris 1943 ff.
Studies and Documents, edd. Kirsopp and S. T. Lake. London 1934 ff.
And others.

#### (ii) Important Editions

*The Apocryphal New Testament,* trans. M. R. James. Oxford 1924.
*The Apostolic Fathers,* ed. and trans. Kirsopp Lake. 2 vols. London 1912–13.
*Die apostolischen Väter,* ed. Hans Lietzmann. Handbuch zum Neuen Testament, Suppl. 4 vols. Tübingen 1920 ff.
Geffcken, Johannes. *Zwei griechische Apologeten.* Leipzig 1907.
Grant, Robert M. *Second Century Christianity: a Collection of Fragments.* London 1946.

HENNECKE, EDGAR. *Neutestamentliche Apokryphen.* 3rd edn. ed. W. Schnee-melcher. VOL. I. Tübingen 1959.

HIPPOLYTUS. *The Apostolic Tradition of Hippolytus,* ed. and trans. Burton Scott Easton. Cambridge 1934.

IRENAEUS. *Sancti Irenaei episcopi Lugdunensis libros quinque adversus haereses,* ed. W. W. Harvey. 2 vols. Cambridge 1857. Still adequate.

*The Odes and Psalms of Solomon,* ed. J. Rendel Harris. 2nd edn. Cambridge 1911.

ORIGEN. *Contra Celsum,* trans. and ed. H. Chadwick. Cambridge 1953.

——— *De principiis,* trans. and ed. George W. Butterworth. London 1936.

——— *Selections from the Commentaries and Homilies of Origen,* trans. R. B. Tollinton. London and New York 1929.

TERTULLIAN. *Apologeticus,* ed. Joseph B. Mayor. Cambridge 1917.

——— *De anima,* ed. J. H. Waszink. Amsterdam 1947.


## F. Early Christian Doctrine

ALLEN, A. V. G. *The Continuity of Christian Thought.* Boston 1884.

BADCOCK, F. J. *The History of the Creeds.* London 1938.

BAUER, WALTER. *Rechtgläubigkeit und Ketzerei im ältesten Christentum.* Tübingen 1934.

BETHUNE-BAKER, J. F. *An Introduction to the Early History of Christian Doctrine.* London 1903, 9th edn. 1951; revised edn. Greenwich, Conn., 1959.

BIGG, CHARLES. *The Christian Platonists of Alexandria.* Oxford 1886; reprinted with additions 1913.

BOUSSET, WILHELM. *Kyrios Christos.* Göttingen 1913; 3rd edn. 1926.

CULLMANN, OSCAR. *Baptism in the New Testament,* trans. J. K. S. Reid, London 1950.

DODD, C. H. *According to the Scriptures.* London 1952.

EHRHARDT, ARNOLD. *The Apostolic Succession.* London 1953.

GRANT, F. C. *Basic Christian Beliefs.* Edinburgh 1960; New York 1961.

——— "Exegesis," in *Encyclopedia Americana,* VOL. x, 1952, pp. 628–36 and bibliography.

GRANT, ROBERT M. *The Bible in the Church.* New York 1948; revised edn. 1954.

——— *The Letter and the Spirit.* London 1957.

——— *Miracle and Natural Law in Graeco-Roman and Early Christian Thought.* Amsterdam 1952.

HARNACK, ADOLF. *Lehrbuch der Dogmengeschichte,* VOL. I. 4th edn. Tübingen 1909. Eng. trans. of 2nd edn., trans. N. Buchanan, in *History of Dogma,* 7 vols. Boston 1895–1903; London 1899. Paperback edn. New York 1961.

——— *Dogmengeschichte (Grundriss).* 6th edn. Tübingen 1922.

——— *Marcion: Das Evangelium vom fremden Gott.* 2nd edn. Leipzig 1924.

HATCH, EDWIN. *The Influence of Greek Ideas and Usages upon the Christian Church.* 1890; paperback edn. New York 1957.

JOHNSTON, GEORGE. *The Doctrine of the Church in the New Testament.* Cambridge 1943.

KELLY, J. N. D. *Early Christian Creeds*. London 1950.
—— *Early Christian Doctrines*. London 1958.
LAMPE, G. W. H. *The Seal of the Spirit*. London 1951.
LOOFS, FRIEDRICH. *Leitfaden zum Studium der Dogmengeschichte*. Halle 1889; new edn. 1950–3.
PRESTIGE, G. L. *God in Patristic Thought*. London 1952.
SEEBERG, REINHOLD. *Lehrbuch der Dogmengeschichte*. 2 vols. Leipzig 1908–17; new edn., 5 vols., 1953 ff. Eng. trans. by C. E. Hay, 2 vols., Philadelphia 1905.
TIXERONT, JOSEPH. *Histoire des dogmes*. 3 vols. 2nd edn. Paris 1905–12. Eng. trans. of 5th edn. Freiburg 1910–16.
WERNER, MARTIN. *Die Entstehung des christlichen Dogmas*. 2nd edn. Bern 1953.

# Index

A. SUBJECTS

*Aberglaube:* v, 4, 76, 176
*aether:* 62
Agdistis: 16
Alexander's Successors: 82
apocalyptic: 23
Apocrypha: 99
Apologists: 26
apostolic books: 130
Asia Minor: 51
*askēsis:* 164
astrology: 11, 16
astronomy: 47
Atonement: 9, 158
atthidographers: 36

Baptism: 24, 153
Bible, the Jewish: Ch. V
*biblia:* 128
biblical theology: 125, 161
Bibliography: 188ff.

Cambridge Platonists: viii
Chassidim: 145
Christology: 157
Chronology: 179ff.
chronology in N.T.: 124
creed: 55f.

*Daemons:* 51
Dead Sea Scrolls: 108
Demeter: 11
democracy: 92
Dionysus: 14
Docetism: 128f., 165
Doctrine: Ch. VIII
dogmatic theology: 125
*Do ut des:* 103

Education, Greek: Ch. II
envy of the gods: 10
Epidaurus: 37
ethics: 91f., 167f.

Euhemerism: 16
existentialism: 127

Form criticism: 120

Geocentrism: 47
Gnosticism: 46, 74, 111, 128f., 150, 166
God-fearers: vi, 99
Gospel, the: Ch. VI
Gospel: 26
Greek: 89, 113ff., 160f.
Greek language: 72, 80

Hades: 47
*Heilsgeschichte:* 13, 122
*Heimarmenē:* 52
Hellenism: 81f.
Hermetism: 46
history in N.T.: 123
holy fear: 10
*homo novus:* 142
Hope, the: 134

Immortality: 78
Incarnation, the: 155
inscriptions: 36
*interpretatio graeca:* 94
*interpretatio romana:* 55
Isis Aretalogy: 16

Jews: 86

Kingdom of God: 24
"Know thyself": 10
*Kyrios:* 156

Law, the: 140
legions: 86
liberal arts: 35
liturgical use of the Bible: 127ff.

*Logos:* 49, 118f.
Love: 24

Maccabees: 87
Magi: 51
magic: 14
*Mar, Mari, Maran:* 155
*Marána thá:* 23
Marxism: 90
Messiah: 24
Mithras: 15, 18, 50, 77
Moira: 11, 58
monotheism: 51, 115
motion: 62
Muratorian Canon: 130
mysteries: 12, 37f., 45
mystery religions: vi, 76ff.
mystery theology: 39
mysticism: 50, 145

Nag-Hammadi: 76
Nazarenes: 149
Neoplatonism: 49
Neoplatonists: 60
Neptune: 104
"Nothing overmuch": 10

Oracles: 38
*orexis:* 63f.
Orphism: 14

*Paideia:* vii
Palestine: 86
Paraclete: 119
Parthians: 87
partiality of evidence: 124
*pax romana:* 89, 97
person of Christ: 164
personal religion: 7
personality: 117
Pharisaism: 136
Pharisee: 134f.
phenomena of religion: 5
Phrygian religion: 16
planets: 59
Platonism: 73
poets: 4, 41
*Pontifex maximus:* 20
population: 84

Poseidon: 104
power and cleansing: 4
*praeparatio evangelica:* 71, 114
primitivism: 108
prosperity: 84
psychography: 133
Pythagoreanism: 50

Qumran: 23

Realism: 117
*religio:* 175
*religio licita:* 172ff.
Resurrection, the: 156
*rhētores:* 32
Ritschlians: 22
*Roma:* 18
Roman Empire: Ch. IV
Roman Hellenism: v
Roman influence: 163

Sacrifice: 109
Sceptics: 67
Septuagint: 21
sin: 8
sin as pollution: 117
social gospel: 92
Solar Monotheism: 95;
*Sol invictus:* 19
  see also SUN WORSHIP
Son of Man: 23f.
Sophists: 10, 14
*sōtēria:* 27
soul: 62
source criticism: 120
Spanish hymn: 61
Sun god: 46
Sun worship: 49f.
superstition: 14
Syncretism: Ch. III

Taormina: 1
*taurobolium:* 40, 78
Testament, Old, and New: 128
textual criticism: 120
Torah: 108
Trinity, the: 152
twice-born: 141
Tyche: 41

Unmoved Mover: 63

Virgin Birth: 165

"We-sections": 134
world-soul: 58

Zealots: 87

## B. Persons

Aedesius: 18
Allan, D. J.: 62
Apollodorus: 36
Aquinas, Thomas: 28, 74
Aristarchus: 47, 56
Aristotle: 28, 57, 62ff.
Arndt, W. F.: 116
Arnold, M.: v
Arnold, T.: 81
Augustine: 57, 145, 177
Augustus: 17
Aurelian: 19

Bacon, B. W.: 130
Baudissin, W. W. von: 155
Bauer, W.: 116
Bayet, J.: 97, 174
Belloc, H.: 48
Beloch, K. J.: 84
Bengtson, H.: 15
Bidez, J.: 40
Boehme, J.: 145
Bousset, W.: 112
Brandon, S. G. F.: 119
Bultmann, R.: 75, 125
Bunyan, J.: 158f.
Burkitt, F.: 170
Burnet, J.: 42
Burton, R.: 68

Caesar: see Julius Caesar
Caird, E.: 64
Calvin, J.: 121
Caracalla: 50, 96
Carrington, P.: 25, 130
Cellini, B.: 20
Chadwick, H.: 177
Chadwick, H. M.: 115
Chamberlain, H. S.: 142
Chesterton, G. K.: 127, 144, 171
Chillingworth, W.: 125
Christ, W. von: 27

Chrysippus: 68
Cicero: viii, 17, 29, 96
Cleanthes: 68f.
Colet, J.: 29, 143
Copernicus, Nicolaus: 58, 167
Cross, F. L.: ix
Cumont, F.: 40, 42, 77

Davies, W. D.: ix
Deissmann, A.: 84, 142
Dessau, H.: 37
Dibelius, M.: 120
Diogenes: 67
Diogenes of Oenoanda: 71
Dionysius the Areopagite: 28
Dittenberger, W.: 37
Dodd, C. H.: 24, 150

Easton, B. S.: 150, 178
Eissfeldt, O.: 155
Eliot, T. S.: 166
Emerson, R. W.: 52
Epictetus: 68, 70
Epicurus: 70
Eudoxus: 47, 58f.
Eusebius: 111, 130
Ezra: 127

Farnell, L.: 35
Festugière, A. J.: 41, 131
Ficino, M.: 27, 143
Field, G. C.: 57
Foakes-Jackson, F. J.: 173
Fowler, W. W.: 173ff.
Frank, T.: 90
Frazer, J.: 5

Gibbon, E.: 84
Gingrich, F. W.: 116
Gladstone, W. E.: 3

Glover, T. R.: 94
Goethe, J. W. von: 113
Goguel, M.: 178
Golding, W.: 127
Grant, M.: 84
Grant, R. M.: 26, 29, 76, 150

Hadas, M.: 44
Harnack, A.: 22, 150f.
Hatch, E.: 22, 54, 151
Heraclides: 47
Herodotus: 10, 34
Highet, G.: ix
Hillis, W. B.: 42
Hipparchus: 47
Hobbes, T.: 9
Hodgson, L.: 144
Holl, K.: 124
Holmes, O. W.: 66
Homer: 43
Hooker, R.: 73
Horace: 3

Ignatius of Antioch: 122
Illingworth, J. R.: 57
Inge, W. R.: 13, 50
Irenaeus: 122, 129
Irmscher, J.: ix

Jaeger, W.: vii, 35, 62
Johnson, H. A.: 156
Johnson, S.: 116
Jowett, B.: 60
Julius Caesar: 36, 85
Juster, J.: 178
Justin Martyr: 49

Kahle, P.: 149
Kahrstedt, U.: 89f.
Kant, I.: 125
Kepler, J.: 60
Kilpatrick, G.: 130
Kittel, G.: 116
Klausner, J.: 91

Lake, K.: 173
Larfeld, W.: 37
Last, H.: 173

Latte, K.: 13, 45, 98, 101, 175
Leclercq, H.: 173
Lieberman, S.: 20
Lietzmann, H.: 173
Livingstone, R.: viii
Livy: 33

Macaulay, T. B.: 3
Manson, T. W.: 118
Marcion: 128
Marcus Aurelius: 68, 85
Marrou, H.: 173
Marshall, J. S.: x
Mattingly, G.: 125
McNamara, K.: 165
McNeill, J. T.: 121
Meredith, G.: 48
Milton, J.: 65
Moffatt, J.: 151
Mommsen, T.: 172
Moore, C. H.: 12
Moore, G. F.: 153
More, P. E.: 22
Murray, G.: 43, 71

Nestle, W.: 41, 44
Nilsson, M. P.: x, 5, 18, 38, 44f., 46,
    49f., 65, 79, 166
Nock, A. D.: 15f., 41, 46, 116, 131

Orsi, P.: 1
Osler, W.: 121
Otto, W. F.: 44, 175

Papias: 122
Pascal, B.: 50, 145
Pater, W.: 19, 100
Paul: 24f., Ch. VII
Pétrement, S.: 52
Philo: 49, 110
Plato: viii, 9, 11f., 27f., 42, 47, 56ff., 142
Pliny the Younger: 32
Posidonius: 32, 70, 167
Preuschen, E.: 116
Protagoras: 105
Ptolemaeus, Claudius: 47, 167
Pyrrho: 67

Quintilian: 33.

Rashdall, H.: 158
Redlich, E. B.: 120
Riccobono, S.: 89
Robinson, R.: 62
Rohde, E.: 42
Ross, D.: 18
Rostovtzeff, M.: 90
Rousseau, J. J.: 68

Sandys, J. E.: 28, 37
Santangelo, M.: 2
Schoeps, H. J.: 75, 113
Scholem, G. G.: 29
Schürer, E.: 178
Seeley, J.: 93
Seneca: 9, 68
Seznec, J.: 20, 83
Sherwin-White, A.N.: 173
Showerman, G.: 77
Socrates: 9
Sostratus of Cnidus: 37
Stanley, A. P.: 81
Streeter, B. H.: 124

Tacitus: 33
Temple, W.: 125
Theophilus of Antioch: 152

Theophrastus: 57
Thomas: see AQUINAS
Thrasyllus: 42
Thucles: 1
Thucydides: 1, 33
Tiberius: 42
Tillich, P.: 126
Toynbee, A.: 55

Vermaseren, M. J.: 40
Virgil: 17
Voltaire, F. M.: 68

Weiss, J.: 150
Wendland, P.: 55, 76, 95, 150
Wheeler, M.: 83
Whitehead, A. N.: vii
Wikgren, A.: 143
Wilamowitz, U. von: 27
Willoughby, H. R.: 143
Wilmer, R.: ix
Windelband, W.: vii
Wissowa, G.: 45, 175
Woodhead, A. G.: 37
Wycliffe, J. : 132
Zeller, E.: 58
Zeno: 68
Zielinski, T.: 10

## C. TEXTS

Pentateuch, *passim:* Ch. V
Genesis II. 2: 64
    XVII. 9–14: 139
Exodus II. 14: 91
    XXIII. 23: 65
Leviticus XVIII. 5: 135
1 Samuel VIII–XVI: 88
    x. 6, XI. 6, XVI. 13: 104
    XIV. 6: 61
Job IX. 12: 60
Psalms XXIV: 7
    XLIX. 12: 137
    XCV. 17: 11
    CX. 1: 155
    CXIX: 135
Isaiah VII. 14: 155
    XIX. 23–5: 139
Zechariah XIV. 9: 13

Judith VIII. 11–17: 62

Matthew: 26
    v. 8: 65
    v. 36: 72
    VI. 34: 72
    XI. 25–30: 75
    XI. 27: 161
    XII. 28: 158
    XIX. 26: 57
    XXIII: 141
    XXIII. 15: 149
    XXVIII. 19: 115, 152
Mark: 25
    III. 22–7: 158
    IX. 29: 49
    IX. 41: 178
    X. 27: 57
    XII. 17: 91
    XII. 35–7: 155
    XIII. 10: 115
    XIII. 14: 129

Mark XIII. 32: 161
  XIV. 37: 57
  XVI. 20: 147
Luke–Acts: 26
Luke I. 1: 120
  I. 1–4: 26, 128, 178
  II. 1–7, III. 1: 89
  X. 21f.: 75
  XI. 20: 158
  XII. 14: 91
  XVIII. 27: 57
  XXIV. 31, 36: 165
John: 26
  I. 3: 65
  I. 14: 22
  I. 18: 65
  IV. 24: 7
  V. 17: 64
  X. 30: 154
  XVI. 12–15: 112
  XVI. 13: 154
  XVII. 15: 75
  XX. 19: 165
Acts I. 8: 115
  II–XV: 149
  V. 33–9: 139
  VIII. 1: 23
  VIII. 4–25: 75
  IX. 2: 23
  X. 1–33: 106
  XI. 19: 23
  XIII. 50ff.: 91
  XIV. 8–18: 16
  XIV. 11: 79
  XIV. 23, XV: 124
  XVI. 10–17: 134
  XVII: 16
  XVII. 22: 41
  XX. 4–16: 134
  XXI. 1–17: 134
  XXII. 3: 139
  XXIII. 6: 134
  XXIII. 23: 86
  XXIV. 10–16: 134
  XXVI. 4–8: 134
  XXVI. 26: vii
  XXVII. 1–XXVIII. 20: 134
  XXVIII. 20: 134
Romans I. 3f.: 135
  III. 1–2: 108
  III. 1–5: 140
  IV. 11f.: 172
  V. 1: 158

Romans V. 8: 71
  VI. 3, 5: 159
  VI. 4: 158
  VII. 12: 135
  VII. 24: 74
  VIII. 3: 161
  VIII. 18: 73
  VIII. 18, 28, 32, 38f.: 71
  VIII. 19–23: 64
  VIII. 20f.: 166
  X. 4: 147
  X. 8: 143
  XI. 33: 145
  XII. 1: 7
  XIII. 1–7: 90f.
  XVI. 7: 112
  XVI. 25–7: 160
  XVI. 27: 162
I Corinthians II. 9: 145
  II. 9f.: 98
  VII: 167
  VII. 19: 139
  VII. 20–4: 139
  VIII: 109
  VIII. 5: 169
  VIII. 6, XI. 3: 154
  XII–XIV: 138
  XIV. 8: 142
  XIV. 18f. 138
  XV. 23–8: 157
  XV. 24–8: 154
  XV. 32: 72
  XV. 54: 71
  XVI. 22: 23, 155
II Corinthians IV. 18: 21, 62, 94
  V. 17–20: 159
  VI. 18: 72
  VIII. 3: 60
  XII. 2: 158
  XIII. 14: 154
Galatians III. 7: 172
  III. 19–IV. 7: 135
  III. 29: 169
  IV. 3: 48
  IV. 3–5, 28: 159
  V. 1: 159
  V. 6: 139
  V. 18: 141
  V. 22f.: 137
Ephesians IV. 4f.: 56
  VI. 5–9: 139
Philippians I. 1: 124
  I. 23: 132

Philippians II. 5–11: 137, 143, 154, 156
  II. 7: 161
  III. 4–6: 134
  III. 4b–11: 135
  III. v: 140
  III. 9: 146
  III. 20: 159
Colossians I. 13: 158
  I. 14: 159
  I. 17: 72
  III. 22–IV. 1: 139
  IV. 16: 129
I Timothy VI. 1–2: 139
  VI. 16: 72, 162
II Timothy III. 16: 129
  IV. 13: 128
Titus II. 13: 163
  III. 4: 72

  III. 4f.: 162f.
Philemon 16: 139
Hebrews I. 1–4: 154
  I. 3: 9
  IV. 14f., v. 2: 79
  VI. 5: 147
  VI. 19f.: 61
  VIII. 13: 106
  XI. 10: 72
James I. 17f.: 65
  III. 6: 74
I Peter II. 13–17: 91
I John IV. 12: 65
  v. 19: 74f.
Revelation III. 9: 178
  XIII. 1, 4ff.: 96
  XIV–XX.: 97
  XXII. 20: 23

Aeschylus, Prometheus: 7
Apuleius, Metamorphoses, XI. 5: 95
  XI. 14: 176
  XI. 25: 7
Aristophanes, Frogs, 454ff.: 12
Aristotle, De Caelo, II. 1: 65
  Eudemian Ethics, 1243b: 60
  Frag., 15: 18
  Metaphysics, IV. 1012b: 65
  XII. 1072a: 65
  Nicom. Ethics, 1177b: 65
Augustan Histories: 33
Cicero, De inventione, II. 161: 176
  De legibus, II–III: 174
  X. 25: 176
  De Natura deorum, I. 24 (§66): viii
  II. 3 (§8): 17
  De officiis: 22, 92
Cleanthes, Hymn to Zeus: 106f.
Cornutus, Outline of Greek Theology: 110
Corpus Hermeticum, I: 6, 131
Digest, XLVIII. 8, 11: 177
Euripides, Hercules Furens, 1252: 7
Herodas, Mime, IV: 7
Homer, Odyssey, XI. 488ff.: 11, 79
  XVIII. 130ff.: 137
Homeric Hymns: 36
Horace, Carmen saeculare: 17
  Odes, IV. 9, 25: 3
Juvenal, Satires, I. 85f.: 34

Longinus, De sublimitate, IX. 1: 103
Lucian, How to Write History: 33f., 68
Lucretius, De rerum natura, I. 101: 176
  VI. 9–42: 137
Phocylides, Maxims: 150
Pindar, Frag., 137: 12
Plato, Apology, 38a: 9
  Epinomis, 987d: 39
  Laws, VIII. 835e: 60
  X. 896e, 897d: 58
  X. 903: 61
  Phaedo, 83b: 60
  Phaedrus, 246e: 59
  Republic II. 362d–367e: 71
  III. 401c: viii
  VII: 74
  Symposium, 190: 106
  202e–203a: 59
  Theaetetus, 176b: 65
  Timaeus, 29d: 74
  29e, 30a: 60
  30ab: 104
  34bc: 104
  40b: 65
Pliny, Letters, X. 96f.: 91
Porphyry, De abstinentia, II. 61: 8
  Sibylline Oracles: 46
Sophocles, Frag., 753: 12
Tacitus, Annals, XV. 44: 91
Theophrastus, Characters, XVI: 41

Thucydides, III. 82f.: 44
    VI. 3. 1: 1
Virgil, *Aeneid*, VI. 851ff.: 102
    *Eclogue* IV: 17


*Oxyrh. Papyri*, XI. 1381: 39


Josephus, *War*, II. 16. 4 (§ 345ff.): 86
    II–VI: 149
    V–VII: 44
    *Antiq.*, XIV: 178
    XX. 2–4: 149
    *Vita:* 140
*Pirqe Aboth*, I. 10: 169
*Shemoneh Esreh:* 87


Ambrose, *De officiis minist.:* 22, 92
I Clement, v. 7: 83
Clement of Alexandria, *Stromata*, v.
    1. 13: 8
Didache, VII. 1–4: 153
    x. 6: 23

Eusebius, *Ch. Hist.*, II. 12. 1–3: 149
    II. 17. 2: 130
Justin Martyr, *Apology* LVI. 11: 152
    LXI, LXV: 153
Minucius Felix, *Octavius*, VI. 1, VIII. 1, 3:
    177
Origen, *Contra Celsum*, VIII. 68: 177
Tertullian, *Apology*, XXI. 1: 177
    XXIV. 27: 173
    *De praesc. haer.*, VII: 20


Dante, *Paradiso*, XXXIII. 145: 63
Emerson, R. W., *Boston:* 52
Tennyson, *Locksley Hall*, 24: 66
    *The Passing of Arthur:* 166


*Brit. Mus. Inscs.*, 894: 96
*Corp. Insc. Attic.*, III. 171a: 8
*Corp. Inscr. Lat.*, VI. 510: 18
Dessau, H., *Inscr. Lat. Sel.*, II. 1. 4152: 18
Dittenberger, W., *Orientis Graec. inscript.*
    *sel.*, II. 458: 96
*Ephem. Arch.*, III. 81: 12